Management Fads
in Higher Education

Robert Birnbaum

Management Fads in Higher Education

in Higher Education

Where They Come From, What They Do, Why They Fail

JOSSEY-BASS
A Wiley Company
San Francisco

Jossey-Bass books and products are available through most bookstores. To contact Jossey-Bass directly, call (888) 378-2537, fax to (800) 605-2665, or visit our website at www.josseybass.com.

Substantial discounts on bulk quantities of Jossey-Bass books are available to corporations, professional associations, and other organizations. For details and discount information, contact the special sales department at Jossey-Bass.

 Manufactured in the United States of America on Lyons Falls Turin Book. This paper is acid-free and 100 percent totally chlorine-free.

Library of Congress Cataloging-in-Publication Data

Birnbaum, Robert.
    Management fads in higher education: where they come from, what they do, why they fail / Robert Birnbaum.
        p. cm.
Includes bibliographical references (p.   ) and index.
    ISBN 0-7879-4456-4
    1. Education, Higher—United States—Management.   2. Fads—United States.
3. Organizational effectiveness.   I. Title.
    LB2341.B49   2000
    378.1'01—dc21

                                                                              00-009722

FIRST EDITION
HB Printing   10 9 8 7 6 5 4 3 2 1

Contents

Preface   xi

The Author   xxi

Part I: Developing Academic Management Fads

1. Seeking the Grail: The Never-Ending Quest   3
2. We're from the Government, and We're Here to Help   33
3. Survival in a Changing Environment   63
4. Higher Education as a Commodity   91

Part II: Understanding Academic Management Fads

5. The Life Cycle of Academic Management Fads   125
6. Organizations and Fads   143
7. Managers and Fads   169

Part III: Working with Academic Management Fads

8. The Legacy of Fads   193
9. Managing Fads   215

References   243
Name Index   267
Subject Index   273

Preface

*"Bennett told me you were working on fads source
analysis. Why did you decide to work with fads?"*
"Everybody else was doing it."
*"Really?" she said eagerly. "Who are the other
scientists?"*
*"That was a joke," I said lamely, and set about the
hopeless task of trying to explain it. "You know, fads,
something people do just because everybody else is
doing it?"*
C. Willis, Bellwether

Americans are traditionalists and pragmatists and enjoy debunking new-fangled ideas. We're from Missouri, and we weren't born yesterday. At the same time, we are intrigued by change and inventiveness. We cheer the ingenuity and stick-to-itiveness of garage inventors who devote their lives to perfecting a perpetual motion machine or a car engine that runs on water. We know from high school physics that perpetual motion is not possible. But listening to the inventor's dazzling arguments, it is easy to become seduced. After all, science is not perfect. Perhaps there *are* some exceptions to the laws of thermodynamics that The Power Company and their conspirators do not want us to know about.

So it is for management fads. The last one did not work, but the new one appears brilliant and failure proof. Yes, it does seem to be inconsistent with our experience of how things actually work, but the world changes. Paradigms shift. Perhaps *this* time someone has found the answer.

We know from experience that it is no easier to get people to implement a management strategy inconsistent with their values than it is to get internal combustion from water. But in the flush of excitement at finally finding the Philosopher's Stone, we forget.

Higher education has to do with teaching, learning, and knowledge. Is it important to focus attention on managerial support activities? If a new academic management technique is adopted and it turns out that it does not do what it claims, so what? Why should we care if decisions about efficiency and effectiveness are made in one way or in another?

I believe management approaches make a difference. As Enarson (1975, p. 172) has said, "Techniques and tools tend not to be the neutral servants we describe them to be. Techniques and tools are used, always, by persons operating in time, place, circumstance, culture, and power relationships." In the case of higher education, innovative management techniques and tools may appear to be value-free technologies, but in fact their deep ideological foundations have been at the core of two academic management revolutions. The first academic management revolution took place near the turn of the twentieth century and lasted for about sixty years. It emphasized means rather than ends. Its goal was to make higher education more efficient and accountable—that is, more businesslike.

This book is primarily about the second academic management revolution that followed and its effects on higher education during the four decades between 1960 and 2000. Its focus was on ends rather than means, and its goal was to produce at the lowest cost goods desired by customers—that is, to make higher education more like a business.

Business and Higher Education

Business corporations and universities are organizations with mission statements, employees, management systems, and physical assets. Although they share many characteristics, they behave quite differently. Businesses usually are directed by professional managers who pride themselves on their market sensitivity, customer orientation, innovativeness, and productivity. Universities are frequently coordinated by professional scholars who have received on-the-job training as amateur managers. Businesses focus on the bottom line, while colleges and universities are criticized for appearing to be insensitive to economic realities.

When critics of higher education ask, "Why can't a college be more like a business?" they are likely to take a narrow perspective. They refer to business's presumed efficiency, but they usually ignore business's penchant for short-term expediency and golden parachutes. They overlook the selection of board members by management, provision of stock options to failed executives, and CEO salaries unrelated to company performance and over four hundred times higher than that of the average factory worker (Anderson and others, 1999). Curiously, the question, "Why can't a firm be more like a college?" is seldom asked, although the American higher education system is considered to be the best in the world, even by business leaders (Immerwahr, 1999), enjoys a favorable balance of trade, is a successful growth industry, has a strong record of fiscal stewardship, offers its customers a bargain, and provides high returns on investment (Woodbury, 1993).

Another way in which business and higher education are similar is their propensity to adopt new management techniques that often turn out to be fads. *Fad* often has a negative connotation, but in this book I use it descriptively rather than pejoratively to refer to something enjoying brief popularity. I do not condemn fads, and in fact, as we shall see, although fads (by definition) fail, they make important contributions to higher education. Remnants of fads may become incorporated into institutional culture and become part of our collective thinking. But fads have costs as well as benefits, and we have to learn how to use them wisely. Fads can be helpful when they provide managers with new insights that can be incorporated into their professional practice. But they can be disruptive when they are applied as formulas and implemented without the support of organizational participants.

Management, too, often has negative overtones, particularly in academic environments where we prefer to use the more professional and genteel *administration.* This antipathy has probably been exacerbated by the clever, but misleading, dictum, "Managers do things right, and leaders do the right thing." In my experience, distinctions among *leadership, management,* and *administration* when applied to higher education are more of degree than of kind. It is easy to differentiate between bean counters at one end of the continuum and visionaries at the other, but in formal organizations, effective leaders cannot be indifferent to beans, and effective managers must have a clear sense of where they want to go, and why. In higher education, good leaders often possess good management skills, and good managers are often considered also to be leaders. So I am going to use the word *management* without apology to refer to the work that administrators and faculty members do when they set objectives, establish policies, organize, motivate, communicate, assess performance, and develop people (Drucker, 1954; Hungate, 1965). In weblike systems typical of colleges and universities, managers can be anywhere, and anyone can be a manager (Mintzberg and Van der Heyden, 1999).

While recognizing the diversity of higher educational institutions, the book does not attempt to differentiate between them. I use the words *college* and *university* interchangeably to refer to all not-for-profit institutions offering two-year, four-year, or graduate programs of instruction and research.

Confessions of a Manager Manqué

At many points in this book, I criticize the proposals and analyses of scholars and administrators of the past who encouraged and defended management innovations that later proved not to be as effective as claimed. Since 1961 as an administrator and 1978 as a professor, I have been involved in most of the changes discussed in this book. Although now an apostate, I empathize with my colleagues who worship at the altar of false gods. I was once myself a votary.

It is not a coincidence that the four decades included in this study almost exactly parallel my own career in higher education, and I use 1960 as a convenient base year from which I measure all subsequent change. The practice of higher education management in 1960 is what I think of as the original or Ur-Management—the foundation on which our current systems have been built. Except for a general discussion in Chapter One of the causes and consequences of what I refer to as the First and Second Academic Management Revolutions, I have not given specific attention to management systems in use before 1960.

When I was a young executive in multicampus and state system administration, I was much more certain about everything in higher education than I am today. I spent a great amount of time and energy trying to convince much more senior campus presidents that the errors of their wasteful ways could be corrected only by adopting a new and scientific management technique. The technique in question changed from time to time, but was usually championed by a midlevel technocrat in our office who then promoted it to the senior executives in central administration. We executives remained somewhat fuzzy about the details of the innovation, although it was not seemly to acknowledge our ignorance publicly. Of course, it was in the details that the devil lurked. We knew the old system did not work well, and so we proclaimed the new technique A Good Thing that, if used wisely, would finally resolve the problems we faced. Mandating implementation of a scientific-sounding system allowed us to appear to have esoteric knowledge and gave us the opportunity to justify our positions and salaries by exercising the authority of our offices. The "if used wisely" caveat enabled us to blame others if the new system did not have the expected outcomes.

We insisted that colleagues at the campus level embrace this new technique. We gave them the Omelet Speech. "Yes," we said, "we know it will require a complete reworking of your planning and budgeting systems, put your administrative offices into overtime mode, and paralyze your day to day operations, but you cannot make an omelet without breaking eggs." The exact procedures by which they were to implement the new technique were not quite ready, but we promised to get them to the president months, or at least weeks, ahead of the date their 500-page budget documents were due. Cornford, that canny Oxbridge don, would have referred to me as a Young Man in a Hurry,

> a narrow-minded and ridiculously youthful prig, who is inexperienced enough to imagine that something might be done before very long, and even to suggest definite things. His most dangerous defect being want of experience, everything should be done to prevent him from taking part in affairs. He may be known by his propensity to organise societies for the purpose of making silk purses out of sow's ears. This tendency is not so dangerous as it might seem; for it may be observed that the sows, after taking their washing with a grunt or two, trundle back unharmed to the wallow; and the purse-market is quoted as firm. [Cornford, (1908) 1964, p. 13]

In academia, where people often move between faculty and administration, labor and management, campus and system, what goes around often comes around. When I became a campus executive myself, I saw things much differently. I was now the *recipient* of the Omelet Speech. The speech seemed quite statesmanlike when I delivered it to others, but from my new vantage point, I could see how wrong-headed it was. Where you stand really *does* depend on where you sit. I responded to the demands of system administrators in the same way presidents previously responded to me: complied ritually, did as little of what was asked as possible, and found ways around the rest. Aside from some localized pain on the part of those who had to collect data or complete forms, little of institutional consequence changed because of the new system procedures; teaching, research, and service went on much as before, and the purse market was quoted as firm.

Having come full circle in the management dance, I now wish to share insights gained over these four decades.

Structure of the Book

The book is divided into three parts. Part One introduces the fad concept and analyzes the development of seven new management systems in higher education. Chapter One proposes a number of different ways of thinking about management fads and traces the development of academic management in higher education over the past forty years. Chapter Two looks at the first three management fads: Program Planning Budgeting System, Management by Objectives, and Zero-Base Budgeting. Each of these rational approaches was first fully developed in government, personally supported by the president of the United States, and disseminated from the federal to state governments, where it eventually found its way into higher education. Chapter Three summarizes the histories of two newer fads, strategic planning and benchmarking, which were born in business and focused attention on how institutions could best fit with their environments. Chapter Four describes the development, diffusion, and consequences of two of the most recent fads: Total Quality Management and Business Process Reengineering. Readers with a scholarly interest in academic management may wish to follow the detailed analyses and historical references in these three chapters carefully. Practitioners eager to cut to the chase will find they can easily follow the book's arguments even if they skim these three chapters and selectively return to them later.

Part Two uses the material in the earlier chapters to answer three questions: How does the fad process begin and end? Why are some organizations vulnerable to fads? Why do some managers adopt them? In Chapter Five, the histories of these seven new management techniques are integrated into a conceptual model describing the life cycle of management fads. We consider how fads are created, developed, move among institutional sectors, and eventually disappear. Chapters Six and Seven use notions developed in the social sciences to offer some speculations about the nature of fads in higher education and business. Chapter Six analyzes how fads function from a sociological perspective. What characteristics of the environment, organizational process, or fads themselves may influence their adoption or abandonment? Chapter Seven considers fads from a psychological perspective to propose why some academic managers may find fads attractive. In particular, we consider how biases in the ways managers make sense of their world may influence the systems they choose to adopt.

Part Three deals with outcomes. In Chapter Eight we review the reasons fads fail, giving particular consideration to their residual consequences. Their negative outcomes may be the most obvious, but their positive consequences may be more enduring. Finally, in Chapter Nine we consider how management fads have contributed to several major problems in higher education and discuss what academic managers can do to maximize the benefits that fads can provide while minimizing their organizational costs.

Audience

This book was primarily written for college and university trustees, presidents, and other managers who constantly find their institutions under pressure to become more efficient and effective, and for faculty who often oppose management innovations even if they are not quite sure why. Knowing what has gone before and why it did not work may help readers resist unwise change, constructively experiment with new ideas, and consider how the experiences of other kinds of organizations may be useful to them.

Scholars and students of higher education should also find the book of interest. Although the higher education literature on these techniques is voluminous, there is surprisingly little critical reflection and even less scholarly evaluation. The book brings together for the first time in one place a diverse literature and a number of uncommon perspectives that I hope may serve as the basis for future research. Although the book focuses explicitly on colleges and universities, its basic ideas may also be applicable to management in other not-for-profit organizations in education, social service, and related organizational sectors. And finally, I should note that scholars who study government and business have given much more serious and extended attention to management fads than have scholars who study higher education. Just as their work has given me insight into a different institutional sector, I hope they will find in this analysis of higher education some materials and ideas to inform their work in their own fields.

Acknowledgments

Several colleagues carefully and thoughtfully read this book in draft form; I thank Dick Anderson, Bill Bergquist, Matt Birnbaum, Ellen Chaffee, Bob Dickeson, Dan Julius, George Keller, and Frank Schmidtlein for their many constructive suggestions. In addition, students in graduate seminars in 1997 and 1999, including Liam Dunfey, Ed Englebride, Amy Ginther, Brett Kennedy, Joel Kincart, Sally McCarthy, Monica Moody Moore, Damon Riley, Stephen Shipp, Lisa Stephenson, Marie Ting, Paul Umbach, Lynn Van Wagenen, Alan Vincent, Catherine Watt, and Nancy Young, offered ideas and helpful criticism.

It is usual in the acknowledgments to absolve from responsibility for error all those who have provided assistance and to accept blame for oneself. However, in this instance I cannot do so. Because this book was written within the parameters of the latest paradigms, using ISO 9000 certified, Six Sigma, zero-defect processes, by definition it is of high quality and error free. Responsibility for any mistakes therefore must be placed on previous authors whose erroneous ideas led me astray, colleagues whose prepublication critiques of the manuscript were not as careful as they should have been, my graduate research assistant Judy Deshotels who should have been more diligent, Jossey-Bass editors whose changes confused rather than clarified, or you, dear reader, who unfortunately has misinterpreted what I have written. How *could* you all have gotten it so wrong?

ROBERT BIRNBAUM
University of Maryland, College Park

The Author

Robert Birnbaum is professor of higher education at the University of Maryland, College Park, where he teaches and writes about higher academic leadership and organization and the role of higher education in society. He has also been professor of higher education and chair of the Department of Higher and Adult Education at Teachers College, Columbia University. He earned his B.A. in psychology at the University of Rochester and his M.A. and Ed.D. in higher education from Teachers College.

Prior to his faculty career, Birnbaum held administrative appointments as vice chancellor of the City University of New York, vice chancellor of the New Jersey Department of Higher Education, and chancellor of the University of Wisconsin, Oshkosh. More recently, on leave from his faculty position in Maryland, he served for two years as the founding vice president and dean of faculty of Miyazaki International College, a new four-year liberal arts institution in Japan.

Birnbaum is the author, coauthor, or editor of nine books and numerous articles in scholarly and professional journals. His previous books for Jossey-Bass include *Maintaining Institutional Diversity* (1983), *How Colleges Work* (1988), and *How Academic Leadership Works* (1992).

He is a past president of the Association for the Study of Higher Education and a recipient of that organization's Research Achievement Award.

Management Fads
in Higher Education

Part I

Developing Academic
Management Fads

1

Seeking the Grail

The Never-Ending Quest

This is a book about academic management fads—where they come from, why they are adopted, what their consequences are for academic institutions and the educational enterprise more generally, and how they can be made more helpful. I use the term *fad* to refer to any higher education management "practice or interest followed for a time with exaggerated zeal" (*Webster's Ninth New Collegiate Dictionary*, p. 444).

Institutions of higher education are always under pressure to become more efficient and effective. In response, many have attempted (either voluntarily or under mandate) to adopt new management systems and processes originally designed to meet the needs of business or governmental organizations presumed to be more efficient. One contemporary observer, referring to "the hum of corporate buzzwords" in the academy, commented, "A person would be hard pressed these days to find a college that doesn't claim to be evaluating or reshaping itself through one of these approaches" (Nicklin, 1995, p. A34). This hum is not new; it has been a feature of the higher education landscape for at least the past forty years.

Among the first of these new processes was Planning Programming Budgeting System (PPBS), initially developed by Rand for use by the Defense Department and adopted by many higher education institutions in the early 1960s. Among the most recent are

Business Process Reengineering (BPR) and benchmarking. In between, business management scholars have documented over two dozen management innovations that were proposed between 1950 and 1990 (Pascale, 1991), some of which were adopted by some institutions of higher education. The development and advocacy of new management approaches in both nonacademic and academic management continues, and at an increasing pace. Today, over sixty different management tools and techniques are in use by one corporation or another (Rigby, 1998).

What Are Academic Management Fads?

Management fads usually begin in the business or governmental sectors and diffuse into higher education through a process we explore in Chapter Five. Widespread adoption is then followed by subsequent abandonment. Books are written, consultants traverse the country, and reorganizations are undertaken in business after business as attention to one fad is soon replaced by attention to another. "The books are all like one another in the sense that they present fat collections of case studies that shore up whatever philosophy is advocated. Some of the fads work for a time, only to be replaced by the next thing that comes along. Some of them don't work at all" (O'Shea and Madigan, 1997, p. 190). With each new idea, "the true path out of the jungle has been found. How could we have been so misguided?" (Baker, 1991, p. 6).

In the business sector, these new ideas are often "presented as universally applicable quick-fix solutions—along with the obligatory and explicit caution that their recommendations are *not* quick fixes and will require substantial management understanding and commitment. As many managers will attest, the result has been a dazzling array of what are often perceived as management fads—fads that frequently become discredited soon after they have been widely propagated" (Eccles and Nohria, 1992, p. 7). Business writers describe "fad surfing in the boardroom" as executives sift through "the seemingly endless supply of programs and mantras for accomplishing 'break-throughs' in performance and achieving 'world-class' results" (Shapiro, 1995, p. xiii). Fads are introduced with "high hopes," only to be fol-lowed by "busted dreams" (Malone, 1997, p. 72).

In higher education, fads have been described as management innovations borrowed from other settings, applied without full con-sideration of their limitations, presented either as complex or decep-tively simple, relying on jargon, and emphasizing rational decision making (Allen and Chaffee, 1981). Management fads in higher education appear to follow the cycle of educational innovations in general: "early enthusiasm, widespread dissemination, subsequent disappointment, and eventual decline" (Slavin, 1989, p. 752). This sequence leads people to ask, "Whatever happened to TQM? For that matter, what happened to MBO, strategic intent, managing for excellence, management by walking around, core competencies, employee empowerment and one minute managing? They were all terrific ideas in their time, many of which were turned into fads and short lived programs" (Taylor, 1995). In the chapters that follow, I analyze why so many terrific ideas eventually fail and suggest what can be done about it.

A fad is a paradox of complexity and simplicity. Its central ideas may appear brilliantly original. Yet at the same time they are so commonsensical as to make us wonder why we had not thought of them ourselves, and so obviously reasonable as to defy disagree-ment. "The case is put so simply, forcefully, and fashionably that any other view sounds untenable, or even politically incorrect. The clarity of the message can lull the listener into uncritical accep-tance. Since everybody is saying these sorts of things, surely they must be right" (Hilmer and Donaldson, 1996, p. 6). A fad may be presented as based on extensive research and accompanied by tes-timonials of satisfied users. Only a cynical apologist for the status quo could fail to be impressed with the need to change and the ability of the innovation to correct the problem. Yet in the world of management fads, things are seldom what they seem.

Portfolio Matrix

Take as one example the portfolio matrix concept developed by Boston Consulting Group. The name *portfolio matrix* itself may not be familiar to today's higher education managers, but the ideas and terminology behind it almost certainly are. The innovation was originally developed to help corporate conglomerates sort out their various businesses, but some higher education planners transformed it into a process to inform strategic planning and academic program review. Stable programs that generated a lot of revenue were *cash cows*. Low-growth programs that brought in little income were *dogs*. Growing programs yet to prove themselves were *question marks*, and high-growth competitive programs were *stars*. The idea in business was to sell the dogs so capital could be invested in stars and question marks, while income from the cash cows kept the whole group humming along.

Some strategic planners in higher education adopted similar terminology. An institution's curriculum and program mix was its *portfolio*, and analyses of quality and centrality could yield a market value that would suggest whether it was best to build, hold, reduce, or terminate (Kotler and Murphy, 1981). The notion that one should stick with winners and drop losers was intuitively appealing, and the matrix was generally taught in business schools despite the lack of empirical evidence that its use could maximize profits (O'Shea and Madigan, 1997). Considering a curriculum as a conglomerate of discrete programs and getting rid of low-enrollment, high-cost dogs such as physics or music—what could be a more obvious way of saving money? Low-enrollment programs are still under scrutiny on many campuses today, of course, but institutions are more likely to base their judgments on quality, centrality, mission, and academic politics than on a purely financial bottom line (Dickeson, 1999; Slaughter, 1995; Eckle, 1998).

Excellence

An even more familiar example is excellence. Based on a multiyear study of forty-three "excellent" American companies, *In Search of Excellence* (Peters and Waterman, 1982) was on the *New York Times* best-seller list for over a year. The book claimed that excellent companies displayed eight characteristics: a bias for action, close to the customer, autonomy and entrepreneurship, productivity through people, hands on–value driven, stick to the knitting, simple form–lean staff, and simultaneous loose-tight properties. These became a mantra for many excellent corporation wannabes. Follow the eight rules and thrive; ignore the eight rules at your peril. Management by walking around (MBWA), one of its technologies, was the order of the day. Once it was explained, it all seemed so, well, obvious. Of *course* that's the way it had to be!

It took a while before follow-up studies of the excellence movement became available, but when they did, their findings were disconcerting. Within two years, fourteen of the forty-three "excellent" companies were in serious trouble ("Who's Excellent Now? Some of the Best-Seller's Picks Haven't Been Doing So Well Lately," 1984); within five years two-thirds had ceased to be excellent (Pascale, 1991; Butler, 1998). Stocks of "excellent" companies underperformed those of "nonexcellent" ones (Clayman, 1987), and it was not clear whether the companies defined as "excellent" were really different from other companies that were not so defined (Hitt and Ireland, 1987).

Several years after the publication of *In Search of Excellence*, one of its authors wrote another book suggesting there were really only four organizational attributes required for excellence rather than eight; still later, in another best-selling book, he recanted the excellence approach altogether and started preaching a new philosophy (Weaver, 1987). More recently, one of the researchers on the original project revealed that the eight attributes of excellence "came not from thoughtful analysis but straight from [the author's] head when he had less than one day to prepare a talk" for a client (Collins, 1996).

In retrospect, "intellectual justification for the excellence approach is surprisingly hard to find. It falls down at the early hurdles of both empirical and theoretical inquiry" (Wilson, 1992, p. 73). Excellence, said one critic, was "'fad management theory' at its best" (Butler, 1998, p. 40).

Does the debunking of excellence suggest its ideas were completely without merit? Not at all. *In Search of Excellence* was a valuable book because it stressed the importance of people and culture—a welcome counterbalance to a previous overemphasis in the management literature on number crunching. The problem was not with many of the core ideas, but rather with the simplification and packaging of these ideas so they were no longer hypotheses to be tested by experienced managers but truths that promised to improve their effectiveness.

Descriptions of the portfolio matrix or of excellence are one traditional way of considering the fad phenomenon, but fads may be more complex than we ordinarily suppose. In this book we explore many other correct yet inconsistent ways of completing the sentence, "A fad is . . ."

A Fad Is a Product

Fads are not themselves new ideas, but rather are specific ways of enacting an idea. Fads are business products. They are promoted by those who have a vested financial, professional, or psychological interest in having their ideas disseminated. For example, U.S. companies have used over nine hundred different, standardized TQM programs, each promoted by a different "manufacturer" (Nohria and Berkley, 1994, p. 130). Fads are processes promoted as solutions to management problems and disseminated by the increasing number of "managers, academics, consultants and journalists who proffer solutions to these problems" (Eccles and Nohria, 1992, p. 7).

A Fad Is a Narrative

Narratives are stories with heroes, villains, and innocent victims involving change or transformation (Stone, 1988). Fads are narratives that try to tell a better and more compelling story than the narratives they are trying to replace (Roe, 1994). Fads tell stories that help a distressed manager understand what is wrong, describe how to fix it, and offer a vision of professional efficacy. They are stories of managerial sin, redemption, and salvation. The narrative of a fad helps people make sense of their organizations and their roles.

A Fad Is Magic

Fads establish procedures for doing things the right way through rites that "make the world seem more deterministic and give us confidence in our ability to cope, . . . unite the managerial tribe, and . . . induce us to take action" (Gimpl and Dakin, 1984, p. 125). The consultant or fad champion, like the tribal shaman, appears to be in touch with the gods. The shaman provides a compelling anchor of certainty and comfort in an otherwise ambiguous world. The rituals that accompany many fads, such as planning retreats or visioning exercises, bring the tribe together and help confirm hope for the future.

A Fad Is Rhetoric

Managers talk and listen in order to influence others. Managers take fuzzy, ill-defined situations and reduce their ambiguity by defining them in certain ways. The essence of management is interaction and conversation (Mintzberg, 1994). Fads reduce ambiguity by developing a specific language that shapes the nature of problems and therefore the nature of their solutions. Fads use language to argue, convince, and change the way people think and act (Eccles and Nohria, 1992, p. 10).

A Fad Is Technology Transfer

Fads are ways of packaging and standardizing a social technology so it can be disseminated among organizations and between organizational sectors. "Every six months, it seems, a new fad sweeps through management circles. First it strikes the business community, then government, and finally education. Think back a few years and the mind stumbles on the carcasses of fads once touted as the newest 'scientific' way to manage an organization" (Baldridge and Okimi, 1982). Management fads transferred to higher education involve both social technologies and process technologies. Fads are knowledge-derived artifacts (Tornatzky and Fleischer, 1990) moving from government and business to higher education (but, curiously, never the other way around).

A Fad Is a Rejected Innovation

An innovation is an idea or practice seen as new by an organization. Not all innovations are fads, but many fads are innovations. Innovations follow well-studied paths of diffusion (Rogers, 1995). Some are eventually accepted by most members of an organizational system. Others, after trial by some system members, are ultimately rejected. Fads follow a standard sequence in higher education: "First, the system will be widely acclaimed in the higher education literature; institutions will eagerly ask how best to implement it. Next, the publication of a number of case studies will appear, coupled with testimonials to the system's effectiveness. Finally, both the term and the system will gradually disappear from view" (Chaffee, 1985, p. 133). Since fads by definition are ultimately not adopted throughout an organizational system, they may be considered rejected innovations.

A Fad Is an Uninstitutionalized Innovation

Colleges and universities are institutions based on legitimation, infused with meaning, and perpetuated because they adhere to common norms, values, and ways of thinking. Their existence and survival depends on something far deeper than their technical success. Those elements of a university seen as proper and legitimate are institutionalized. Those elements seen as illegitimate and unrelated to core values and ways of thinking are not institutionalized; they do not endure. Even when a fad is temporarily adopted by a university, it is almost never incorporated into the institution's culture and therefore remains uninstitutionalized.

A Fad Is a Meme

Memes are self-propagating ideas that move through a host population like electronic viruses through a computer network or biological viruses through the countryside (Lynch, 1996). The concept of memes focuses not on how organizations acquire ideas, but on how ideas acquire organizations. Management fads are ideas diffused throughout an environment looking for organizations that can serve as their hosts. Fads, like all other memes, need not necessarily assist their host; memes are primarily interested in reproduction and self-survival.

A Fad Is a Political Process

Innovations involve political and social processes of change. The success of an innovation, or the failure that marks it as a fad, is a consequence of the application of power by various interest groups at numerous levels. The technical outcomes of a proposed innovation are of less significance than the costs and benefits seen by self-interested individuals and groups (Frost and Egri, 1991). Particularly in settings of ambiguity, the fate of an innovation may depend on the ability of one ideology to gain ascendance over another within an existing system of organizational influence.

A Fad Is a Placebo

A fad is a treatment prescribed in order to cure an institutional illness. Sometimes institutions improve after a "treatment," even when there is no evidence that the fad had anything to do with it. "When an intervention is followed by improvement, the intervention's effectiveness stands out as an irresistible product of the person's experience" (Gilovich, 1991, p. 128). When this happens, fads may function as placebos, seen by managers who implement them (and sometimes by other institutional participants as well) as having a positive effect.

A Fad Is an Alternative to Management

Good management depends on a thorough knowledge of the university as an institution and an organization, experience in administration, and knowledge of management practices. Sound managers apply judgment to context-specific situations in order to define problems in ways that may lead to effective action. By specifying a structure and a rhetoric through which problems should be viewed, fads may disconnect a problem from the context in which it occurs, and thus prematurely reduce uncertainty. In so doing, fads may restrict the pragmatism that is the heart of management (Eccles and Nohria, 1992). Fads do not strengthen the discretion of management; they are an alternative to the exercise of managerial judgment.

A Fad Is a Post Hoc Social Construction

Not all higher education management innovations are fads. Some (for example, fund accounting) may diffuse, be adopted rapidly through institutional networks, and become an accepted part of the educational system. Whether an innovation is a fad cannot be known before it reaches its adoption peak and then begins to fade. Nevertheless, as we shall see, there are some cues that should alert potential adopters to the possibility that a proposed innovation is a fad, as well as some steps that can be taken to make constructive use of new ideas while minimizing the risk of unnecessary disruption.

Fads and the Higher Education Environment

By definition, academic fads come and go. As we shall see in later chapters, even when a fad appears to be in widespread use, its direct influence on educational processes is usually negated or moderated by institutional cultures and organizational processes. If fads are so impermanent and ineffective, why is it important to understand them?

Fads are important not so much because of what they do to an organization, as because of what they say about our changing beliefs of what an organization is and how it should function. The indirect consequences of fads are usually more important than the direct ones. We have known for a long time that the technology of management has consequences for the technology of education. Any management innovation "may have far-reaching implications for other parts of its formal and social organization, for the people who work in it, and for the organization's relationship to its environment" (Peterson, 1971, p. 3). Management systems can affect *how* decisions are made as well as *what* decisions are made. They can influence what data are collected and how they should be interpreted. The decision to structure information in one way rather than another is important: "Some categories conceal; others will reveal. Some categories foster certain kinds of comparisons; others foster other kinds of comparisons. The decision to conceal or reveal information and to foster some kinds of comparisons rather than others, is dependent on our purposes" (Hammond and Knott, 1980, p. 17). The study of management fads helps us to understand the values that undergird the educational system and the purposes people believe are important.

The effects that management systems have had in the past on American society demonstrate the importance of the relationship. The emergence of new technologies and theories of organization and management has been accompanied by changes in the way we all think about the world. We take for granted analytic approaches to organizations and concepts such as orderliness, predictability, and definable purposes that at an earlier time might have been considered "novel states of consciousness" (Scott, 1995, p. 48). Techniques that are claimed to further these objectives are acclaimed. These changes can be seen in briefly reviewing some of the major changes in higher education management over the twentieth century.

Management Revolutions

Management in the twentieth century has gone through two revolutions. Both successfully overturned previous social norms and values and had profound effects on American, and subsequently world, culture. The first revolution can be traced back to the diffusion of scientific management at the turn of the century, leading to the Triumph of Managerialism. The second had its genesis after World War II in the growing use of operations research and systems management in government (Rourke and Brooks, 1966), leading to the Triumph of Rationality. It would not be an exaggeration to say these new approaches to management had as great an influence on how we live our lives, enact our roles, and perceive our world as any of the more widely celebrated and dazzling technical achievements of our era.

The First Revolution: The Triumph of Managerialism

In 1880, a young supervisory engineer named Frederick W. Taylor started to measure work. Taylor's observations about how much work *was* done over a specific period of time soon developed into an interest in discovering how much work *should* be done. This led him systematically to separate out the various components of a task, determine through measurement the proper amount of time required for each, and combine each of these elements into a set of instructions describing the One Best Way the task should be performed. Taylor's instructions were not based merely on his assessment of past practice or his own judgment, but on data he collected through controlled experiments (Kanigel, 1997).

The system, as elaborated over time, came to be known as *scientific management* or simply *Taylorism*. Taylorism worked. The factory tasks to which the method was originally applied became more efficient; productivity increased rapidly; the quality of output was regularized, permitting standardization and (later) assembly line methods; and workers' salaries dramatically improved as incentives were offered on a piecework basis. Taylorism was referred to by some as magic, because it simultaneously increased production, raised wages, and lowered prices. It was "American mechanical genius at its best, solving the problems of competition from Germany, the high cost of living, and the conservation of national resources at one blow" (Callahan, 1962, p. 20).

The costs were less visible but no less profound. Worker autonomy was severely diminished as decisions were no longer made by
the craftsman but by the manager. As the need for competent managers grew to exceed the supply, managers' jobs were simplified,
requiring coordination by yet higher-level managers. Jobs that had
been sources of pride became drudgery, to be endured only as sources
of income. Workers made more money, but only by rigidly following orders. Skilled craftsmen and artisans whose judgment was
honed through years of dedicated apprenticeship were now mere
tools in the hands of the young and inexperienced time and motion
engineers. As Kanigel (1997) describes the Faustian bargain, "You
do it my way, by my standards, at the speed I mandate, and in doing
so achieve a level of output I ordain, and I'll pay you handsomely
for it, beyond anything you might have imagined. All you have to
do is take orders, give up your way of doing your job for mine"
(p. 214). In the world of the efficient business, planners would think
through everything beforehand, lower-level managers would super-
vise the detailed instructions, and workers would do as they were
told. Work no longer had a moral or spiritual dimension. The benefits of scientific management required only one thing: "the ir-
reversible and complex handover of all planning, control, and
decision making from the workmen to the new class of scientific
managers" (p. 372). In the past, said Taylor, man was first. In the
future, the system must be first.

Taylor believed his principles were universally applicable, as
valid in the university as in the factory. *Efficiency* was the new
watchword. It was scientific. It was progressive. It was the road to
prosperity. And it required a revolutionary new way of thinking on
the part of both workers and managers. Today these notions of efficiency are so familiar and accepted that it is difficult to understand
now why they were thought then to be revolutionary. What better
sign can there be of a successful revolution?

Taylor helped make productivity and efficiency the gods we
worship today—gods all the more powerful because their unques-
tioned acceptance as part of our culture makes them invisible to

us. Management gurus and social critics have characterized Taylorism as "the most powerful as well as the most lasting contribution America has made to Western thought since the Federalist Papers," and Taylor as "having a greater effect on the private and public lives of men and women of the twentieth century than any other single individual" (Kanigel, 1997, pp. 11, 8).

Scientific Management and Education

The concepts of scientific management in the industrial sector rapidly diffused into higher education. In 1910, the Carnegie Foundation for the Advancement of Teaching asked Morris Llewellyn Cooke, a mechanical engineer, to study the efficiency of American universities. Cooke was selected for the job because Carnegie explicitly wanted a view through the eyes of a businessman familiar with modern management practices. The purpose of his study, titled *Academic and Industrial Efficiency* (Cooke, 1910), was to help institutions "gain from an intelligent study of college forms of organization a real help from those who conduct industrial enterprises" (p. v).

After visiting several well-known universities, Cooke reported, "There are very few, if any, of the broader principles of management which obtain generally in the commercial world which are not, more or less, applicable in the college field, and as far as was discovered, no one of them is now generally observed" (p. 7). Cooke was shocked by the absence of uniformity among the institutions, and he suggested standards should be set by experts who were familiar with the best way of doing things. Decision by committees, department autonomy, and lack of functional management came under particular attack. Presaging calls for accountability in our own time, Cooke suggested that institutions use a novel approach he called the "credit hour" as a unit with which to measure efficiency. The days of academic autonomy were over. "The college professor must take the position that he is not an individual set apart, and that in the long run he must be governed and measured by the same general standards that generally obtain in other occupations" (p. 21).

The pressure on educational institutions to adopt management practices considered both more modern and more efficient was irresistible; colleges increasingly added businessmen as trustees and began the road toward efficiency. Colleges all over the country conducted self-surveys designed to collect data on every aspect of their functioning, and books provided lists of questions to be asked and the forms to be used (Allen, 1917). Thorstein Veblen castigated college presidents as "captains of erudition" who were responsible for governing a "corporation of learning" which "set [its] affairs in order after the pattern of a well-conducted business concern" (1957/1918, p. 62). Veblen recognized that when business principles are accepted by a university as a matter of habit, they have a major influence on academic affairs as well. Just as higher learning is incompatible with business shrewdness, he said, so business practice is incompatible with the spirit of higher learning. The consequences for higher education were that "the intrusion of business principles into the universities goes to weaken and retard the pursuit of learning, and therefore to defeat the ends for which a university is maintained. This result follows primarily from the substitution of impersonal, mechanical relations, standards and tests, in the place of personal conference, guidance and association between teachers and students; as also from the imposition from a mechanically standardized routine upon the members of the staff" (p. 165).

The elementary and secondary school sector, less prestigious and more hierarchical, was even more vulnerable than the colleges to the diffusion of scientific management processes, and Taylorism proceeded apace. In his classic *Education and the Cult of Efficiency*, Callahan (1962, p. 6) said, "The procedure for bringing about a more businesslike organization and operation of the schools was fairly well standardized from 1900 to 1925. It consisted of making unfavorable comparisons between the schools and business enterprise, of applying business-industrial criteria (e.g., economy and efficiency) to education, and of suggesting that business and industrial practices be adopted by educators." By 1930, school administrators saw themselves primarily as executives and business managers rather than educators. "The whole development produced [administrators] who did not understand education or scholarship. Thus they could and did approach education in a businesslike, mechanical, organizational way" (p. 247). Education was changing not only in response to pressures to be more businesslike, but also because business and education leaders were coming to share common ideals of what "proper" management was supposed to be (Tyack and Cuban, 1995).

In higher education, the changes were reflected in the appointment of business-oriented trustees, growing cadres of technically trained middle managers, and increased emphasis on data-based decision making. New administrative positions proliferated, and procedures were regularized. Activities formerly performed by faculty amateurs were increasingly being administered by nonteaching professionals newly outfitted with master's or doctoral degrees in educational administration. In some institutions, even deans and presidents were being selected from among professional administrators with Ed.D. degrees. This first revolution marked the triumph of managerialism in higher education.

Ur-Management: Doing It the Old-Fashioned Way

Management has never been a popular term in colleges and universities, but the rapid acceptance of scientific management in business made inevitable the adoption of more extensive managerial control systems by other social institutions. When the twentieth century began, there was no standardized format for reporting institutional income or expenditures, no standard way to count students, and no agreed-on process for measuring faculty workload. Organizations could request budgets as lump sums, without at the same time submitting a justification for the request or indicating clearly the purposes for which the funds would be used (Wanat, 1978). Some institutions had no budgets at all. More than one college treasurer kept a shoe box labeled "unpaid bills" that were dealt with sequentially as funds became available, thence to be transferred into an identical shoe box labeled "paid bills."

When managerialism came to higher education, all that changed. An encyclopedic two-volume handbook of college and university administration (Knowles, 1970) advised that seat-of-the-pants management was no longer good enough, and provided over twenty-eight hundred pages of examples of how scientific management could be applied to academic institutions. Smaller private institutions could continue for a while as mom-and-pop operations, and even larger private institutions were able for a time to ignore management problems and paper over their inefficiencies. But the growing complexity of larger institutions and the demand for increased accountability in public institutions receiving increased levels of public funding soon led to general acceptance of two critical processes. One, increasingly used even before World War II, emphasized incremental line-item budgeting. The other, which came into prominence to deal with enrollment expansion after World War II, focused on planning. I shall refer to the general combination of line-item budgeting and planning as the Ur (meaning original, prototypical, or foundational) management system of higher education. Ur-Management was a product of the First Academic Management Revolution that would have been familiar to institutional administrators of the 1960s. Although its simplicity may give it an air of quaintness to today's managers, it was itself an innovation that represented a significant departure from the informal and unstructured management systems of earlier years.

Line-Item Budgeting

The line-item budget identified—often in minute detail—the specific items for which funds were requested. Such a budget might literally have a separate printed line that indicated the numbers and salaries of all clerks. Another line might account for assistant professors, and still another for all maintenance workers. Alternatively, it could devote an individual line to a subgroup of such persons or even to an individual. In the same way, lines could also identify requested expenditures for telephone, travel, printing, and other nonpersonnel costs. A line-item budget usually included expenditures and estimates over a three-year period. Requests for the future could be compared with similar expenditures of the past and current years, and increases in requests were easily identifiable. Such a budget focused attention on changes over time and made it easy to determine whether funds were being expended on the objects for which they were appropriated.

Although line-item budget formats differed among institutions, they all began with the "base," a sum usually equivalent to the previous year's budget. The philosophy of incremental budgeting assumed that last year's budget was properly distributed among the various programs of the institution (Why shouldn't it be, since it was a continuation of the year before that?) and little programmatic change was necessary. As long as the university was continuing to operate as in the past, no additional justification was required to continue base funding.

Institutions could also request increments of different kinds to be added to the base. Requests for certain budget increments, such as increases resulting from inflation, might ordinarily be approved without requiring detailed justification other than reference to the consumer price index. But while the base and inflation were given little scrutiny year to year, a great deal of attention was paid to other requested increases, and most of the decisions in the Ur-Management budget process dealt with how to allocate these increments (Caruthers and Orwig, 1979). Institutions might ask for additional funds to pay for workload changes (such as enrollment increases), improvements in current programs (such as adding faculty positions to reduce class size), or new programs (such as adding an academic major or support service). Each such request required elaborate written documentation that would be subjected to intense scrutiny both inside and outside the institution.

Planning

If each year is only incrementally different from the previous one, looking ahead one year at a time makes sense. But the GI Bill after World War II changed social expectations of who could go to college and led to a flood of new students. Existing institutions expanded, and new institutions were created. Growth appeared uncontrollable: new community colleges were founded on a weekly basis, four-year colleges were expanding into university work, and university facilities were inadequate to cope with the demand for graduate education. State and federal agencies searched for ways to coordinate and control growth. Long-range plans were proposed as one response to growth, and some institutions developed them. But individual plans were not enough. In 1960 California developed the first statewide master plan for higher education. Master planning came to be a sign of good public stewardship, and other states followed. In New York State, the Board of Regents not only developed a statewide plan but also required each institution to develop for review and approval by the Regents its own four-year master plan displaying enrollment and facilities projections and intentions for developing new programs. The Regents had authority to review all new programs and degrees in both public and private institutions, and would consider for approval only those that had been previously included in the institution's master plan. Some institutions used the required planning to think seriously about their future. Others seemed more intent on writing complex and opaque plans they could later interpret in various ways depending on the arguments they were making to the Regents at the time. Planning was required in New York and many other states, and everywhere the existence of a long-range plan was accepted by external audiences as a sign of managerial competence and accountability.

Deficiencies and Benefits of the Ur-System

Line-item budgeting and long-range planning marked a great step forward in the management of academic institutions. Line-item budgets ensured that funds could be expended only for the specific objects for which they had been appropriated, thus establishing a clear system for legal accountability. Later variants, such as performance budgeting, permitted analyses of the unit costs of specific activities over time, thus establishing a consistent system for assessing efficiency as well as providing a simple basis for making budget decisions (for example, "reduce travel expenses by 10 percent"). Planning helped an institution think more carefully about the future.

And yet Ur-Management suffered from basic problems. Line-item budgets told you what you were paying for, but did not indicate the nature of the programs they were designed to support. As one analyst put it, they were "devoid of any conceptual representation of what the institution is doing" (Balderston, 1974, p. 210). Performance budgets indicated whether the unit costs of certain outputs were improving, but not whether the costs were "right," or whether the outputs being measured were related to institutional purposes. Long-range planning schemes helped project the future as long as it was assumed that the future was going to look pretty much like the past. Each process was done by different people and with different intentions. Budgeting was "conservative and constraining"; planning was "innovative and expansionist" (Schick, 1971, p. 38). Budgeters had one-year horizons, worked retrospectively to fund ongoing activities, experienced an environment of scarcity, and focused on costs; planners had multiyear perspectives, planned prospectively for change, worked in an environment of opportunity, and focused on benefits.

But the problems of Ur-Management were even more fundamental. Ur-Management gave a great deal of attention to deviations from the previous year's budget, but seldom analyzed the base itself—and the base was the major portion of the budget. This meant that after being initially approved, most expenditures continued year after year with little reconsideration. Moreover, Ur-Management was basically linear, incremental (or sometimes decremental), and additive. Next year's budget, or next year's plan, looked remarkably like that of the current year, except it was likely to ask for more.

Despite its weaknesses, Ur-Management was remarkably resilient, and for good reasons. Organizations are complex, administrative time and attention are limited, and understanding all the items in a budget, much less the relationship among the items, is an enormous (in fact, an impossible) task. Incremental budgeting made it possible for humans with limited rationality to make sense of their institutions' expenditures. In many ways, it is an extremely attractive technical and political approach to budgeting (Caruthers and Orwig, 1979). Consider its advantages. It is based on previous experience, permits attention to simple and solvable subproblems, permits budgeters to find acceptable solutions rather than demand they search for optimal ones, relies on history so every program need not be reviewed every year, and reduces the burden of calculations by considering only the alternatives feasible at a specific time. Moreover, the processes of bargaining and compromise that typify the Ur-Management increase agreement among the parties to the process, and they are repetitive, so budgeters become experienced and can predict consequences (Wildavsky, 1974). Ur-Management worked in higher education because it reflected in many ways the political processes of universities themselves.

But some policy analysts saw a major flaw. Ur-Management dealt with inputs rather than outputs. You could tell how much something cost, but that did not answer the question of whether it was worth it. That question—whether the costs of a program were worth the benefits—led to the adoption in education of new management techniques that had their intellectual roots in scientific management but far exceeded it in analytic sophistication.

The Second Revolution: The Triumph of Rationality

Prior to the end of World War II, there was not much research on higher education management, and "even in the postwar years little attention was paid to the need for efficient and effective management of the institution's resources. The pressure was on expansion, not on management efficiency" (Bogard, 1972, p. 7). But growth in size, complexity, and cost of higher education was accompanied by demands for greater accountability. The problem was that "traditional management techniques do not provide educational executives and administrators with a systematic and orderly method of analyzing policy and the means of implementing it, nor do these techniques, in most cases, offer rational criteria for weighing the range of available options and the resources each will require" (McManis and Parker, 1978, p. vi).

The solution was to follow the lead of business and the military by adopting new ways of assessing cost-effectiveness. There was a need to collect more information about more things, and the new availability of computers made it possible for the first time to manipulate immense quantities of data rapidly. The starting point was the development of management information systems (MIS), for without them, the data and information that top-level managers needed to plan, manage, evaluate, or make optimal decisions soundly would not be available.

Ur-Management was put on notice "to hasten the conversion of academic administration from folk to systems methods" (Cheit, 1977). Books with titles such as *The Managerial Revolution in Higher Education* (Rourke and Brooks, 1966), *Quantitative Approaches to Higher Education Management* (Lawrence and Service, 1977), *Implementing Management Information Systems in Colleges and Universities* (McManis and Parker, 1978), *Management Science: Applications to Academic Administration* (Wilson, 1981), and *Applying Corporate Management Strategies* (Fecher, 1985) documented the growth of the approach and encouraged its dissemination. Organizations such as the National Center for Higher Education Management Systems (NCHEMS) promoted the cause.

Of course, in order to use an MIS effectively, certain modest requirements had to be met. Institutional goals and objectives had to be clearly defined, measurable standards of performance set, ways of assessing alternatives developed, and a common database using agreed-on definitions constructed. It did not sound that difficult. Consider goals. If an institution wanted to assess its progress toward quantitatively assessing outcomes, all it had to do was to prepare "a limited number of goals that serve to define the broad and vague mission statements that are the rule in postsecondary education" (Lawrence and Service, 1977, p. 48). But could that be done? Responsible advocates of quantitative approaches acknowledged that "many higher education outcomes are simply not susceptible to description in quantitative terms." They cautioned against giving precedence to quantitative over qualitative data, or considering quantitative data more valid because it appeared to be more objective. They also mentioned there were no data to confirm that the quantitative approach led to better decisions or more effective management, because "no one has developed measures of 'decision quality' and then proceeded to evaluate quantitative management approaches on the basis of the impact of such measures" (Lawrence and Service, 1977, pp. 45, 65). They even went so far as to warn that "quantitative information cannot and should not replace any of these other sources or types of information—experience, intuition, judgment, and plain old gut-level feeling" (p. 68). But these warnings were often lost in the rush to embrace science and progress.

With an integrated data system and the ability to crunch the numbers it produced, effective decisions could finally be made. It would be possible for institutions to plan their own development consciously, to "relate means to ends, and to seek to obtain the maximum return from the university's resources" (Rourke and Brooks, 1966, pp. vi–vii). And this could happen, it was promised, without altering the basic nature of the academic enterprise. What occurred in many places, of course, was somewhat different. Managing information led to increased centralization of authority and increased uniformity in language and definitions; sometimes educational definitions or practices had to be altered because they could not be accommodated by the computer (Rourke and Brooks, 1966; Cheit, 1977). "Without really understanding the decision process, or knowing what information was required, we therefore began to collect and store massive amounts of data because the technology became available and it seemed like a reasonable approach" (Parden, 1978, p. 12).

Academic management was adopting the language of business and becoming more of a quantitatively driven enterprise. Academic leaders would join the search for the grail identified by managers in other organizations: an MIS system that could provide "exactly enough of the most relevant information at precisely the right moment to produce an infallible management decision—and, of course, at the least possible cost" (Spencer, 1978, p. 26). A summary of the state of the art in 1977 (Lawrence and Service, 1977) showed some progress already made. Common program classification structures had been created, with each program (instruction, research, and so on) capable of being further disaggregated. These common program classifications and common data elements could support program planning, accommodate many different kinds of institutional data, permit comparisons among institutions, and be linked to external data sources. By 1974, 26 percent of all institutions claimed to make extensive use of management information systems, 17 percent were extensively involved in program budgeting or Management by Objectives, and 36 percent were extensively analyzing institutional goals. Institutional projections for the next five years indicated that by 1980, 55 percent would be making extensive use of management information systems, 47 percent of program budgeting, and 63 percent of goals analysis (Lawrence and Service, 1977).

Sophisticated, complex, comprehensive computer-based planning models that attempted to model institutions or entire systems of institutions were soon available. We will not explore here the development and structure of the Resource Requirement Prediction Model (RRPM), System for Evaluating Alternative Resource Commitments in Higher Education (SEARCH), and Comprehensive Analytic Methods for Planning in University/College Systems (CAMPUS), among others (Lawrence and Service, 1977), but the alert administrator of the 1970s could hardly avoid hearing their advantages touted. The message was clear: if you did not adopt one of them, you were not doing your job. By 1978, 55 percent of administrators claimed to have used a computer model, and about the same percentage thought they were successful (Masland, 1983). As it turned out, the models did not have the predicted effect. They were too complicated to be operated, maintained, or understood; managers did not want them and did not use them. Budget decisions continued to be made for essentially the same political reasons.

But even if the systems did not work, they helped change the way people thought about their institutions. A college no longer needed to be considered as an organic whole—a place, an idea, an alma mater or nurturing mother. The new analytic systems made it possible for the first time to consider an institution as a collection of interchangeable parts. In theory, one could deconstruct the university, analyze and optimize each of its components, and then put it back together. Parts no longer considered necessary could be abandoned. Parts considered weak could be strengthened. Parts considered less related to mission could be subcontracted to other agencies.

Management Fads

The development of MIS and computer modeling paved the way for the management fads that are the subject of this book. Program budgeting and its progeny have been the symbols of education's Second Management Revolution, which began in approximately 1960 and continues to this day. This second revolution marks the ascendance of rationality in academic management.

I consider myself to be a rational person, and yet a major argument of this book is that rational approaches to academic management often have not been effective. How can I believe both things? The apparent discrepancy is due to different ways of defining the concept of rationality—one emphasizing action and the other emphasizing decision processes. In everyday language, to be rational is to be sensible—that is, to respond to problems using reason rather than emotion and superstition. A decision is rational when it leads to action that gets things done (Brunsson, 1982). Academic managers must exhibit action rationality if they are to be effective, because managers whose decisions lead to poor outcomes are properly seen by others as incompetent, if not foolish. It is in this ordinary sense of the ability to take effective action that I can think of myself as a rational person.

But a much different meaning of rationality is used in management and decision theory (and in this book) to refer to making decisions among alternatives through the use of formal models whose elements are related by logical consistency. There are many formal models of "decision rationality," but most of them share some or all of several characteristics: they are normative (this is how decisions *should* be made), they specify decision rules and the type of information system to be used, they attempt to measure the value of alternative outcomes to select the one with the maximum payoff, and they assume a hierarchical social structure (Friedland, 1974). Systems of this kind are considered rational as long as they are internally consistent, *even if they do not consider social norms or context, even if their elements are not consistent with external reality, and even if they do not lead to the desired outcomes.* Using this definition, it is possible to think of academic managers making a rational decision even if it does not lead to rational action and desired outcomes. It is possible that rational decision making in a complex environment may be *less* likely than irrational decision making to lead to rational action (Brunsson, 1982). It is this difference between decision rationality and action rationality that led March (1984) to comment that managers act more sensibly than they talk, and Wildavsky (1974) to explain the paradox that rational systems can be irrational.

The hallmarks of decision rationality in higher education management have included a commitment to cost-benefit analyses and the importance of measurement, a pro-innovation bias, and a neo-Darwinian belief that change and improvement are closely related (if not identical). The revolution marked the replacement of incremental, remedial views of higher education management with comprehensive, prescriptive approaches (Schmidtlein, 1974). The successive limited comparison mode of "muddling through" (Lindblom, 1959) was yielding to rational cost-benefit analyses made possible by the power and speed of the computer. This would not be remarkable if in fact the comprehensive analytic approach had been effective in other settings. But there was little evidence it was. As one observer commented, "After successive disasters of comprehensive planning in other areas in which it has been applied, it is somewhat peculiar to see these techniques optimistically and unselfcritically grasped in educational policy making, an area in which knowledge is even more inadequate and the system if anything even more complex" (Dresch, 1975, p. 249).

The decision to adopt or implement a new management technique may frequently be seen as an issue of technical neutrality and understood as surface politics, akin to other political processes through which interested groups or individuals attempt to expand or defend their power bases. But some proposed innovations may be more usefully understood as deep structure politics, which attempt to change perceptions of social reality (Frost and Egri, 1991). Management techniques that emphasize rationality at the expense of ritual, for example, use a technical process as a guise under which to try to change the cognitive frames and interpretations of what a college is and how it should behave.

The Perfect Management System

A perfect institutional management system would have mechanisms to ensure that institutions were operating legally, efficiently, and effectively. The perfect system would satisfy the interests of managers, those to whom the managers were responsible, and those who were subject to the system itself. Some of the many systems that have been developed in higher education have met some of these criteria. Some have met none. No system has met—or can meet—all, in part because the demands of legality, efficiency, and effectiveness may be mutually inconsistent and in part because the interests of the various groups participating in institutional management are often in conflict. Different systems serve different purposes. The acceptance of a specific management system is as much a political judgment about whose interests are to be served as it is a technical decision.

In the next three chapters we review the development of seven different management systems. The literature for this review was selected to include foundational works for each of seven techniques both in and outside higher education, repeatedly cited journal articles, conference presentations and fugitive materials identified through the ERIC database, and a sample of other references cited in these materials. The literature is skewed toward recency. The fact that I have written more extensively about some systems than others may not reflect their relative importance as much as it does the availability of writing about them. In 1960 higher education was not yet a legitimate field of scholarly inquiry. Aside from a handful of distinguished sociologists, economists, and political scientists, only a few people studied or wrote about higher education, and relatively few journals existed to publish work in the field. Today, more than fifty university programs offer doctorates in higher education and hundreds more offer master's degrees. The number of programs, the number of faculty members, the number of students, and the number of consultants have burgeoned, as have the number of journals created to disseminate the results of their research labors.

The fads are presented in chronological order so the reasons for their development, their use by higher education, and their outcomes can be seen sequentially and in social context. Each new management system has arisen from the perceived shortcomings of its predecessor. Even the Ur-Management system of line-item budgets and incremental planning, whose deficiencies led to the development of its successors, was in its time an innovation. The three older management innovations considered in Chapter Two are Planning Programming Budgeting System (PPBS), Zero-Base Budgeting (ZBB), and Management by Objectives (MBO). Chapter Three reviews two newer innovations: strategic planning and benchmarking. Finally, in Chapter Four we consider Total Quality

Management/Continuous Quality Improvement (TQM/CQI) and Business Process Reengineering (BPR).

My descriptions of the development of each fad and its infiltration into higher education are based primarily on the statements of contemporaneous observers whose assessments and claims are often in conflict. Their observations are important not because they are necessarily accurate (indeed, subsequent analyses demonstrate that many were quite wide of the mark), but because they reflect the rhetoric used at the time. I do not necessarily share their sometimes unflattering assessments of academic institutions or their managers.

It is often easy to identify the year in which a fad starts. Determining the year it ends is more difficult, because references to it may linger in the literature years after the fad itself has expired. Occasionally there will be an authoritative article or book that claims the fad is dead. Sometimes the setting of a date is a matter of judgment. The dates I cite in the following chapters are therefore somewhat arbitrary but not capricious.

Now attend to the Bestiary of Academic Fads that awaits you.

2

We're from the Government, and We're Here to Help

We begin with three academic management fads that were important in higher education during the period 1960–1985. In addition to the many similarities in their evolution, these fads are also noteworthy because of their sponsorship. Each one was championed by an incumbent president of the United States. Of course, the fads might have been widely adopted even in the absence of public presidential support. But the imprimatur of the leader of the free world ensured that the fads would be disseminated and at least some public organizations would be legally forced to adopt them.

Planning Programming Budgeting System: More Bang for the Buck (1960–1974)

It all started with the cold war. The federal government needed to analyze the costs and benefits of military weapons. Traditional budgeting could calculate how much it would cost to add an infantry division, but it could not help decide whether the nation would be better off spending those dollars on new bombers or on intercontinental ballistic missiles. Which alternative would provide more bang for the buck?

Development of PPBS

The Rand Corporation, using new economic theories and the data-crunching power of the computer, proposed an answer (Caruthers and Orwig, 1979). It was called Planning Programming Budgeting System (PPBS), and it promised a "comparison of all the relevant alternatives from the point of view of the objectives each can accomplish and the selection of the best (or a good) alternative through the use of appropriate economic criteria" (Hitch and McKean, 1960, p. 118). Robert McNamara, the secretary of defense first appointed by John F. Kennedy, was so impressed with the Rand analysis that in 1961 he hired one of its creators, Charles Hitch, to implement PPBS in the Department of Defense.

Very little is known about how well this new system actually worked in the Department of Defense, but government publicity created the image of considerable management success (Schick, 1971). President Lyndon B. Johnson called PPBS "a very new and very revolutionary system" (Gross, 1969, p. 114), and in 1965 he issued an executive order requiring its use by all federal agencies. So it was that a highly publicized but nonvalidated management system, developed for a specific purpose in the Defense Department, was imposed on other government systems for other purposes.

Each of the letters in PPBS had significance. The first P stood for Planning: the identification of long-range objectives over a period of five to ten years and the assessment of the costs and benefits of alternative means of achieving those objectives. The second P was Programming: taking the alternative with the best cost-benefit ratio and deciding exactly how it should be implemented over the intermediate term of perhaps one to five years. The B was for Budgeting: the process by which financial plans would be made over a short one-year period in order to support the program. And finally, the S reinforced the notion that planning, programming, and budgeting were not discrete activities but part of an integrated System.

PPBS required the identification and classification of all activities into discrete programs, the preparation of detailed narratives with a multiyear time frame, and quantitative evaluation of alternative proposals (Wanat, 1978, p. 99). Managers had to identify the costs of inputs, specify desired outputs, and analyze the effects of applying those inputs to get the desired outputs as well as the alternative ways in which those outputs could be achieved (Gross, 1969). This rational process allowed a manager to assess the costs and benefits of alternative programs so the one with the most favorable cost-benefit ratio could be selected. The concept was brilliantly sensible: analyze your goals, compare the costs and benefits of various ways of achieving them, and choose the most effective alternative. What could be more reasonable?

President Johnson made extraordinary claims for the new system. Program budgeting, he said, would enable the government to "(1) identify our national goals with precision and on a continuing basis, (2) choose among those goals the ones that are most urgent, (3) search for alternative means of reaching those goals most effectively at the least cost, (4) inform ourselves not merely on next year's costs but on the second, and third, and subsequent years' costs of our programs, (5) measure the performance of our programs to insure a dollar's worth of service for each dollar spent" (Schick, 1971, p. 1). The notion that national goals could be determined by analysis rather than by politics was breathtaking, particularly when proposed by a master politician. PPBS technology seemed to offer the promise of transforming politics from an art to a science.

Two years later, Johnson, without presenting any evidence, reiterated his support for "this system—which proved its worth many times over in the Defense Department" and which would now "bring to each department and agency the most advanced techniques of modern business management" (Gross, 1969, p. 114). The system, said the president, would correct a number of deficiencies in existing budgeting systems, including their failure to define objectives clearly, propose alternatives, provide sufficient time for review by upper levels, specify accomplishments, consider future-year costs, and use formalized planning and systems analysis (Hartley, 1968).

The claims were bold. But in 1968 a study by the Bureau of the Budget found that planning, programming, and budgetary functions were not being performed any differently in federal agencies after the implementation of PPBS than before. "Observers of the budgeting process agree that PPB[S] has had limited influence on major resource allocation decisions," primarily because it did not give attention to the political processes that had characterized budgeting and planning in the past (Harper, Kramer, and Rouse, 1980, p. 101). Whether PPBS was successful in the Department of Defense was debatable; whether it could be effectively implemented in civilian agencies with less centralized command and control structures was another matter altogether (Balderston and Weathersby, 1972). Nevertheless, PPBS spread rapidly under the presidential imprimatur, and by 1969 it was reported in wide use in the federal government. It was also formally adopted by over half of state governments, which then imposed it on all state agencies, including higher education (Balderston and Weathersby, 1972).

Interest in the new system started to recede by mid-1970 (Schick, 1971) as presumed successes in the Department of Defense were not seen in other agencies, "where quantification and program analysis proved more elusive" (Freeman, 1978, p. 38). PPBS was essentially abandoned by the U.S. government in 1971 (Caruthers and Orwig, 1979, p. 28). In 1973 federal agencies were no longer required to submit their budgets in PPBS format, a tacit recognition that the costs of the process exceeded the benefits (Balderston and Weathersby, 1972). By 1974 PPBS in the government was dead.

PPBS in Higher Education

One part of PPBS that seemed to work was the publicity campaign supporting it. If it was good enough for the president, it was good enough for higher education. Because of recurrent crises of confi-

dence, relevance, and finance, as well as the pressure to demonstrate accountability, trustees and state governments started to give
greater attention to higher education management (Balderston and
Weathersby, 1972), and many saw PPBS as the answer to their problems. Since advocates could present no evidence that PPBS actually worked, they instead argued it should be implemented because
no one had discredited PPBS with evidence that it did *not* work.
The higher education community, they said, "has little choice except to explore PPBS and similar planning systems, or lose their
credibility as legitimate managers of a vital social function" (Farmer, 1970, pp. 5–6).

The American Council on Education (ACE) published a book
(Williams, 1966) suggesting that the Defense Department's publicized success could be transferred to higher education. The Ford
Foundation supported PPBS-related research and development activities at several prestigious institutions in 1968 (National Association
of College and University Business Officers, 1975), and in 1969 the
U.S. Office of Education (USOE) funded a multistate interinsti-
tutional PPBS developmental program. The USOE program later
became the National Center for Higher Education Management Systems (NCHEMS), a major champion for the use of PPBS in higher
education (Balderston and Weathersby, 1972). By 1972, 31 percent
of colleges and universities of all sizes, types of control, and degree
level claimed they were using some form of PPBS (Bogard, 1972).
In 1975, four years after the federal government had essentially terminated its PPBS support, the National Association of College and
University Business Officers (NACUBO) published a handbook
incorporating PPBS principles (National Association of College and
University Business Officers, 1975).

How could PPBS be adapted to higher education? The foreword
to an explanatory booklet advocating the use of PPBS to the higher
education community acknowledged that "its advantages are not
casually obvious. One must struggle with its concepts until they are
understood. All too frequently these fundamental concepts of PPBS

have been buried in systems lingo and computer jargon" (Farmer, 1970, p. iii). The booklet noted that PPBS would require a significant commitment of already stretched financial and personnel resources, and many current users were not satisfied with it. It also recognized that certain characteristics of higher education made the application of PPBS problematic, in particular the difficulty in identifying outputs, the fact that no single organizational unit produces any specific output, and the reality that the production functions of higher education are unknown. PPBS, an exercise emphasizing cost-benefit analysis, was being touted even as it was being recognized as having high costs and uncertain returns!

Some educators warned that PPBS could "lead in the direction of economically optimal, yet potentially educationally unsound courses of action" (Thompson, 1971, p. 690). Those familiar with higher education recognized that the imposition of a complex system such as PPBS could cause organizational and governance problems as well. It could diminish faculty voice in governance, polarize decision making, increase administrative workload, require more specialized staff, and increase the potential politicization of educational program issues in state legislatures and central coordinating offices (Peterson, 1971).

But the cautions went largely unheeded. PPBS was hailed as a framework for "intelligent planning which is a substantial improvement over conventional educational planning procedures," and educators were assured "the conceptual simplicity of . . . PPBS is such that it can be applied, with judicious concern, to nearly any type of human organization" (Hartley, 1968, p. iii). The same conclusion was reiterated four years later in a report issued by the Carnegie Commission on Higher Education (Bogard, 1972, p. 28). Many institutions were swept along. While some colleges and universities were adopting PPBS because of state mandates, others voluntarily adopted it to improve their own administrations and "reverse the decline in public confidence and the ever-deepening fiscal crisis for higher education" (Caruthers and Orwig, 1979, p. 46).

The Ohio Board of Regents' efforts to establish a statewide PPBS program illustrated both the promise and the problems. Ohio's extensive planning documents recognized the difficulty of the task, but argued they could be overcome with dedication and hard work. "One should not be discouraged," they said, "if initial attempts to develop and agree upon goals and objectives are less than satisfactory. Through repeated efforts, coupled with an educational program, the goals and objectives will become more useful and meaningful" (Ohio Board of Regents, 1973b, p. 23). Measuring inputs was (relatively) easy, but outputs were problematic. PPBS required that outputs be measured (Peterson, 1971), and the Ohio Regents recognized that their outputs included such ephemeral things as an "educated person" and "social justice." Since they could not measure these, they settled for student credit hours and degrees earned as proxies.

Then there were the data. "Anyone attempting to compile all of the data desirable for program budgeting faces a nearly impossible task," agreed the Regents, citing major problems related to measuring real outputs, benefits, or added value, among others. And finally there were the programs themselves, "a group of coordinated activities" that were to be developed by analyzing alternative courses, technologies, admissions and related programs, and other elements (Ohio Board of Regents, 1973b, p. 34). But what really was a program? Experts defined a program as "a package which encompasses each and every one of the agency's efforts to achieve a particular objective or set of allied objectives" (Greenhouse, 1966, p. 273), so programs were to be stated in terms of objectives and outcomes— for example, "student intellectual development." But most institutions instead defined them within existing institutional structures (Balderston and Weathersby, 1972). The systemwide program in Ohio, for example (Ohio Board of Regents, 1973b), made planning units coterminous with budget units such as departments—a sensible economic decision perhaps, but one inconsistent with the basic philosophy of program budgeting.

Higher education continued to adopt PPBS in the late 1960s, but enthusiasm frequently was greater among the legislatures and state coordinating boards that mandated the program than in the institutions required to implement it. Often the imposition came without planning, resources, or warning; in 1971, for example, all agencies in one state were given fifteen days' notice to revise two years of historic budget data and prepare five years of projected budgets in PPBS format (Thompson, 1971).

Institutions that began using PPBS soon found that "program budgeting was far more costly in time, effort and money than had been expected. Even at the University of California, which spent enormous time, energy, and dedicated talent on designing and implementing a comprehensive PPB[S] system, the administration concluded reluctantly that PPBS had not really been very effective in achieving the objectives for which it was designed" (Freeman, 1978, p. 39). The supreme irony of California's rejection was that Charles Hitch, the original developer and champion of PPBS, by then had become the president of the University of California system.

Whatever Happened to PPBS?

PPBS was initiated in "a burst of grandiose claims of breakthroughs" (Gross, 1969, p. 115). Many institutions claimed to be using PPBS, but subsequent analysis indicated that implementation was in name only. "Some ten years after program budgeting was implemented on the federal level, virtually no institutions of higher education have viable program budgets. There is little evidence that full program budgeting can be implemented in the next few years" (Farmer, 1970, p. 6). Two years later, a study of PPBS found that no institution had implemented PPBS in a comprehensive way (Balderston and Weathersby, 1972). Early reports that half of all university libraries in 1971 were using PPBS were proved false in 1976 when a study found that none of them had actually implemented anything even close to PPBS, and libraries, "with their usual sense for ill-timing, were jumping on the PPBS bandwagon just as it was leaving town" (Koenig and Alperin, 1985, p. 27).

"Like other major innovations," said Wildavsky (1974, p. 182), "PPBS took on the status of a fad. Everywhere PPBS was praised; everywhere it ran into serious difficulties." PPBS was an example of the "confusion that new techniques are bringing to college and university administrators. The confusion arises not only from the inexperience of planners, but also because the technical experts advocating the system use the term with different meanings" (Harvey, 1971, p. 3). PPBS was expensive, programs were unclear, and assessing alternatives too easily turned into management game playing.

PPBS was the opening salvo in the revolution of rationality. By the mid-1970s PPBS was in retreat in higher education, as "study after study documented the pitfalls of introducing overly ambitious, rigid, centralized analytic formats into diverse, loosely coupled, decentralized, academic administrative settings" (Backoff and Mitnick, 1981, pp. 73–74). In California, the same legislature that in 1966 initiated the PPBS movement in public education as a technical issue to be handled by accountants abandoned it in 1972 when it became clear that input-output analyses and production functions could not be applied to education (Kirst, 1975). Financial considerations also played a role. As one economic researcher said, "The striking characteristic about all these PPB[S] systems is their unbelievable complexity, the attention to the minutiae of budgetary classifications, and their costliness" (Kirst, 1975, p. 538).

Many reasons for the failure of PPBS were offered, ranging from administrative foot dragging to technical issues of theory and data. The definition of PPBS itself was "a source of disagreement and confusion" (Gross, 1969, p. 115). Some thought it was a revolutionary development in management, others said it was not much different from what they had always done, and a third group saw it as part of a continual evolution of budget reforms (Schick, 1980). PPBS was difficult to accept because it was antiorganizational, operating at cross-purposes to the existing organizational structures and constantly forcing the institution to question its own purposes and existence (Schick, 1980). In higher education, as elsewhere, there were serious problems related to the lack of quantifiable objectives and the difficulty in assigning either costs or benefits to programs with multiple and joint processes (Balderston, 1974). But the real reason for failure was most effectively captured by Wildavsky (1974): "No one knows how to do program budgeting. . . . Program budgeting cannot be stated in operational terms. . . . Failure is built into its very nature because it requires the ability to perform cognitive operations that are beyond present human (or mechanical) capacities. PPBS sacrifices the rationality of ends to the rationality of means; that is why seemingly rational procedures produce irrational results" (pp. 201–207). "Basically, the concept was a success," said one observer, even though "as an application . . . PPBS was a failure" (Newton, 1976). PPBS's epitaph was memorialized in Wildavsky's comment (1974, pp. 200, 205) that "I have not been able to find a single example of successful implementation of PPBS. . . . PPBS has failed everywhere and at all times."

In retrospect, the difficulty of successfully applying PPBS to higher education was obvious to anyone who knew anything about how colleges work. Program budgeting required an incredible degree of integration. Department planning had to be merged into college planning, to be merged into institutional planning, and finally to be merged into statewide planning. All goals of the comprehensive system had to be clearly defined and divisible into objectives. Objectives had to be measurable or observable, and they had to specify the criteria by which they would be evaluated and the measurement method used. And analysis had to be exhaustive, because "to require that every expenditure in the budget produce a benefit which is worth its cost, it is necessary to view both the benefits and the cost of each budget item in comparison to the benefits and costs of other possible ways to utilize the same resources. An ideal budget is one that produces more valuable results than would be achieved if resources were allocated in any other way" (Ohio Board of Regents, 1973a, p. 37). It was a glorious ideal, but one doomed to failure in both government and higher education, and for the same reason: it was inconsistent with the necessary politics of budgeting.

Although PPBS failed as a system, some still believed that its implementation had had positive consequences for higher education, and "the influence of PPBS as a way of looking at management problems . . . has been far greater than its influence as a formal structure for decision making" (Freeman, 1978, p. 40). PPBS led institutions to begin thinking about programs as well as about structures, focus more attention on goals and objectives, and legitimate the concepts of comprehensive planning and quantitative analysis. As Freeman put it in 1978 (p. 42), "Although PPBS may be dead, its spirit lives on."

Management by Objectives: The Illusion of Empowerment (1965–1980)

In 1954, Peter Drucker suggested that complex organizations were too large to be managed by controlling their activities. Instead, they should be managed by controlling results. His concept of "management by objectives and self-control" (p. 119) was that managers should create their unit's objectives within the context of the objectives of the units above them and the goals of the organization itself, and should receive enough data to enable them to measure progress toward their objectives.

Development of MBO

The concept of objectives was elaborated in *Management by Objectives: A System of Managerial Leadership* (Odiorne, 1965), which gave the movement its name and marked its formal introduction into the world of business. Management by Objectives (MBO) is based on a simple idea: "manage with long-term objectives clearly in mind, and state them frequently to keep people aware of them.

Each objective should have a deadline; when the deadline comes, the organization assesses to see if the objective was achieved and, if not, why not" (Robbins and Finley, 1996, p. 146).

MBO was proclaimed as "the single most successful concept ever to have been picked up and put into practice in all of management history" (Barrett, 1973, p. 79). Although there was no real evidence that it was successful, advocates argued that because MBO was in use around the world and in major corporations, including GM, RCA, and General Foods, "there must be something to it" (Reddin, 1970, p. 12). From the beginning, MBO was somewhat undefined. Different practitioners proposed various ways of doing it. "To hear some talk, MBO is primarily an attitude, a state of mind, a philosophy. To hear others, MBO is primarily a matter of filling out forms or meeting deadlines. Still others seem to imply MBO is limited to a new appraisal system, an executive development program, or a modern compensation scheme. Actually MBO is all of these" (Deegan and Fritz, 1975, p. 15).

MBO viewed organizations as a hierarchy of goals. Based on goals established by their superiors, managers formulated subgoals for their subordinates, who used them as the basis for formulating objectives for those further down the line. The notion that effective managers must act with reference to organizational goals was not a unique contribution to management theory. What made MBO different from just "good management" was the "assumption that certain formal mechanisms . . . can improve managerial performance" (DeFee, 1977, p. 39). MBO was based on the premises that organizational goals could be made concrete, organization processes were stable and predictable, the organization could deal openly with conflict over goals, and managers were willing and able to take risks and make trade-offs. Successful implementation depended on strong support from the top to integrate MBO into budgeting and reward systems (DeFee, 1977).

MBO had both macro and micro aspects. At the macrolevel, it was an integrated management system in which goals defined at the highest level were further refined and used to drive the plans of those at lower levels. At the microlevel, it was a process in which subordinates had regular meetings with their superiors to negotiate the objectives to be undertaken by the subordinate in support of the unit's goals, and later to assess progress toward those objectives. Subordinates were not expected merely to carry out directives from above, but were to be partners with their superiors in designing how mutually agreed-on objectives should be best pursued. In MBO, "manager and subordinate sit down at the beginning of each period and talk until agreement upon job goals are reached. During the period, the subordinate is given wide latitude in choice of method. At the end of the period the actual results are jointly reviewed against agreed upon goals and an assessment of the degree of success made. The process is begun again" (Odiorne, 1971, p. 14). It is this continuing process of negotiation that allowed the advocates of MBO to advertise the process as empowering subordinates, because objectives would have to be mutually approved before they could become part of a subordinate's responsibilities.

MBO was a total system of management, encompassing planning, appraising, and motivating (Deegan and Fritz, 1975). It focused management's attention on purpose, reduced discrepancies in expectations of superiors and subordinates, clarified responsibilities, improved overall performance, enhanced opportunities for participation, and improved communications (Deegan and Fritz, 1975; Lasher, 1978). MBO was concerned only with improving performance: "MBO is not concerned about the past. It is not concerned about the present. MBO is concerned about tomorrow, whether tomorrow be next week, next month, next year, or ten years hence" (Barrett, 1973, p. 66). The focus was not on activities but on outcomes. As the flyleaf of one book asserted, "When you put its simple but astonishingly effective guidelines for management-action to work for you, you can't help but attain a new high level of effectiveness and accomplishment" (Reddin, 1970).

MBO was used by several government agencies as early as 1970, but it was not until 1973 that an attempt was made to establish it on a systemwide basis. Just as PPBS was promoted by President

Johnson, MBO found a presidential sponsor in Richard Nixon. Facing continuing criticisms of management deficiencies in government, the Nixon administration wanted to get a handle on federal programs and better coordinate the work of the White House and federal agencies (Rose, 1980). Nixon's corporate advisers suggested MBO as the remedy, and they were clearly less concerned with empowerment than with control. "The attitude of the Nixon top management was one of low trust and contempt toward civil servants. Control and dominance of the system became particularly central concerns during his second term" (Sherwood and Page, 1976, p. 7).

Governmental directives identified MBO as "the answer to your managerial problems. MBO would produce better strategies, higher quality decisions, less red tape, enhanced motivation, and a better ability to control things by the governmental executive" (Sherwood and Page, 1976, p. 5). To be acceptable to the White House, agency MBO programs had to respond to issues important to the president and had to include a means of determining whether objectives had been achieved. No additional financial or legislative resources could be required (Rose, 1980). The federal Office of Management and Budget (OMB) initiated the MBO cycle by asking the agencies to develop their lists of objectives. The theory was that OMB would hold quarterly meetings with the agencies, the agencies were expected to hold regular internal management conferences to prepare for these meetings, and managers were to ensure that the agreed-on milestones had been met. In practice, the objectives that the agencies set were so noncontroversial that OMB lost interest in attending the meetings, leading managers to lose interest in their internal sessions (Rose, 1980).

Whether MBO was not effective because "the Federal bureaucracy 'spit it up' as it had PPBS before it" (Harvey, 1977, p. 39) or whether it did not have continued support from the top is unclear. But by 1976 the government had essentially given up, and there was "a noticeable disenchantment with MBO as a panacea" (Sherwood and Page, 1976, p. 11). Its failure in government led to some reconsideration of the practice in business as well. On further examination, it turned out that many firms claiming to use MBO really were not doing so, and "by far the majority of attempts [to implement MBO in business] end in what must be called failure" (Reddin, 1970, p. 121). Among the reasons cited for failure were a lack of commitment, lack of involvement of top managers, and poor implementation methods.

Advocates called MBO the most widely practiced systematic management system in current use (Barrett, 1973; Eddy and De-Cosmo, 1977). But in 1974, a survey of Fortune 500 companies indicated that only 120 had ever tried MBO, and of those, only 10 thought they had been highly successful. Anecdotal stories of dysfunctional and countermotivational applications of MBO were appearing as early as 1970. "Just as disappointing as the limited coverage of MBO has been its superficial effects on organizational climates," said West (1977, p. 33) in his analysis of why MBO failed.

MBO in Higher Education

One of the first references to MBO in higher education was by the president of a public two-year college. MBO, he said, required the development of job descriptions, expression of performance objectives by subordinates, negotiation and agreement with superiors, continuing appraisal of progress, and establishment of new objectives. His very own college was in the second year of MBO implementation, which was "yielding positive results" (Lahti, 1971, p. 31).

Lahti's 1973 book, *Innovative College Management*, touting the value of MBO, was subtitled "Implementing Proven Organizational Practice," suggesting that MBO had been successfully implemented in other settings. Higher education, said Lahti, was suffering from a crisis in public confidence that could be corrected only by reforming its failed management systems. MBO was given a further impetus in higher education with the publication of a workbook, *MBO Goes to College* (Deegan and Fritz, 1975). Written by two management consultants who previously had been academics, the book argued that the "national scandal of rising educational costs" (p. 5) was due primarily to poor management. The book provided step-by-step instructions to correct the situation. First, an institution had to clarify and obtain agreement on its ultimate purposes as reflected in its charter, mission, and philosophy (for example, "the development of the student as an individual"). Then multiyear statements of institutional goals or objectives consistent with the clarified purpose were to be developed (for example, "Implement a tutorial program for students requiring academic support"). Based on this list, a statement of objectives for the coming year would be prepared quantifying the outcomes to be achieved and the indicators of success to be used (for example, "Freshman retention at the end of the year will be improved 10 percent from last year"). The process to this point was the primary responsibility of the president, in consultation with trustees and senior staff. Once the annual goals and objectives had been approved, department heads worked with their staffs to formulate their own goals and indicate how they would support the goals at the institutional level. Each goal had to identify the specific program to be changed, a way of measuring the change, and the specific amount of change desired in the time period specified (Deegan and Fritz, 1975). If it could not be measured, it could not be part of MBO.

The involvement of higher education in MBO increased rapidly. "Prior to 1970 there were possibly half a dozen colleges which had tried anything like MBO in a formal manner. From 1970 to 1975, as management consultants, university continuing education programs, professional administration associations, the Department of Health, Education and Welfare and others encouraged the spread of this system of management, many colleges have sought to follow suit." As a consequence, "it is hardly possible [in 1975] to attend any management conference without hearing some reference to Management by Objectives" (Deegan and Fritz, 1975, pp. 8, 15).

MBO was seen as being useful in all organizational settings (Odiorne, 1971), although those who supported its use in the academy knew the task might not be easy. On the plus side, "Academe and

MBO appear to be quite compatible" (Lasher, 1978, p. 107). MBO was said to be particularly useful for academic institutions because it was based on a belief in participative management (Deegan and Fritz, 1975; Cigler, 1979) and led to "more democratic participation, less superordinate-subordinate gap and more shared authority" (Njoku, 1977, p. 209). Its supporters claimed that it would facilitate participative management, focus on outputs and goals rather than day-to-day operations, coordinate the activities of the organization, strengthen faculty-administrative relationships, and reinforce management effectiveness goals.

There were potential costs as well. MBO required significant commitments of staff time and energy, it was difficult to write performance objectives, it created snowstorms of paperwork, quantitative goals could overwhelm quality goals, and many administrators lacked the requisite management skills to implement it (Lahti, 1973; Chronister, 1974; DeFee, 1977). Some thought MBO might be particularly difficult to implement in higher education because of "the fervent attachment of the persons employed there to activities" (Odiorne, 1971, p. 15) rather than to outcomes. And MBO was a top-down system whose hierarchical structure could be incompatible with traditional academic culture (Lahti, 1973, p. 57).

There was almost no research evidence about the effectiveness of MBO. Lacking data, advocates relied instead on rhetoric describing MBO as a "proven concept which has already realized considerable success in business and industry" (Njoku, 1977, p. 200). MBO's use and success in business and government proved later to be exaggerated, as did reports of its use in higher education. Only a handful of institutions ever totally implemented MBO—the University of Tennessee claimed in 1973 to be the only one to have done so at that time (Temple, 1973). But there is no way of knowing either the actual extent of adoption or the impact on institutions with any certainty. Among other problems, there were few well-designed studies, and most "research" was based on interviews with administrators. A handful of studies suggested that MBO had marginal effects in some institutions (Baldridge, 1979; Shetty and Carlisle, 1975). One researcher who tried to construct a study of the effectiveness of MBO in small colleges gave up after discovering that "what was being called 'MBO' was not MBO at all" (Cigler, 1979).

Although there was little evidence of success, the academic allure of MBO continued. MBO might not be easy, but the rewards after, say, two years, would be great. Once "unrestricted communication occurs, meaningful performance-improvement sessions between administrators and faculty and other administrators occur, and a reward system is fair and equitable, one can expect personal commitment to organizational and individual goals to increase and long-run improved performance to result" (Lasher, 1978, p. 111). In 1979, long after business and government had thrown in the towel, educators were still calling MBO "a widely used tool both in the private and public sectors" (Cigler, 1979, p. 1), which, when "done properly," could provide many advantages to organizations employing it.

Whatever Happened to MBO?

It is difficult to state authoritatively why MBO died because there were few serious attempts to study the phenomenon or its demise. Apologists offered mostly tautologies. For example, there were really *two* versions of MBO: "good MBO," which helped an institution to be accountable and solve problems of ambiguity and uncertainty of purpose, and "bad MBO," which emphasized cost analysis and ignored human needs (Eddy and DeCosmo, 1977, p. 79). When MBO failed, it was due to defects in design and implementation rather than flaws in the basic idea itself (Cigler, 1979). The problem was not with the system but with those who abused the system through malpractice and failure to accept participative decision making (Deegan and Fritz, 1975).

A more realistic appraisal suggests that MBO foundered in part because its assumptions of a hierarchy of mutually acceptable goals did not accurately reflect how the complex social systems in which it was tried actually worked. In the political environment of higher education, it was difficult to define goals in operational terms and virtually impossible for institutions to reach consensus on them. The same issue bedeviled MBO in government, where "there are no commonly accepted standards for monitoring performance or measuring achievement of many public objectives," and where there were many political advantages to keeping things fuzzy (Sherwood and Page, 1976, p. 9).

Perhaps even more important, the claim of subordinate empowerment was in many cases hypocritical. MBO was supposed to make superiors and subordinates collaborators. Instead, "The typical MBO effort perpetuates and intensifies hostility, resentment and distrust between a manager and subordinates. Obviously, somewhere between the concept of MBO and its implementation, something has gone seriously wrong" (Levinson, 1970, p. 125). Rather than increasing freedom, MBO could be used to tyrannize. "A system which places so much emphasis on planning, goal setting, the designation of objectives, and quantitative evaluation can distort and even subvert the expressed humanistic goals of the organization" (Saurman and Nash, 1975, p. 179). While theoretically everyone could participate in MBO, folks at the top of the organization participated more equally than others, and not all managers were able to accept a participative philosophy (Raia, 1965). The promise of shared decision making conveniently overlooked the natural power imbalance between the parties, and "although proclaimed as a participative process, government-wide MBO should be more properly identified as a strategy for hierarchical control. Proposals were made from the lower to higher echelons, but it was up to the boss to decide" (Sherwood and Page, 1976, p. 7).

So MBO did not work. It was "used as a public relations gimmick with little or no impact on the organization itself" (Saurman and Nash, 1975, p. 184). When MBO finally ended, the only legacy of this widely acclaimed innovation in government was a "piecemeal form of decentralized management teams in the agencies"

(Rose, 1980, p. 110). The death of MBO in higher education is undocumented, but references in the literature peak between 1975 and 1980 and virtually disappear by 1985.

Zero-Base Budgeting: Denying History (1970–1985)

In 1970, Peter Pyhrr described a process through which Texas Instruments was making resource allocation decisions and having "a considerable measure of success." The new process was based on a form of analysis called "zero-base budgeting," commonly referred to later by its initials, ZBB. The technique was "simple in principle and easy to apply" (Pyhrr, 1970, p. 111).

ZBB, like PPBS, emphasized analyzing inputs and outputs of specific programs. ZBB divided a company into discrete activities and required managers to put activities and alternate ways of implementing them into rank order based on cost-benefit analyses. Resources were then allocated according to the rankings. Unlike the Ur-System, which assumed continuation of the base, ZBB assumed that the starting point for each budget was zero. Budgets of the past inevitably had built-in fat related to tradition and history. Programs once started became part of the "base" and were likely to remain even after they were no longer needed. ZBB responded to that reality. Every program, new or old, had to justify both its existence and "each and every expenditure" each year (Harvey, 1977, p. 4). "ZBB can then be defined as a part of the budgeting process which starts from a zero base, disregarding previous years' budgets, and leads to the definition and selection of the most efficient and effective activities and expenditures consistent with meeting the institution's goals and objectives" (Harvey, 1977, p. 5).

Development of ZBB

ZBB started out as "an approach, not a fixed procedure or set of forms to be applied uniformly from one organization to the next" (Pyhrr, 1977, p. 2). As interest in the idea grew, different people defined it in different ways and constructed products designed to implement it. As a consequence, "There are as many definitions of zero-base budgeting as there are articles and books written on the subject" (Connors, Franklin, and Kaskey, 1978). Some of the products were structured and elaborate. But the very elaboration may have obfuscated more than clarified. One observer commented, "I was specifically asked what was so unique about zero-base budgeting that it couldn't be accomplished by a strong dose of good old-fashioned tough-minded management. My answer is . . . reduced to its essentials, nothing" (Cheek, 1979, p. 156).

Jimmy Carter, the governor of Georgia, was impressed by Pyhrr's article on MBO in the *Harvard Business Review*, and he invited Pyhrr to join his staff (Anthony, 1977). Carter became a ZBB convert. In his 1971 budget message to the Georgia General Assembly, he said, "No longer can we take for granted the existing budget base and simply be responsible for reviewing proposed increases to continue programs and add new ones. . . . I will insist that the entire range of State services be re-examined and will cut back or eliminate established programs if they are judged to be ineffective or of low priority" (Lauth, 1980, p. 115).

Carter was confident ZBB was working, and advocates (Pyhrr, 1977) insisted the program had led to major reallocation of resources in Georgia and elsewhere. A study of actual budgeting practices in Georgia in 1977 disagreed. None of the agency heads interviewed indicated that ZBB had led them to reevaluate every program every year. In fact, ZBB as actually implemented was not much different from the old incremental budgeting approach it replaced, with the "base" in ZBB turning out to be the historic base rather than the zero base. A study done after three years of implementation in Georgia found that no shift of resources could be attributed to it, and not a single instance could be identified in which a function received less funding than in the previous fiscal year (Lauth, 1980). The failed implementation of ZBB in Georgia might have sunk into obscurity had not Governor Carter subsequently been elected president of the United States.

Carter's presidential campaign pledged to zero-base the federal budget (Hammond and Knott, 1980, p. 72). Even before his inauguration, Carter was promising to replicate Georgia's "success" on a national scale through an executive order requiring ZBB in all federal departments. One justification for his position was that implementation of ZBB in Georgia had resulted in major benefits to taxpayers. Another was that "some 500 businesses and a dozen state governments are now utilizing the concept" (Carter, 1977, p. 25). The claims of wide and successful use, though unsubstantiated, helped to promote the idea, and ZBB took on a life of its own. Zero-base budgeting was "rapidly becoming a highly prestigious term" (Anthony, 1977, p. 26). And why not? It "is the most popular budget reform of the decade" (Hammond and Knott, 1980, p. ix). "Since it scored several impressive successes in state and local government as well as in the private sector, interest in applying zero-base budgeting at the federal level has grown" (Cheek, 1979, p. 253).

It was difficult to argue against the principles of ZBB. They seemed so obvious. "What could be wrong with specifying objectives, grouping activities together, setting priorities on programs, and then funding only the most important? If we were to *define* rationality in budgeting, we would come up with something like these procedures. Indeed, it might be said that such procedures *embody* the concept of rationality in government" (Hammond and Knott, 1980, p. 9). From Carter's perspective, any naysayers were "bureaucrats who thrived on confusion, . . . special interests that preferred to work in the dark, . . . and a few legislative leaders who did not want to see their fiefdoms endangered" (Carter, 1977, p. 25).

Could ZBB succeed in the 1970s when PPBS failed in the 1960s? Some advocates said it could because ZBB had the advantage of having been tried in state governments before being implemented in the federal government (Hammond and Knott, 1980). But others argued that the claims of success in the states were bogus. An article in the *Wall Street Journal* proclaimed, "Zero base budgeting is a fraud." The original claims of success at Texas Instruments were based on the use of ZBB in only a fraction of their activities, and the "judgment that the system was a great success was entirely the author's and based on a single year's experience" (Anthony, 1977, p. 26). Moreover, when it was applied in Georgia, ZBB never built a budget from scratch as claimed. Instead, a tacit agreement was reached that the first 80 percent of department requests would not be examined closely. Zero base immediately became 80 percent base, and the system started to look incremental in nature. And finally, the system itself did not lead to large shifts in resource allocation, and the ranking procedures were unmanageable. About Carter's claim that ZBB led to improved government efficiency in Georgia? "Compared to the antiquated budget process which Georgia had at the time," opined Anthony (1977, p. 26), "zero-base budgeting was probably an improvement—almost any change would have been."

Perhaps of even greater importance was that ZBB was introduced in Georgia at the same time the state passed the 1972 Executive Reorganization Act, and even Carter admitted the act was the primary factor influencing resource reallocation in the state (Hammond and Knott, 1980). When all was said and done, "There has not been a single verifiable instance where the new budgeting system has caused a shifting of financial resources other than during reorganization" (Minimer, 1975, p. 157).

In the federal government, some agencies claimed ZBB had been implemented "with dazzling results." But further analysis suggested some of the claims were false, and other reports of changes were not due to ZBB but to the fact that "President Carter's appointees had different concerns from Republican predecessors" (Hammond and Knott, 1980, p. 64). An extensive analysis of ZBB in the Department of Agriculture indicated that although the process could be described, it could not actually be practiced. The calculations required could not be done, the consequences of removing programs could not be reasonably estimated, no one had confidence in the bulky reports produced, and no one could integrate them. A great deal of effort produced almost no changes attributable to the process (Wildavsky and Hammond, 1965).

It is difficult to know precisely the extent of adoption of ZBB. Advocates suggested it had been "adopted by a variety of organizations in many sectors of the economy, as well as state and local government" (Pyhrr, 1977, p. 1), yet others simultaneously indicated that only a few organizations—perhaps thirty to one hundred— had used ZBB in one or another of its many forms, and "it has not worked" (Suver and Brown, 1977, p. 76). The process led to few decisions and insignificant savings.

ZBB in Higher Education

Because ZBB was claimed to be effective in business and state government and was being promoted by the new president for the federal government, advocating its use in higher education was a natural next step. A major impetus was provided in a how-to book by a higher education management consultant (Harvey, 1977). The leadership of higher education, said Harvey, was losing public confidence and was under greater pressure than ever before to be more efficient and effective. The old style of seat-of-the pants administration would no longer be acceptable. ZBB was the answer.

Harvey's book provided a complete description of ZBB, including sample forms. In Harvey's product, institutions begin by determining their general goals and setting measurable objectives to meet these goals. The budget is then divided into decision units, which are natural groupings of institutional activities. A decision unit might be an activity, program, institutional unit (such as the English department), or even subunits of a department (such as English 101). Each decision unit prepares "decision packages," in which it demonstrates it has considered alternative ways of providing the service or activity (for example, English 101 could be offered by lecture, lecture-discussion, small groups, or individualized instruction) and has selected the "best" one. The costs and benefits of the alternative selected are then analyzed for each of three budget levels—

minimal, maintenance, and desired—and a written narrative prepared for each level. Decision units may be given specific budget targets, so the first decision package (minimal funding) could be no more than 85 percent of the previous year's budget, the maintenance level the next 10 percent, and one or more proposals to reach a higher desired level could be added at the unit's discretion.

Decision unit managers then rank each of their packages from most to least important and forward them to their supervisors. Supervisors review the rankings of the units under their control and consolidate them into their own rankings, which are then forwarded still further up the line. Thus, a department chair with four decision units, each providing three decision packages, would have to place all 12 packages in rank order. A division director with 6 departments might have to place 6 times 12 or 72 packages in rank order, a dean with 4 divisions might have to place 4 times 72 or 288 packages in rank order, and so on. At the top of the hierarchical pyramid, a president might have literally thousands of items to be placed in rank order. Theoretically at least, the 85 percent minimal funding request of one decision unit might be given lower priority than the additional 10 percent maintenance funding of another and receive no funding at all. The requests were to be funded in rank order until the money ran out. The lower the ranking of a decision package, the less likely it was to be funded.

There are no reliable data that indicate the number of colleges and universities that used ZBB. There are few examples in the literature of adoption by private institutions, and adoption for the most part appeared limited to the public sector in states where it was governmentally imposed. Some colleges may have adopted it because it led to good publicity and was seen as a sign of good management. A community college that claimed ZBB had been a catalyst for significant change was lauded in the press for implementing it (Hardin and Lee, 1979).

The benefits of a well-designed ZBB budget were being promoted in higher education as late as 1984 (Pinola and Knirk, 1984).

Despite a lack of any evidence that it really worked, the idea behind it appeared to be so potent that people were reluctant to admit it was not effective. Even after reciting the failures of ZBB to do what it said it was going to, some still proposed, "If you are dissatisfied with your present budgeting system, or are uneasy about the magnitude of some or all of your administrative programs, you will find that zero-base budgeting provides you with a systematic method of addressing your problems" (Suver and Brown, 1977, p. 84). Some people claimed to like ZBB, but that may be because what they were really doing was incremental budgeting (Hammond and Knott, 1980, p. 76). Still others compromised ZBB principles by implementing so-called modified ZBB approaches

Whatever Happened to ZBB?

"Why has ZBB failed where it has been tried? . . . Our judgment is that, when all is said and done, little is changed. Few resources are reallocated due to ZBB, and few decisions are made differently. And in the process of following ZBB's complex procedures, officials spend a huge amount of time, energy and money which could be used more fruitfully elsewhere" (Hammond and Knott, 1980, p. 1). Yet as late as 1981, in an article coauthored by Pyhrr, a medical school was using the "success" of its ZBB as the basis for suggesting it might also be useful for other medical schools (Herrmann, Pyhrr, Thomas, and Gronvall, 1981). Librarians were commenting on the possibilities offered by ZBB, even while recognizing there were no data available that could be used to assess its usefulness (Crowe, 1982; Koenig and Alperin, 1985). Libraries were among the institutions that enthusiastically embraced the idea of ZBB in the 1970s but discarded it in the 1980s (Koenig and Alperin, 1985). Just as universities lagged behind government, so libraries lagged behind universities, and "the major work devoted to the use of ZBB in libraries appeared in 1980, just as the Carter administration, ZBB's champion, was being voted out of office" (Koenig and Alperin, 1985, p. 27).

The difficulties of implementing ZBB were acknowledged by advocates and critics alike. It required twice the paperwork of PPBS (Hammond and Knott, 1980) and enormous staff time, there was no objective way of defining a decision unit—although Pyhrr (1977, p. 2) described it as "straightforward"—and ranking the packages they produced was difficult. ZBB advocates proposed a number of offsetting advantages, including saving money, reviewing each program each year, developing a cost-conscious staff, reducing empire building, and increasing communication, among others. Harvey (1977) was able to list fifteen advantages and only four disadvantages, supporting his conclusion that the former outweighed the latter. ZBB often failed for many reasons, including lack of support from the top, trying to do too much in too little time, and the lack of a clear decision-making structure. And perhaps of greatest importance, "If an institution is highly political, meaning that major decisions are made more on the basis of power, self-interests, and political forces inside and outside the institution, then forget ZBB" (Harvey, 1977, p. 29). Trying to assess the value of intangible outcomes was also difficult, although (begging the question) advocates assured potential users that "if a cost/benefit analysis can be performed on a function, it is a candidate for a zero-based budgeting package, even if the benefit is intangible" (Cheek, 1979, p. 13).

ZBB did not work in state government because of statutory requirements for certain programs, public expectations of continued services, differences in the budgeting systems used by executive and legislative agencies, and the demands of interest groups (Lauth, 1980). Pyhrr (1977) surmised that the major problem was that bureaucrats felt threatened by a process that evaluated the effectiveness of their programs. Less obvious were some of the basic conceptual assumptions that clearly could not be met in practice. For example, ZBB assumed each decision package should stand alone and all costs of producing a product could be identified (Cheek, 1979). In an institutional world of joint costs and joint benefits, stand-alone decisions, except perhaps in the most trivial cases, were not possible. And the concept that decision units were discrete, so changes in (or indeed elimination of) one such unit would have no effect on another, was contrary to the experience and reality of interdependence. ZBB assumed it was possible to rank-order such diverse items as increasing salaries, reducing class size, and building a new laboratory—even though when ZBB was attempted in the federal government, some cabinet officials refused to rank their decision packages on the grounds that ranking made no sense (Hammond and Knott, 1980). And ZBB was based on the presumption that it was possible for the budgets of some programs to be reduced to zero. Unless this is a real possibility, noted Balderston (1974, p. 216), then "the zero part of zero-base budgeting may simply be an agonizing charade and would not be worth the trauma that raising such questions would entail."

The Past Is Prologue

A review of the use of PPBS, MBO, and ZBB in the federal government stated, "Despite optimistic claims, they have not been panaceas for nonprofit organizations. Each technique has been (PPB[S] and MBO) or may be in the process of being (ZBB) rejected by governmental decision makers" (Dirsmith, Jablonsky, and Luzi, 1980, p. 310). Proving experience may not be a good teacher, some advocates recommended that ZBB should be used to complement and supplement PPBS and MBO rather than replace them (Harvey, 1977, p. 2).

If they did not work, why did some scholars advocate them? Perhaps because they sounded as if they *should* work, even though "numerous hortatory pieces espousing the use of PPBS or ZBB were written by people who had no experience with either system or, indeed, frequently no significant experience in budgeting or administration at all" (Koenig and Alperin, 1985, p. 26). If they did not work, why did three U.S. presidents support them? Perhaps because "effecting an appearance of concern about government inefficiency and ineffectiveness is an important electoral strategy" (Hammond and Knott, 1980, p. 102). Ineffective innovations could also be adopted for other reasons: state governments followed federal leads because it was prestigious to do so, new administrations look for new techniques to control the bureaucracy, and administrators try to control internal processes because they cannot control external ones.

It might be thought that the almost uniform failure of three highly publicized and celebrated management innovations over a relatively brief period would have given pause to those who were interested in improving efficiency and effectiveness. To be sure, some admitted they might have been duped. Looking backward from the vantage point of 1985, Koenig and Alperin (1985, p. 26) confessed, "Much of [the] literature of the 1970s seems rather naive to us now." What advocates should have been learning from previous failures was that management systems based on rational models do not work. What they appeared instead to be learning was that things had not yet been finely tuned, but with a little tweaking, rational models would come into their own. It was as much marketing as substance, and "one of the basic precepts of marketing is that if a product has bombed but is believed to still have potential, then it should be relaunched with a new name. The basic precepts of PPBS and ZBB will probably be repackaged under a new label, and the pendulum will swing again . . . and of course the bandwagon should have a new gimmick" (Koenig and Alperin, 1985, pp. 35–36). In Chapters Three and Four we examine some of the new bandwagons and the "gimmicks" on which they were based.

3

Survival in a Changing Environment

The failure of PPBS, MBO, and ZBB everywhere it was tried might have served as a cautionary tale. It could have reminded us of how complicated universities are, how little we know about how they work, and how well-intentioned but misguided attempts to rationalize their affairs could lead to confusion rather than improved effectiveness. Instead, we attributed our failures to lapses in leadership, institutional intransigence, and flaws in implementation. The evidence of our own experience was overwhelmed by our belief in the virtues of rationality and the legacy of the first management revolution. If one form of rationality did not work, let's try another, and another, and still another. And so we did.

Strategic Planning: The Grand Name Without the Grand Thing (1972–1994)

As Ur-Managers, we constructed long-range blueprints for the future based on existing campus power structures and assumptions that past trends would continue. The blueprints failed because they were not rational enough. So we rationalized planning using computers and sophisticated algorithms that ignored traditions and values. Rational planning failed as well because it was not political enough. In response to successive failures, a new generation of planning systems was developed in the world of business. Called strategic planning, it represented "a third way in planning, one that eschews the arrogant excesses of the highly quantitative management science experts, their disregard for human frailties and politics, and their reams of computer printouts, but also the supine accommodations of the highly political brokers, their neglect of costs, values and the future, and, their excuses about how so-and-so 'won't buy it'" (Keller, 1983, p. 108). Although grounded in theories of rational decision making (Swenk, 1999), strategic planning attempted to merge rationality and politics. Rather than emphasizing internal operations, it focused on fitting the organization to the environment in which it functioned.

Development of Strategic Planning

The concept of strategy began to appear in the business literature during the 1940s (Chaffee, 1985), was given prominence through the publication of a book about successful business practices (Chandler, 1962), and was in frequent use in business from about 1965 on (Mintzberg, 1994). Strategic planning was a simple and sensible process of "matching the threats and opportunities of the present and future external environment with the distinctive competencies of an organization in such a way as to develop a differential advantage. Its purpose is to carve out a niche in the external environment in which the organization can successfully compete and improve its performance" (Arns, 1982).

If the environment was munificent and stable, there would be no need for strategic planning. It would be easy to predict both the needs of the future and the availability of resources to survive effectively. But organizations in the 1960s were living in a blizzard of discontinuities, unprecedented threats, and surprising changes (Keller, 1997). In a world of competition and external threats, survival itself depended on taking a strategic approach. "The strategic concept is at once simple and complex. Simply put, . . . strategic planning is what an enterprise does to position itself favorably relative to resources in the environment" (Cope, 1987, pp. 1, 3). It could be simply put, but could it be simply done? Mintzberg's (1994) display of a number of elaborate flowcharts, planning models developed as products, and theories suggested that it might not be so simple at all.

To plan, one had to have some idea of what the environment looked like now and what it might look like in the future. One of the major elements of strategic planning was "continuous and comprehensive environmental scanning" (Cope, 1981, p. 31), a distant early warning system to peer into the world "out there" and detect minor blips that might be precursors of future trends. To anticipate the future (and, some said, to control it), organizations had to be aware of environmental, market, and competitive threats and opportunities. The kind and amount of information needed to scan the environment for blips turned out to be formidable. Social problems, emerging social needs, scientific breakthroughs, economic changes, cultural evolution, and "major new opportunities in general" were on the list of things to watch for (Cope, 1981; Keller, 1983). How would organizations be able to do what governments and astrologers could not? The strange response by some planning advocates, who recognized the difficulty of forecasting even one dimension of change, was to compound the complexity by proposing the development of two-dimensional matrices that predicted not only the probability of certain changes but also their level of diffusion throughout the nation and the rest of the world (Cope, 1981). Further elaborations (Morrison, Renfro, and Boucher, 1984) called for the construction of "impact networks," "policies-to-events matrices," and other analytic methods.

Business adopted strategic planning, but by 1978 its effectiveness was already being questioned. Mintzberg (1978, p. 948) argued that explicitly stating goals, assessing strengths and weaknesses, and systematically planning to achieve the goals was "at best overly general guidelines and at worst demonstrably misleading precepts to organizations that face a confusing reality." *Strategic planning* was replaced by around 1980 with *strategic management*, which was different (according to some) because it included operational as well as planning elements. Neither term, nor the others that used *strategic* as a modifier, had generally accepted definitions. Because "the concept of strategy is difficult to define yet can be understood intuitively" (Cope, 1981, p. 5), it was "overused and frequently incorrectly applied" (Cope, 1987, p. iii) and meant different things to different organizations, consultants, and scholars.

By the 1980s, the business literature began to ask whether there was any evidence of a relationship between planning and organizational performance and to suggest that formal strategic planning can sometimes impair rather than improve an organization's competitive position (Hayes, 1985). The problem was that quantitative goals often drove out nonquantitative ones, and economic forecasts were wildly off the mark (as were the strategies they produced). Some suggested that organizations might do better to base their strategy on the expertise of their current staff rather than recruit new staff to implement new strategies (Hurst, 1986).

One discouraging estimate was that fewer than 10 percent of business strategies were successful, although some called 10 percent "wildly inflated" (Mintzberg, 1994, p. 25). *Business Week* reported on the strategic plans of thirty-three companies in 1979 and 1980 and found by 1984 that only fourteen had been successful (Schmidtlein and Milton, 1988–1989). In his extensive analysis, *The Rise and Fall of Strategic Planning*, Mintzberg (1994) criticized planners for failing to study the effects of their own plans and for the shoddy methodology that characterized what little "research" had been done. Analyses were based more on wishful thinking than on evidence of improved outcomes, he said. In summary, "A number of biased researchers set out to prove that planning paid, and collectively they proved no such thing" (Mintzberg, 1994, p. 134).

Strategic planning sounded so reasonable. Yet "we have no evidence that any of the strategic planning systems—no matter how elaborate, or how famous—succeeded in capturing (let alone improving on) the messy informal processes by which strategies really do get developed. . . . Take apart any model of strategic planning, box by box, and at the heart of the process where strategies are supposed to be created, you will find only a set of empty platitudes, not any simulation of complex managerial processes" (Mintzberg, 1994, p. 297). By the mid-1980s, articles with titles such as "Why Strategic Management Is Bankrupt" (Hurst, 1986) argued that interest in strategy was waning because its results were disappointing and because it encouraged short-term views of management. By the late 1980s, "corporate America ceased practicing strategic planning as its mantra for success" (Presley and Leslie, 1998, p. 234). But wait. In 1996, *Business Week* announced that strategic planning was back: "Reengineering consultants with stopwatches are out. Strategy gurus with visions of new prospects are in. . . . Business strategy is now the single most important management issue and will remain so for the next five years" (Byrne, 1996, p. 46).

Strategic Planning in Higher Education

Although some academic institutions had been engaged in strategic planning since 1972 (Cope, 1987), the publication in 1981 of Kotler and Murphy's article, "Strategic Planning for Higher Education," and in 1983 of Keller's book, *Academic Strategy*, marked its formal introduction to higher education. "Strategy, having shown its usefulness in business [sic!], was borrowed by higher education" (Chaffee, 1985, p. 135), and "by the mid-1980s, strategic planning dominated both scholarly literature and the literature oriented towards practitioners" (Cope, 1987, p. 2). A survey in 1985 reported that 88 percent of postsecondary institutions were using it (Cope, 1987). Even jaded scholars, surveying the graveyards of previous fad failures, were impressed. "What about it?" asked Baldridge and Okimi (1982, p. 6). "Is strategic planning just another gimmick destined to join the ghosts of past management failures and institutional do-dads?" And their answer: "For once, the newest movement—strategic planning—does seem to have promise." Strategic planning in higher education was championed by NCHEMS (Cope, 1981) and a professional association, the

Society for College and University Planning (SCUP). These groups, and their publications, provided champions for the process and forums for its dissemination.

The impetus for strategic planning in higher education in the 1980s was the "new era of massive and widespread social, economic, demographic, and technological change and new international competition" (Keller, 1997, p. 160). Institutions should not wait for crises to provoke changes in their strategies, but instead should engage in thoughtful adaptations in advance of crises by following the strategic process: environmental and resource analysis, followed sequentially by goal formulation, strategy formulation, organizational restructuring, and the design of information systems (Kotler and Murphy, 1981). The process should be hierarchical in nature, with strategic plans completed first by administrators at the higher institutional levels and then in turn by lower units.

George Keller's influential manifesto, *Academic Strategy*, warned that "the specter of decline and bankruptcy" (Keller, 1983, p. 3) was haunting higher education. "Experts predict that between 10 percent and 30 percent of America's 3,100 colleges and universities will close their doors or merge with other institutions by 1995. On many campuses the fear of imminent contraction or demise is almost palpable" (p. 3). The only solution, according to Keller, was "a rebirth of academic management . . . that has an agreed-upon strategy for an institution's role and objectives for action" (p. 176). The prospect of an extended enrollment decline, together with changes in the nature of the student body itself, the disintegration of the curriculum, increased competition among colleges, the growth of technology, the problems of a faculty that was aging and losing commitment to their institutions, and increased external pressures, mandated that "the era of laissez-faire campus administration is over. The era of academic strategy has begun" (Keller, 1983, p. 26).

Higher education jumped on the strategic planning bandwagon. There were only a handful of institutions engaged in strategic planning in the late 1970s. In 1988, Keller, then the senior vice president of a strategic planning consulting firm, reported that half of the campuses he visited were doing strategic planning; overall, perhaps 10 to 15 percent of all colleges either had or were working on a strategic plan (Keller, 1988). He estimated that use was still growing: "Perhaps as many as one-fourth of America's 2,160 four-year colleges and universities and several hundred two-year colleges may have attempted to realign or restructure themselves for the future" (Keller, 1997, p. 159). Keller's estimates were significantly lower than the 88 percent claimed by Cope in 1985, suggesting either a dramatic decline in use or else (and more likely) that either or both estimates were guesses and used different definitions.

The literature identified four basic elements of strategic planning: scanning the external environment, assessing internal strengths and weaknesses, analyzing data drawn from both the institution and its environment, and identifying major directions that would promote institutional vitality (Schmidtlein and Milton, 1988–1989). Done properly, wonderful outcomes were predicted. It could permit an institution to "make decisions about missions, goals, markets, priorities, and programs. It promises adaptive management" (Steeples, 1988, p. 1). It could clarify institutional purposes and directions and set out action steps for their achievement through a vision that unites the institution's mission, target audiences, program mix, comparative advantages, and principal action steps (Arns, 1982). After determining one's mission and aspirations, the next step is to "see and foresee the nature and extent of turbulence and change in [twelve different] sectors of the external environment," including social trends, technological development, and political, legal, and regulatory forces (Arns, 1982).

If predicting turbulence was not enough of an oxymoronic challenge, one could go further. "It is not only necessary to resolve conflict between the economic ends and the internal values of the culture of the institution, but also to calculate the ever-changing cross-impacts and trade-offs among economic, social and political forces" (Hollowood, 1981, p. 18). Unfortunately, research found that universities could not really implement the kind of environmental scanning the theorists recommended (Hearn, Clugston, and Heydinger, 1993). "Analysts of higher education in the second half of the 20th century cannot take great pride in their ability to predict the path which the enterprise took in recent decades. Several major trends have either not been predicted or the predicted results have been quite contrary to what actually happened" (Hauptman, 1993, p. 212). Keller's inaccurate prediction that up to 30 percent of all institutions would merge or close by 1995 was a case in point.

There were different flavors of strategic planning. Environmental scanning could become segmented and complex, with each segment requiring different forecasting methods (Peterson, 1980). Some approaches involved elaborate models, systems, and data sets, requiring twelve to eighteen months to prepare comprehensive documents with decisions laid out for the next five years (Cope, 1987). Others suggested that gathering too many data and subjecting them to too much analysis was counterproductive because "most of the information needed to make strategic choices is already in the minds of the participants" (Cope, 1987, p. iv). Perhaps strategic planning was not so much a matter of data and paper as a way of articulating current thinking.

Cope's definition of strategic planning (1981, p. 8) was reasonable enough: "an institution wide, future-examining, participative process resulting in statements of institutional intention that synergistically match program strengths with opportunities to serve society." But what did it mean in practice? In the end, strategic planning had no fixed meaning and "could be defined in such a way as to affirm virtually any arbitrarily-chosen course of action, including no change from present procedures—which leads one to wonder whether it provides any substantive guidance at all" (Allen and Chaffee, 1981, p. 24). Summarizing a number of descriptions by leading authorities in the field, Tan (1990, p. 3) commented, "It appears that almost anyone can come up with his or her own definition."

Because there was no agreement on what strategic planning was, it was difficult to determine the extent to which it had been effective. Keller's book (1983) described successful use of strategic planning by joint big decision committees (JBDC). Later analysis by others (Schuster, Smith, Corak, and Yamada, 1994) suggested that some JBDCs worked and some did not, although none fully performed the functions Keller envisioned, and few were able to function as strategic planning entities. The tautological implication seemed to be that "strategic planning could be done successfully if the right methods of structure and process could be arranged" (Leslie, 1996, p. 111). If strategic planning was not successful, then the "right methods and structures" obviously had not been selected. It was easy enough retrospectively to list the reasons a strategic plan might fail (Shirley, 1988), but that did not provide a clue as to when it might work. Keller (1997) proposed several "basic ingredients" for success, including a senior-level champion of change, buy-in by other important institutional administrators and faculty leaders, disciplining of campus authorities who oppose the new initiatives, good communication, making hard decisions, allocating funds for some new ideas, attending to the financial implications, and increasing confidence through successfully implementing incremental changes. This is probably good advice, although it could be applied with equal confidence to many different kinds of organizational processes and is not limited to strategic planning.

As usual, the literature had many case studies of successful strategic planning, written by the institutional presidents or deans who implemented them (Steeples, 1988; Flack, 1994) and by scholars promoting the process (Cope, 1987). One of the very few empirical analyses of the effects of strategic planning found no differences in several measures of financial condition between institutions that did, or did not, engage in strategic planning (Swenk, 1998). Perhaps improvement in fiscal condition is not a valid measure of planning outcomes, but then what is, and how could it be measured?

Planning sometimes worked and sometimes did not. "At some institutions planning has transformed the life, financial strength and direction of the school. At other institutions, the planning has been frustrating, inconclusive, and forgettable" (Meredith, 1993, p. 28). In general, "colleges and universities have not had particularly positive results from their experimentation with strategic planning" (Rowley, Lujan, and Dolence, 1997, p. 40). Was success or failure due to the approach used, unusual organizational or environmental contingencies, or chance? Claims of the outcomes of strategic planning were neither well documented nor well described, nor were the costs and benefits assessed. If it is true that "it has lifted up dozens of U.S. colleges and universities, and saved others from decline" (Keller, 1997, p. 159), it suggests a success rate of perhaps 10 percent of the seven hundred institutions that Keller estimates tried it. And while helping dozens of institutions is worthy, it is not possible to know the costs of the failures. Advocates of strategic planning have little beyond individual case studies and advocacy pieces to point to (Cope, 1981; Chaffee, 1985). The problem remains today that "much of what has been written is basically prescriptive advocacy for a particular approach based on little or no systematic analysis of actual campus-planning environments and experiences" (Schmidtlein and Milton, 1988–1989, p. 5). Even its strongest advocates acknowledge that "the literature on academic strategy making is skimpy, and empirical findings about successful strategies are nearly nonexistent" (Keller, 1997, p. 163).

Whatever Happened to Strategic Planning?

At its rational best, "planning makes the implicit, inarticulate, and private explicit, articulate and public. It brings decision making out of the closet. It replaces muddle through with purpose" (Keller, 1983, p. 70). But strategy was particularly problematic in colleges and universities because most of them were too complex to explicate the implicit; in a world of contending values, clarity can cause rather than diminish conflict. Moreover, the most important strategic variables for most organizations—price, location, and program— were not under institutional control in much of higher education.

The options available to public institutions in particular were quite limited (Rowley, Lujan, and Dolence, 1997). Even if colleges and universities wanted to respond to their environment and identify a niche, they did not know what to change since "the number of variables an organization might manipulate in creating a management strategy is almost limitless" and the patterns for successful strategic management are "as idiosyncratic as fingerprints. What worked for the college down the road has no necessary correlation with what will work here" (Chaffee, 1984, pp. 232, 233). Even successful implementation could have unanticipated negative consequences. Some institutions that were able intentionally to change their missions to become more attractive to a wider audience could find short-term enrollment and fiscal benefits followed by long-term erosions of identity (Anderson, 1977). Strategic planning was not as much a technique as a state of mind and an art form composed of "a subtle blend of facts, hunches, assessments, experiences, and trial and error experiments" (Baldridge and Okimi, 1982, p. 18). No formal, structured planning product could implement it; "planning is not so much a subject for the social scientist as for the theologian" (Wildavsky, 1973, p. 153).

It was not as if campuses were not planning. In one way or another, all institutions plan all the time. The problem was that formal planning did not seem to do what its proponents said it should. Campuses first tried one approach and then, when it failed, another. When scholars visited institutions to assess the consequences, "few interviewees could enumerate specific outcomes or substantive benefits of the processes conducted at their campuses" (Schmidtlein and Milton, 1988–1989, p. 7). Yet the need to feel in control through planning was so strong that the failure was often rationalized, and despite persistent failure, "most persons interviewed believed that planning was important but not being properly implemented at their institutions" (Schmidtlein, 1990, p. 164).

The fundamental fallacy of strategic planning, in business or education, was the implicit assumption that the analytic processes of planning can lead to the synthesizing process of strategy—that "decomposition of the process of strategy making into series of articulated steps, each to be carried out as specified in sequence, will produce integrated strategies." But, said Mintzberg (1994, p. 13), "Organizational strategies cannot be created by the logic used to assemble automobiles." There is no more basis for believing that objectives can stimulate the development of strategies than there is for PPBS's assumption that analysis can create goals.

Higher education brought some unique planning problems to the table as well. The theoretical notion that one first plans strategy, then designs structures, and finally implements "stands almost totally at odds with what really happens" in a university, leading to the conclusion that "either the universities 'have it all wrong' or that the strategy theoreticians do" (Hardy, Langley, Mintzberg, and Rose, 1983, p. 407). Given traditions of shared authority, some on campus saw a "fundamental conflict between the concept of planning and pluralistic democratic forms of decision making" (Schmidtlein, 1990, p. 164). Although many institutions devoted extensive resources to strategic planning, most people on campus were unhappy with the outcomes. As a result, "many campuses had tried various processes for one to three years, then dropped them because of perceptions that they were not worth their costs or revised them when a new president arrived" (Schmidtlein and Milton, 1988–1989, p. 10).

Institutions that wanted to try strategic planning had many models to choose from and no way to select among them. "There is no fixed protocol for academic strategic decision making, and even less similarity across institutions about how they implement and enforce the strategic changes agreed upon. Not only is strategic management too new to have settled on a proven set of procedures but also the colleges and universities across the United States are too varied" (Keller, 1997, p. 163). But the lack of proven procedures does not inhibit the continuing development by consultants of prescriptive products. Take, for example, the "strategic planning engine" (Dolence, Rowley, and Lujan, 1997, p. 2), a ten-step cyclical model. Using a "theoretically simple method" and decision trees for each of the ten steps, the engine requires, among other things, the development of key performance indicators (KPI); a strength, weakness, opportunity, and threat analysis (SWOT); and a KPI/SWOT cross-impact analysis. The system was claimed to be generally applicable to all administrative levels, from departments through whole institutions.

Even as different institutions thought they were adopting different approaches, many plans turned out to be quite similar, thus demonstrating "the difficulty of composing a formal plan that provides meaningful direction to a college or university, that commits it to a course of action, while it also solves the problem of 'legitimacy and commitment' or acceptance by a critical mass of constituents" (Presley and Leslie, 1998, p. 225).

So what have we learned from studies of strategic planning? Chaffee wrote in 1985, "At this early stage, the only conclusion one may draw confidently from the higher education studies is that radical departure from the organization's mission is probably an unwise strategy—a conclusion many observers have drawn without the benefit of research" (p. 162). The attempt to impose strategic planning models on colleges and universities resulted in "a great deal of waste, trying to fit the square pegs of planning into the round holes of organization. At best, the pegs were damaged—the planners failed, they merely wasted their time. . . . At worst, the holes were damaged—the planners succeeded and the *organization* wasted its time, possibly becoming dysfunctional in the process" (Mintzberg, 1994, p. 405). In the final analysis, the strategic plans of many institutions turn out to be, in Matthew Arnold's phrase, the grand name without the grand thing.

Benchmarking: Why Not the Best? (1979–)

An organization's environment includes other organizations similar to itself. While strategic planning emphasized interorganizational competition, benchmarking focused on how organizations could learn from each other. Some organizations do certain things better than other organizations. For an organization wishing to improve itself, what could be more sensible than finding out what the more efficient and effective organizations do that leads to their superiority? Benchmarking means finding and implementing best practices (Camp, 1995, p. 247) that have been developed and implemented elsewhere. Comparing an organization's operations to those of competitors is nothing new. Ur-Managers often compared their output measurements to those of other companies and established quantitative targets in areas they believed could be improved. The targets were usually set by assuming the desirability of improving productivity and projecting future trends based on historical practices. Once the targets were established, managers had to figure out how to meet them. For example, a university with 10 percent of its budget dedicated to administration could decide to reduce this figure to the 8 percent expended by a comparable institution. In Ur-Management, metrics came first, and change in practice followed (Camp, 1989a).

The innovative aspect of benchmarking was that it established a structured process of comparison that emphasized practices over metrics. In benchmarking, managers have to identify other organizations that appear to have superior processes so "their practices, processes, and methods can be studied and documented" (Camp, 1989a, p. 66). Only after understanding how these practices work can quantitative targets for one's own organization be set. Best practices must be determined before analytically derived benchmark metrics can be developed. Benchmarking is the process of analyzing best practice; benchmarks are the outcomes of benchmarking. "Benchmarking metrics are seen as a result of understanding best practices, not something that can be quantified first and understood later" (Camp, 1989a, p. 68).

Development of Benchmarking

Benchmarking was pioneered by Xerox Corporation in 1979. It is one of a group of quality techniques, such as 360-degree evaluation, hoshin planning, and learning organizations, that sprang from the

TQM movement discussed in Chapter Four. "Among these, (and given reengineering's decline) benchmarking has so far won the most acceptance" (Marchese, 1995, p. 3).

There are many approaches to benchmarking. One influential model defined a sequential ten-step process, divided into four stages. In the first stage, planning, organizations identify what is to be benchmarked, determine the comparison organizations, and determine how data will be collected. In the second stage, analysis, the performance gap is determined and future performance levels projected. In the third stage, integration, the benchmark findings are communicated in the organization and functional goals are established. In the fourth stage, action, plans are developed, progress is monitored, and benchmarks are recalibrated (Camp, 1989b). Other benchmarking models suggested a different number of steps, ranging from five to twelve (Alstete, 1995). For all the models, "Benchmarking implies measurement . . . of the industry best practices. [Then] the practices can be quantified to show an analytical measurement of the gap between practices. This metric is often the single-minded measurement that most managers want" (Camp, 1989a, p. 67).

Benchmarking standards can be set in four different ways. Internal benchmarking examines similar processes in other parts of the same organization, competitive benchmarking looks at the processes of peers or competitors, functional benchmarking considers similar processes in organizations different from one's own, and generic benchmarking (also called "best-in-class" or "world-class" benchmarking) seeks out best practices regardless of the industry in which they are found (Alstete, 1995). Some benchmarking advocates emphasize the world-class approach, on the grounds that anything less automatically sets limits to an organization's ambitions (Hammer and Champy, 1993). Others argue that what works best for one corporation in one setting may not work best for another. As one information system consultant to corporations put it, "Every firm is different, every organization has different needs and therefore every information system implementation must fit the particular conditions of a particular enterprise" (Strassmann, 1995).

Benchmarking begins with an organization's mission statement, from which a list of "deliverables" expected by the customer can be derived by breaking down "broad purposes into the specific outputs to be benchmarked" (Camp, 1989c, p. 63). Experts have suggested that when firms break down their processes in detail, fewer than two hundred are usually identified. Once identified, they should be put in priority order. "From a benchmarking viewpoint the projects undertaken should be prioritized to ensure that they are the vital few contributing to results. If the set of business processes cannot be identified, how can they be prioritized to select the vital few? If the full set is not the basis for prioritization, then the selection of the vital few is simply a matter of judgment and visceral feel, not informed, fact-based selection" (Camp, 1995, p. 35). And what can be benchmarked? "Every function of a business has or delivers a product. The product is the output of the business process of the function, whether it's a physical good, an order, a shipment, an invoice, a service, or a report. Benchmarking is appropriate for these and all other outputs" (Camp, 1989b, p. 72). Products, processes, levels of customer satisfaction—if it can be measured, it can (and should) be benchmarked.

In 1989, benchmarking was being increasingly used in U.S. business (Camp, 1989a), and by 1992 there were over one hundred articles and several books on the topic (Camp, 1995). By 1995, 80 percent of the Fortune 500 companies were reported to be practicing it (Marchese, 1995). Business had to find a way of expanding its vision of what could be done, and benchmarking, "the discipline of searching out and learning from 'best practices' elsewhere," was "the reigning answer" (Marchese, 1997, p. 509). It was being touted as a necessary prerequisite to corporate excellence and built into the criteria for the Malcolm Baldrige National Quality Award. "Directly or indirectly, benchmarking affects up to 50 percent of the award's scoring, and, therefore, is seen as a critical quality tool" (Camp, 1995, p. 4). Firms that do not benchmark are, for all practical purposes, precluded from winning the award. The enthusiasm for benchmarking led its advocates to declare, "Benchmarking is clearly more than a fad" (Alstete, 1995, p. 27). "It is a winning business strategy. . . . Benchmarking is a new way of doing business. It removes the subjectivity from decision making" (Camp, 1989b, p. 71).

But as enthusiasm for benchmarking increased, thoughtful analysts began questioning whether the concept could really be empirically supported. As one put it (Strassmann, 1995), "I have a large collection of 'best practices' from consultants and professors. Their fundamental flaw is that none of these lists have ever been publicly validated by any independent measure of performance, such as profitability or gains in market share. Each list contains different items, in varying order of importance. Where a list has been appearing for several years, it changes every time." Students of corporate benchmarking warned against thinking of benchmarking as a panacea or using it to develop simplistic measurements for single-minded managers. They cautioned that benchmarking was a process of learning and discovery, and it required continual sorting and sifting of best practices and performance into the communications and decision-making processes of the organization (Camp, 1989a). They questioned whether it was really possible to aggregate numbers and reduce the understanding of an organization's processes to simple quantitative terms. As Mintzberg pointed out (1994, p. 264), "Anyone who has ever produced a quantitative measure—whether a reject count in a factory as a surrogate for product quality, a publication count in a university as a surrogate for research performance, or estimates of costs and benefits in a capital budgeting exercise—knows just how much distortion is possible, intentional as well as unintentional." Moreover, the process of aggregating data may provide a misleading sense of objectivity and validity even as it may destroy the essence of the information it is presumably transmitting. Finally, they warned, there was danger in deciding to whom you should be compared and on how many criteria. "One of the most common failures of benchmarking exercises results from managers trying to compare themselves in too many dimensions. By erecting

'the world's best' standards against which managers and their organizations are to be judged across all activities, benchmarking guar-
antees that almost everyone can feel like a failure!" (Hilmer and
Donaldson, 1996, p. 107). Despite the warnings and concerns, the
use of benchmarking in business increased between 1993 and 1997,
with 86 percent of companies claiming to use it in some form or another (Rigby, 1998).

Benchmarking in Higher Education

The success of benchmarking in business prompted its introduction
in higher education, where it was called "not only acceptable but
almost mandatory. . . . Through benchmarking, not only can time,
energy and money be saved, an institution can also maintain a continuous competitive edge and enhance their national reputation. . . .
Benchmarking in the future may not be optional" (Alstete, 1995,
pp. xi-xii). Higher education managers were told that to make benchmarking work, they had to understand their own work processes,
compare them to other organizations getting superior results from
similar processes, study the differences between the processes, and
adapt the better process to improve performance (Marchese, 1995).
In what charitably can be described as a triumph of hope over experience, one advocate of benchmarking declared it "may find more of
a home in higher education than the other recently adapted management improvement techniques, due to its reliance on research
methodology and hard data" (Alstete, 1995, p. 9).

On the one hand, there was the usual disclaimer that "benchmarking is not difficult" (Alstete, 1995, p. 26); on the other hand,
it was acknowledged that to do it properly requires extensive preparation, training, study, homework, and "extraordinary effort" (Marchese, 1995, p. 3). What ultimately found a home in higher education
(although often not a happy one) was not benchmarking at all, but
a half-sibling called *performance indicators* and a kissing cousin called
performance funding. The superficial similarities among the three
were striking. They often appear to casual observers to be identical,

and the terms are often used interchangeably. The differences between them, however, are profound.

Benchmarking requires an institution to study the processes of others and then use these understandings to set future goals or benchmarks for itself. For example, staff from one admissions office could visit another admissions office considered to be more efficient or effective, study those processes, revise its own processes, and set a goal of reducing its costs by 10 percent based on this revision. In so doing, it is engaged in benchmarking (studying superior processes) and setting a benchmark (10 percent reduction in cost). When an institution decides it should reduce its costs by 10 percent to bring it into line with the costs of another institution but does not study the processes that led to the lower cost, it is not benchmarking. Instead, it is developing performance indicators. When a portion of an institution's budget depends on whether it has achieved stated goals, such as the 10 percent reduction in costs, it is being subject to performance funding.

Performance indicators, which are ratios of operational statistics, can be major tools for management control and decision making in nonprofit organizations, but because they deal with outcomes and not processes, they cannot be used by themselves to improve processes (Elkin and Molitor, 1984). "Performance indicators are essential attributes of benchmarking" (Honan, 1995, p. 10), although benchmarking is not an essential attribute of either performance indicators or performance funding. Indicators ignore the basic questions inherent in benchmarking: "How are we doing compared to others? How good do we want to be? Who's doing the best? How do they do it? How can we adapt what they do to our institution? How can we be better than the best?" (Rush, 1994, pp. 84–85).

Performance indicators and performance funding grew out of the accountability and assessment movement of the mid-1980s (Gaither, Nedwek, and Neal, 1994). Performance indicators were often established because data were available rather than because they reflected something of importance. "What was available was collected and measured, what was measured—or measurable—was given value, and what was given value was reviewed for accountability and funding" (Gaither, Nedwek, and Neal, 1994, pp. 6–7). The value of indicators was sometimes based more on academic folklore than research, so that some systems considered senior faculty "better" than junior, and small classes "better" than larger ones (Gaither, Nedwek, and Neal, 1994, p. 7). Performance measures "often lack validity and reliability" (Gaither, Nedwek, and Neal, 1994, p. 8), using criteria that have not been empirically shown to be related to quality and emphasizing institutional contributions to state economic growth rather than to learning. Performance indicators are a growing phenomenon in higher education, increasingly used by institutions and state systems to assess performance against a standard, but "they are not selected with a view to what actually matters to the long-term well-being of the institution" (Honan, 1995, p. 9).

The confusion between benchmarking and performance indicators is exacerbated by the terminology used by several authoritative organizations that were among the prime movers of the innovation. Higher education organizations involved with and promoting benchmarking include the College and University Personnel Association (CUPA) ("University and Corporate Representatives Determine Focus of CUPA-Led Benchmarking Study," 1998), the National Association of College and University Business Officers (NACUBO) (Blumenstyk, 1993), and the Association of Governing Boards (AGB).

NACUBO has for several years collected, analyzed, and made available to subscribers data from a large number of institutions as part of what it calls a benchmarking process. The purpose of the program is to provide "objective, fact-based information to be used in the prioritization and decision-making processes of the institution" (Douglas, Shaw, and Shepko, 1997, p. 30). The NACUBO data are really performance indicators unrelated to benchmarking, because they were not developed as part of a multistep benchmarking process (Alstete, 1995). NACUBO aggregates data from par-

ticipating institutions so they can compare their cost and performance in specific programs to those of other (not necessarily
exemplary) institutions. No attempt is made to determine which
institutions have programs that are "better" or to identify criteria by which such a judgment could be made. By 1997–1998, the
NACUBO program contained forty modules of data, with each
module containing four to fourteen "benchmarks." An institution
wanting the most comprehensive benchmarking service for managerial use can opt for even greater depth and receive up to forty
benchmarks for each area ("The NACUBO Benchmark Program,"
1997–1998). An institution subscribing to the comprehensive version would receive at least 870 different "benchmarks." By 1997,
over three hundred institutions were participating in the NACUBO
program (Douglas, Shaw, and Shepko, 1997). Basic fees for institutional participation range from about $1,500 to $3,500 annually,
providing NACUBO with a steady stream of income and its clients
with a steady stream of data. NACUBO has never conducted an
empirical study to determine the effect its indicators have had on
participating institutions.

The AGB cosponsored the publication in 1993 and 1996 of the
results of a national survey reporting more than a hundred "key
indicators" that would allow an institution "to compare its position
in key strategic areas to competitors, to past performance, or to goals
set previously" (Taylor and Massy, 1996, p. xii). "Included among
the indicators [in] this book are most of the measures most institutions should monitor, but this is not an exhaustive list" (Taylor and
Massy, 1996, p. xii). Although the book's subtitle referred to benchmarks, benchmarking was not part of the process. The books merely
displayed distributions of measurements of respondent institutions,
sorted into six "peer groups," and presented as ratios or percentages.
The analyses therefore were limited comparisons of outcomes of current practice, and were not based on assessments of best practice.

Interest in benchmarking and indicators was driven by the belief
that clarifying goals and measuring progress was the royal road to

accountability and efficiency. But "if a higher education system's goals are not known and are not clear, then how can a set of performance indicators be adequately applied to measure, evaluate, and reward progress toward desired goals?" (Gaither, Nedwek, and Neal, 1994, p. 42). A good point, but instead of recognizing that higher education's most critical goals are difficult, if not impossible, to measure, institutions and systems responded by setting as goals those things that *could* be measured. Measurement was the key. As one advocate argued, "If you cannot measure or characterize something in some fashion, you cannot even demonstrate it exists. If we academics persist in asserting that our academic enterprise has grand and noble products (learning, perpetuating knowledge and culture, or whatever), but that the quantity and quality of those products are intrinsically indeterminate (and thus, it may be noted, unobservable), then we risk revealing ourselves to be the clueless fools some of our critics claim we are" (Langenberg, 1996, p. 2).

The availability of performance indicators meant that institutional managers could adopt fifty, or one hundred, or even eight hundred of them if they wished. But should they? Some participants in the pilot NACUBO project said it took more time than they had thought it would, complained the results were not presented in a helpful way, and believed the mountain of data it collected made it difficult to draw useful conclusions. One institution had to hire a statistician to figure out what the numbers meant (Blumenstyk, 1993). Is more better? Is increasing the number of indicators a blessing or a curse? If there is no consensus on goals, the number of indicators must be extremely large (and often in conflict) to satisfy constituents. But "the sheer number of indicators in some settings can serve more to confuse decision makers than to simplify the task of making choices. . . . How to convert this plethora of data to information that decision makers can use remains problematic" (Gaither, Nedwek, and Neal, 1994, p. 489).

Even supporters of indicators are pessimistic about their effectiveness. "Given the fads that have marked higher education management circles—management by objectives, zero-base budgeting, planning/programming/budgeting systems, for example—it remains highly unlikely that performance indicators in institutions will create enough broad-based support to sustain a reform movement" (Gaither, Nedwek, and Neal, 1994, p. 42). As with past fads, the tendency is not to question the conceptual basis for indicators but instead to blame the way they have been used. One serious problem, which may become even more pronounced if trustee boards become more involved in campus administration, is that "techniques such as 'benchmarking'—intended to guide continuous improvement—are instead rolled out as high stakes, hard-point objectives against which unit and individual performance will be judged. The result is a predictable return to control-oriented management, countered by statistical gamesmanship on the part of those assigned to obtain such targets" (Ewell, 1993, p. 55).

Regardless of the costs or benefits, "In 1994, 18 states had a performance indicator system in place, the majority of them developed and implemented in the previous three years" (Gaither, Nedwek, and Neal, 1994, p. 33). In different states, performance indicators are either based on past practice rather than best practice (Trombley, 1998) or on negotiations between institutions and state agencies (Floristano, 1996). There is no indication that analysis of best practice has preceded the establishment of such performance indicators. The growing use of performance indicators to support performance budgeting appears to meet political demands for accountability, but has little effect on what actually happens on a campus (El-Khawas, 1998). Institutions continue to get funded at historic levels regardless of performance, since large-scale funding changes are politically unsustainable (Schmidt, 1997; Trombley, 1998).

Whatever Happened to Benchmarking?

There is disagreement as to whether the use of performance indicators and performance funding is increasing or decreasing, and whether it will lead to lasting innovations or "pass quickly through higher education in this country, leaving only a modest residue" (Gaither, Nedwek, and Neal, 1994, p. iv). What is clear is that several states are using or considering performance indicators as part of the basis for funding public institutions. According to one study, as of 1998 eight states have some kind of performance budgeting system, and two-thirds of the states either have or are planning to adopt some performance-based elements in their higher education budgeting systems. The author of the study said, "We don't know yet if this is a trend or just a fad. The rationale makes sense but the implementation details are very difficult" (Trombley and Sevener, 1998, p. 14).

Some summaries of various "benchmarking" processes and studies may characterize the outcomes as showing "many positive results" or as being "highly effective" (Alstete, 1995), but there are few, if any, studies that demonstrate in quantitative terms the consequences of these projects. Statements of positive results appear to be based on the subjective comments of project champions heavily invested in the concept. In the same way, supportive statements made by senior participants in benchmarking projects on HEPROC CQI-L (a listserv active in the early 1990s but no longer being archived by the American Association for Higher Education) present numerous testimonials but few data. Assessing the value of performance indicators is difficult because the factors they measure may not be important to institutional viability or goal achievement. Even when indicators are relevant, they provide no insight into explaining their magnitude and may be misleading (Honan, 1995). And they offer no wisdom at all on whether the most effective response to poor performance is to cut one's losses or increase one's investment.

A study of benchmarking project failures found that the top four reasons cited were poor planning, no top management support, no process-owner involved, and "insufficient benchmarking skills" (Alstete, 1995, p. 85). "Insufficient skills" is a classic tautology used to attribute the cause of a fad failure to implementation rather than the concept itself. Thus the problem is that "the clueless fools" are not clever enough to measure outcomes, not that the outcomes were not measurable. It has proven very difficult to measure productivity in the service sector in general, at least in part because there is no agreement on what is being produced or what its costs actually are. Despite the appearance of rationality given to performance indicators and the like, much of what higher education produces cannot be measured in money, and productivity may not correlate with quality. As one analyst observed, "If you're going to measure the service sector by productivity, and the future of America is supposed to hinge on that, then you'd better give up the best hospitals, the best schools, the best newspapers—because none of these is [productive] if you apply an industrial standard" (Johnston, 1989, p. H2).

Some objections to benchmarking in the literature (which its proponents claim are unfounded) are that it may lead to only marginal improvements, may not be applicable to all university processes, is simply copying and so stifles innovation, and exposes institutional weaknesses (Alstete, 1995). Less frequently mentioned is that little attention is given to the trade-offs (political, programmatic, and analytical) that created the existing campus situation. For example, one institution that increased its student-faculty ratio to be more cost-effective was then penalized when that ratio turned out to be a funding indicator (Trombley, 1998). Benchmarking may also discourage institutional diversity, attenuate distinctiveness that may be conferred by "less than best" practices, and put institutions in no-win situations when the processes required for best practice in one area are incompatible with those required for best practice in another. But perhaps the most problematic aspect of benchmarking is the notion that only that which is measurable is real and worthwhile, when "the value of the truly educated person is no more to be weighed and measured than is a sonnet or a smile. The true values we seek in higher education are, at bottom, matters of faith. Why pretend that the teaching-learning enterprise lends itself to simplistic analysis?" (Enarson, 1975, pp. 172–173). Benchmarkers, like other advocates of increased productivity, "didn't know what they wanted, couldn't accept the logic of trade-offs, couldn't decide how much of anything was enough, and couldn't agree on how much progress had been made. There was therefore no way that any level of campus performance could be judged as satisfactory" (Birnbaum, 1989). And benchmarking may give little consideration to the unhappy statistical reality that regardless of how hard they try and no matter what process or outcome is being measured, half of all colleges and universities will always be below the median.

So what is the future of benchmarking? "The cynic will dismiss or deny the movement, calling accountability and quality assurance yet one more fad foisted on an underpaid faculty by a burgeoning bureaucracy. The hard-pressed, sincere policy maker will wonder whether performance systems improve the quality of the learning environment enough to justify their increasing costs" (Gaither, Nedwek, and Neal, 1994, p. 83). Proponents claim that "despite these concerns and criticisms, benchmarking is currently being used successfully in colleges and universities" (Alstete, 1995, p. 38). Yet "faced with the temptation of complexity, added administrative costs, resistance from faculty, and a less forgiving political culture, the probability increases that by the turn of the century most indicator systems will be viewed as too costly and ineffective as primary management tools" (Gaither, Nedwek, and Neal, 1994, p. 91). Whether performance funding itself has had any real effects in improving higher education is not clear (Serban, 1998), and the future is equally uncertain (Burke, 1998). Supporters predict it will become a standard way of allocating state funds (Carnevale, Johnson, and Edwards, 1998), while critics believe it will die out because its assumptions do not accurately reflect political or organizational realities (Schmidtlein, 1999).

Existing data cannot indicate whether benchmarking in higher education has been successful or unsuccessful, because benchmarking has seldom been tried. This may change with the creation of

new groups, such as the Consortium for Higher Education Benchmarking Associations (CHEBA), which plan benchmarking site
visits and emphasize the comparison of processes. Unless such initiatives prove successful, performance indicators and performance
budgets of dubious validity may continue to be used as proxies for
the achievement of ephemeral goals.

4

Higher Education as a Commodity

Have you heard the story of the inspector on a machine assembly line who uses quality management concepts to improve performance and asks the rhetorical question, "If we can do it for widgets, why not for students?" ("A New Aim," 1993, p. 47). This kind of thinking supports new management techniques on the grounds that "higher education has the same operating characteristics as a bank, an airline, or a restaurant. The fact is that we do have customers. We provide them with a service and an exchange takes place" (Seymour, 1992, p. 128).

Institutions of higher education and their "customers" have always engaged in a process of exchange, but by the 1980s, the process was becoming less of an educational, social, and moral one and more of a utilitarian and economic one. Seen as businesses, colleges and universities take in raw materials, process them, and produce outputs. They have faculty "workers" in "manufacturing facilities" composed of classrooms and laboratories. As with any business, survival depends on producing what the customer wants, and education is a commodity that customers can purchase from many sources on the open market. The commoditization of the research enterprise has transformed research knowledge into intellectual capital and intellectual property. This has been going on for decades. The commoditization of the teaching enterprise has just started, "transforming courses into software, the activity of instruction itself into commercially viable proprietary products that can be owned and bought and sold in the market" (Noble, 1998).

So the customer is king, and universities are engines of the economy. If colleges and universities are doing their job, according to these perspectives, institutions would not have to support programs with few career prospects, students would be trained for the jobs available, business could avoid the cost of retraining new employees, and public funds could be adjusted to regulate appropriations so institutions could change as the market changed. To commodify higher education, we must downsize faculty, replace lectures with Internet sessions, reduce the need for campus facilities, eliminate useless scholarship, charge faculty and others for support services, end tenure, and use economic criteria to assess faculty performance (Margolis, 1998). And if the existing structure, staff, and programs cannot do it right, then perhaps it is time to scrap them and start over.

Total Quality Management/Continuous Quality Improvement: Every Day, in Every Way, Getting Better and Better (1985–1996)

In the early to mid-1980s, distressed American companies losing market share to Japan discovered "quality" as a way of responding to competitive pressures in a global marketplace (Melissaratos and Arendt, 1995, p. 17). Quality concepts, spread by written materials and consultants, were rapidly disseminated and came to be known as Total Quality Management (TQM). Only if every sector of society practiced it could we remain a leading world-class nation (Schmidt and Finnigan, 1992). Newt Gingrich (R-Georgia), the powerful Speaker of the U.S. House of Representatives, identified Total Quality Management as one of the five pillars of American civilization (Ferguson, 1998). "No other management philosophy in recent memory has captured the fancy of American business like

Total Quality Management" (Brigham, 1993, p. 42). Because of TQM's success around the world, "it cannot be dismissed as another management fad" (Seymour, 1992, p. ix).

TQM is "a comprehensive philosophy of living and working in organizations, emphasizing the relentless pursuit of continuous improvement" (Chaffee and Sherr, 1992, p. 3). Its focus is on quality. But what *is* quality? Different gurus offered different definitions, from which Seymour (1992, pp. 13–21) abstracted eleven basic elements. Quality was meeting or exceeding customer needs, everyone's job, continuous improvement, leadership, human resource development, in the system, fear reduction, recognition and reward, teamwork, measurement, and systematic problem solving. Quality was, well, *everything*.

Development of TQM/CQI

From a technical perspective, quality depends on having processes "in control," because quality is "conformance to requirements." "In this context, 'conformance' means reduction in variation, while 'requirements,' of course, are principally shaped by customers" (Ewell, 1993, p. 54). W. Edward Deming, the father of TQM, developed statistical control and sampling processes at Bell Telephone Laboratories. Deming exported his quality processes to Japan, which then reexported them back to their country of origin. Among his widely known notions are the Seven Deadly Diseases, the Fourteen Points, and the Plan-Do-Study-Act (PDSA) process known as the Deming Cycle (Sims and Sims, 1995). The Fourteen Points are considered foundational, although some have labeled many of them "old management elixir in new containers" (Dill, 1992, p. 42).

Because quality is what the customer says it is (Marchese, 1997), customer satisfaction is the essential criterion of quality. TQM emphasizes the need to measure and improve continually the processes that lead to customer satisfaction. TQM's aim is to reduce variation in output. Believing 85 percent of all errors are the result of system design (common cause variation) and only 15 percent are caused by individual performance (special cause variation), emphasis is placed on assessing systems rather than individual performance. TQM's motto is "quality comes first," and its core concepts include process control (consistent and predictable output), management by fact (relying on measurement and data), problem solving using statistical tools, and the use of cross-functional teams leading to employee empowerment and teamwork (Heilpern and Nadler, 1992; Marchese, 1997). Quality is not based on hunches or slogans; it requires numbers and checkpoints (Schmidt and Finnigan, 1992, p. 42).

TQM relies on the metaphor of the production line, "an ordered sequence of defined operations resulting in a specified product or service . . . that is replicable and can be documented. If it cannot be *described*, it by definition cannot be improved; hence a major preoccupation of TQ[M] practitioners lies in identifying core processes and determining exactly how they work" (Ewell, 1993, p. 52). It also requires that "all their goals from the top of the firm to bottom must be congruent. Therefore, firms that have embarked on a TQM journey have well-developed mission statements, priorities, and objectives. More importantly, these firms can show a direct relationship between the company's goals to every employee's objectives" (Camp, 1995, p. 7).

TQM was embraced by corporate America from the mid-1980s on (Marchese, 1997, p. 502). It was hailed as "not just a repackaging of old ideas or the latest 'flavor of the month' in management technology" but as "a revolution in the way Americans manage and work in organizations" (Schmidt and Finnigan, 1992, pp. xviii, xi). It was a new paradigm, and it was claimed that "companies who follow this new model of management are demonstrably more successful than those who tread the traditional paths. TQM companies exhibit greater profitability, increased customer satisfaction, lower costs, higher productivity, and superior products and services" (Melissaratos and Arendt, 1995, p. 17). Congress was so impressed with the potential of the quality movement that it created the Malcolm Baldrige National Quality Award in 1987 to recognize companies with exemplary quality practices. The Department of Defense required its agencies and contractors to adopt TQM, and 68 percent of federal installations reported using it by 1993 (Hoffman and Summers, 1995). The *Wall Street Journal* reported in a survey of the use of a number of management techniques that TQM received the highest satisfaction ratings (Bleakley, 1993). One measure of business interest in TQM was the number of corporations requesting applications for the Baldrige Award. In 1988, 12,000 requests were received. By 1990, there were 200,000 requests (Schmidt and Finnigan, 1992).

Although TQM was seen as the best way of managing, some asked questions: "Will most managers view TQM as a temporary phenomenon that will fade, or will it be seen as a new way of life for building world-class organizations?" (Schmidt and Finnigan, 1992, p. xiv). It was easy to be in favor of quality but tough to implement it. The Baldrige Awards themselves provided a metaphor for the problem: the application forms were so detailed and the process so lengthy that while hundreds of thousands were distributed, only sixty-six organizations in 1988 and ninety-seven in 1990 completed and submitted them (Schmidt and Finnigan, 1992).

The difficulty of implementing TQM in the private sector paled beside the problems in the public sector with its long history of failed management reforms. These reforms could not deal with the multiple actors in the public arena and often led to conflict between the bureaucracy and the managers who wanted to control it. Still, there was a lot of interest in public sector TQM: the fad appeared to respond to diminished resources, it appeared to be successful in the private sector, others seemed to be doing it, top management wanted it done, and agencies could dispel criticism by looking as if they were actively seeking improvement (Radin and Coffee, 1993).

Initial enthusiasm began to ebb in the early 1990s. Some businesses retained their commitment to TQM, but others abandoned it in part on the grounds that they needed more dramatic change. "Clearly American corporations, which have spent hundreds of millions of dollars in the past decade . . . have divergent feelings about their expenditures" (Keller, 1992, p. 48). Corporate skeptics saw TQM as "a mania from management hell, at best a waste of time and at worst harmful to organizations." They called it a fad, supported by a fanatical army of zealots. TQM champions, on the other hand, rejected all criticisms and defended it as "manna from management heaven, essential to the future competitiveness of any organization." What did the evidence show? "There is ample data to support both views" (Shapiro, 1995, p. 174).

By 1993, there were publicized examples of major organizations whose quality programs were in tatters and winners of Japan's Deming Prize who slashed their highly publicized quality programs. At least one Baldrige Award winner filed for bankruptcy protection. Industry surveys indicated that while large numbers of organizations had TQM programs, most had failed to make any substantial quality improvements (Mathews, 1993). "In more cases than not, TQM has failed to produce its promised results" (Brigham, 1993, p. 42). The TQM failure rate was claimed by some to be as high as 80 percent (Schmidt and Finnigan, 1992, p. 335), and "the wreckage of TQM programs has spawned a new kind of ambulance chaser: consultants who specialize in turning around failed quality programs" (Jacob, 1993, p. 66). These consultants helped firms repair the "miscarriages and abortions" that resulted from TQM, "the business fad of the 1980s and the business rehabilitation project of the 1990s" (Mathews, 1993, p. H1).

Articles with titles such as "Ten Reasons Why TQM Doesn't Work" (Harari, 1993a) began to appear in the business literature. "Many managers are beginning to rethink their love affair with TQM. . . . No doubt successful programs exist. But for every success story, I'll show you two disappointments or more. . . . Only about one-fifth—at best one-third—of TQM programs have achieved 'significant' or even 'tangible' improvements" (Harari, 1993a, p. 33).

"Signs of disappointment are everywhere. [TQM] was supposed to have had all the answers" (Rahul, 1993, p. 66).

By 1997, business commentators analyzing the latest annual survey of management practices could write, "What's dead as a pet rock? Little surprise here: It's total quality management. TQM, the approach of eliminating errors that increase costs and reduce customer satisfaction, promised more than it could deliver and spawned mini-bureaucracies charged with putting it into action" (Byrne, 1997, p. 47).

TQM/CQI in Higher Education

A small number of higher education institutions pioneered TQM in the 1980s, but the formal introduction to a larger national audience came in Ted Marchese's 1991 article, "TQM Reaches the Academy." The opening paragraph set the stage:

> Total Quality Management . . . an American set of ideas, engine behind the Japanese economic miracle, agent for the dramatic turnabouts at Ford and Motorola. . . . Suddenly it's at work in more than half the Fortune 1000 firms. . . . It's the "preferred management style" of the federal government. . . . You'll find it in hotels, city government, your local hospital. . . . It's in the air. . . . Can the academy be far behind? [p. 3]

The answer to the rhetorical question was obvious. The academy would follow the trend, prompted by organizations such as the American Association for Higher Education, which made TQM a theme at its 1992 national conference. In the same year, a survey by another organization of institutions identifying themselves as involved in TQM commented, "All at once it's like monitoring the flurry of swirling gasses and exploding matter during our Earth's creation and like watching grass grow. So much quality improvement seems to be occurring in the education sector, but it is so difficult to observe, decipher, and explain" (Axland, 1992, p. 41). The *Chronicle of Higher Education* proclaimed, "TQM: Colleges Embrace the Concept of 'Total Quality Management,'" and went on to assert, "Across the country, colleges and universities are reporting success with the technique" (Mangan, 1992, p. A25).

TQM was promoted as a way of "restoring the pillars of higher education" and overcoming the threat that competition from foreign institutions and the corporate sector would reduce "market share" (Bemowski, 1991, p. 37). By 1992 articles were asking, "What should colleges do about the TQM mania?" (Keller, 1992, p. 48). The "mania" was driven not so much by the numbers of participants as by the intensity of their rhetoric. What Keller (1992, p. 48) called "a small but growing number of academic zealots, true believers, and leaders at several dozen institutions" were arguing that TQM itself could solve higher education's ills. "The presentations are often rich in principles, slogans and invocations and short on specifics, costs and candor" (Keller, 1992, p. 48). The eventual adoption of TQM was accepted by its promoters as a certainty, since "educational organizations are recognizing that they must adopt the tools utilized by business and industry in order to remain in the business of providing education" (Jelinek, Foster, and Sauser, 1995, p. 107). Some advocates of TQM in higher education took an apocalyptic and universalistic view: higher education must accept TQM or go out of business.

The rationale for introducing quality notions to higher education was the need to remain competitive in a changing environment. "The challenges that face higher education today and in the near future require a new set of philosophies and methods. Our work environment is in a continual state of flux. Many of the operating assumptions of the past simply don't apply now. . . . Developing a lot of happy, satisfied customers—whether they are students, parents of students, alumni, professors, or industry employers—should be a primary goal of causing quality in higher education. . . . Quality is defined by the user in terms of 'the capacity to satisfy wants'" (Seymour, 1992, pp. 24, 42, 43).

By 1993, A TQM bible had appeared in *On Q: Causing Quality in Higher Education* (Seymour, 1992), workshops were springing up all over the country, and an entire issue of *Change* was devoted to TQM: "By now it's hard to find a campus without a knot of people trying to implement the thing" (Marchese, 1993, p. 10). Seven of every ten higher education institutions claimed they were using TQM groups and procedures, and one of every ten said the use was extensive (El-Khawas, 1993). By the end of December 1994, a bibliography of articles written about TQM in postsecondary institutions contained 192 items (Work Environment Research Group, 1995), a Baldrige Award for higher education was proposed (Seymour, 1994), and the CQI listserv sponsored by AAHE had six hundred subscribers (Brigham, 1995). CQI was everywhere: "Pick almost any campus in the country and you'll probably find a knot of people trying to figure out how to make it work for their unit or department" (Brigham, 1995, p. 6).

Business corporations were major champions of academic TQM. A Westinghouse executive proclaimed, "My experience is that every one of the TQM principles we use in industry can be appropriated and usefully applied to a college or university" (Melissaratos and Arendt, 1995, p. 30). The university was just another business organization, and "educating people is a process, just like making a car is a process" (Nicklin, 1995, p. A34). TQM proponents used metaphors suggesting that the process for meeting specifications in assembly lines for electronic equipment was comparable to the process for ensuring all students meet specifications ("If we can do it for computers, why not for students?"), or that "sailing a ship across the Pacific is no different from organizing a college or university for performance improvement. In both instances, it is immensely helpful if we can come to some agreement on which way to aim the pointy end" (Seymour, 1995, pp. xix, 6). Differences between technical and social systems were ignored. While some acknowledged that universities and businesses were different, they often argued that these differences could be accommodated if there was a will to do so. Because of this, "Higher education can use these companies as models to design a quality program to fit its unique character" (Waters, 1995, p. 34).

Businesses offered seminars on campus, entered into collegiate partnerships, and provided start-up funds for quality programs in business schools. IBM established a competitive award program in 1992 and funded nine campuses to speed up the teaching and use of quality principles, and a consortium of "leading-edge" companies started the TQM University Challenge to provide expertise to other institutions (Seymour, 1993). Why was business interested in academic TQM? "It's self interest all the way. . . . We want to hire students who are better prepared for our world" (Milbank, 1992, p. B1). After all, "American businesses should not have to spend money . . . to retrofit American workers with TQM skills that should be acquired in American schools" (Schargel, 1993, p. 68). The chairman of IBM was candid about his desire to speed up TQM use in education and industry: "That will mean that graduates, particularly in business and engineering, will be ready to apply the principles of quality management from the first day they are on the job" (Seymour, 1993, p. 14). The way to do that was to make the study of quality a part of the curriculum, and toward that end higher education and business representatives in 1991 formed the National Educational Quality Initiative (NEQI). In addition to working to incorporate quality principles into all aspects of higher education administration, its mission was also "to obtain the inclusions of appropriate portions of the quality sciences and associated arts into every course anyone takes in the United States from preschool through graduate school and in continuing education" (Caplan, 1992, p. 64).

The Q part of TQM seemed a natural for higher education. Even the meanest institutions saw themselves as offering a quality education, and not without some justification. The T part was more problematic. Because of their loosely coupled structures, the strength of the academic guilds, and faculty claims of autonomy, few institutions could easily point to anything that could be considered to be "total." But the hardest nut to crack was the M part. Although institutions *were* managed, even the putative managers would not willingly admit to the fact. Instead, those in the hierarchy euphemistically administered, or served. What to do? If you cannot change the product, change the name—and so they did. TQM in industry became Continuous Quality Improvement (CQI) in higher education.

As early as 1991, the TQM/CQI "success" stories of a handful of institutions were being publicized (Bemowski, 1991) and there were "glowing accounts of its adoption and early success in model institutions, plus 'how-to' stories about TQM/CQI techniques" (Entin, 1993, p. 28). A study of TQM at "twenty-two pioneering colleges and universities" by a quality management consultant (Seymour, 1991, p. 10) focused on their successes. Even as questions were being raised about the effectiveness of TQM in industry, advocates were assuring higher education that its success in industry had demonstrated TQM's ability to improve educational processes as well (Hittman, 1993), and case studies of "CQI Successes" were being disseminated to bolster the claim (Brigham, 1995). Many of the articles and chapters advocating TQM/CQI were written by campus champions or institutional presidents describing their own successes (Hoffman and Julius, 1995), and higher education was being told to "take advantage of the empirical knowledge gained in business of what works and does not work" in developing their TQM programs (Melan, 1995, p. 186).

TQM/CQI was alleged to work in higher education, although "it is surprising how scant the documented evidence for its best practice remains" (Brigham, 1993, p. 48). The glow of initial success was somewhat tempered by other stories of difficulty or failure. One study of ten institutions in the Boston area that had adopted TQM/CQI between 1990 and 1992 reported that "a few minor systems have been analyzed and have definitely improved, but major problems have not yet been solved" (Entin, 1993, p. 31). Still, TQM/CQI advocates remained enthusiastic and confident, and there was "an aura of 'true believer' about these champions" (Entin, 1993, p. 31). A follow-up study of the ten institutions a year later (Entin, 1994) found that TQM had been abandoned at five of the campuses, implemented in selected units at four, and one (a college of business) was attempting to institutionalize it in its major divisions. "Much of the optimism about TQM expressed on these campuses last year now seems unwarranted, if not naive. Arguably, there is now some basis to the charge by TQM's early skeptics that it will go down as the latest management fad" (Entin, 1994, p. 7).

Still, TQM/CQI use appeared to continue growing. In the 1995 American Council on Education "Campus Trends" survey, 65 percent of all campuses reported TQM/CQI activity. However, the annual listing by *Quality Progress* magazine in September 1995 found just under three hundred campuses to profile. A more recent analysis of TQM/CQI in higher education estimates that no more than 13 percent of colleges and universities used TQM for any purpose or any length of time, descriptions of widespread acceptance were acknowledged to reflect only limited local application, and most institutions that adopted it later abandoned it (Birnbaum and Deshotels, 1999). As Marchese put it (1997, pp. 511–512), "If one asks, 'on how many campuses is the pursuit of quality a fact of daily life?' the number may be closer to 100. If one asks further, 'On how many campuses has a "culture of quality" taken root as a new dominant norm?' the number falls below 10."

Does TQM/CQI work in higher education? One book promoting the success of an institution's quality program over a five-year period (Spanbauer, 1992) displayed data showing small, positive changes in several areas of institutional functioning. Sixty percent of respondents to a 1994 survey reported benefits of improved communication and customer satisfaction. A study of ten campuses that had been successful in their CQI efforts said, "Our qualitative, in-depth interviews confirmed that quality principles work, that they are reflected in different practices, and that they do make a difference. Even though it is often difficult to arrive at specific measurements or indicators of some outcomes, our interviewees said that people feel that processes and systems have been improved" (Freed and Klugman, 1997, p. 199). A research study (Levin, 1998) described a community college in which administrators and faculty thought that the introduction of TQM had improved morale, enrollment, retention, and internal harmony.

Testimonials were abundant, but evidence and data were few and far between. Still, reports such as these suggest that TQM/CQI may be effectively used at some places and at some times under some conditions, but "quality management's track record, so far, has been spotty. In some organizations, it has transformed the culture and had a dramatic impact on efficiency and effectiveness. In others, it has been an outright failure" (Seymour, 1993, p. 8).

Although the numbers indicated significantly reduced interest in TQM/CQI, true believers argued that "CQI is alive and well on campus" (Engelkemeyer, 1998, p. 11) and could profile a small number of institutions whose programs apparently had been successful. Further recognition was provided when educational institutions at all levels finally became eligible for the Baldrige Award in 1999. The application procedures included twenty-three pages of specific criteria (*Baldrige National Quality Program,* 1999), following the same framework used for business organizations but with changes in issues and language. Over 16,000 applications were requested by educational institutions at all levels. Only sixteen institutions completed the application process; none of them were colleges or universities. No educational awards were given.

Marchese, who welcomed TQM in higher education in 1991, noted (with sadness) its departure in 1996. Although still believing TQM/CQI works, he was realistic enough to note that thousands of institutions never became involved at all, "dozens of institutions that began a quality journey ended it; others persisted but have little to show for it. . . . In sum, the most important management development of the past two decades has so far had only modest impacts on American higher education" (Marchese, 1996, p. 4). It may not have been an obituary, but it put academia on notice that, at the very least, CQI was in hospice care. As is customary, academic institutions rather than the idea itself were the problem. "In the academy, the odds against any 'three-letter management idea from industry' will always be daunting. More substantially, CQI's emphasis on customer focus, data, teamwork, and systems thinking runs counter to the internally focused, opinionated, problem-chasing world of campus life" (Marchese, 1996, p. 4).

Whatever Happened to TQM/CQI?

If it is true that "the basic assumptions of many U.S. corporations are quality-hostile" (Heilpern and Nadler, 1992, p. 149), it should not be surprising that the basic assumptions of educational institutions, which are more professional, less hierarchical, and more loosely coupled, would be even more so. "Even in companies that have been pursuing TQM for several years, senior executives often report that they are not getting the return they anticipated for their efforts" (Heilpern and Nadler, 1992, p. 137). Business leaders warned, "Given the degree of difficulty, the time demands, and the financial investment, one can say—with a certain degree of certainty—that TQM should not become every company's cup of tea" (Secor, 1995, p. 89). A number of reasons for failure were offered: failure to link TQM to strategic priorities, making some decisions without concern for market performance, employee confusion, underestimating the difficulty of cultural change, lack of project management, failure to set up support systems, and overemphasizing technical tools (Schmidt and Finnigan, 1992, pp. 336–337). When managers say that they have not benefited from the latest fad, such as TQM, it "almost surely says more about the poor quality of their leadership than it does about the quality movement" (Jacob, 1993, p. 66). TQM was sound; it was the implementation that was at fault.

Scholars studying TQM in business organizations, after commenting on the difficulty of engaging in the large-scale change required, warned organizations: "Do not do it unless a. the current state is intolerable, b. you are willing to make the needed investment over time, c. you are prepared to stick with it permanently, d. it is important to the success or survival of the business" (Heilpern and Nadler, 1992, p. 150). Few academic institutions could meet all four criteria. Implementation was thought most likely to be successful when it was accompanied by pain and crisis and when it was consistently applied across the institution and over time by managers at all levels who were fully committed to its ideas. TQM involves cultural changes in the basic mind-set and values of the organization, and probably requires at least five to seven years to implement fully.

Organizations preparing for TQM had to ask themselves, What is our mission? and Who are our customers? (Schmidt and Finnigan, 1992, p. 96). These, of course, are the questions for which many academic institutions, particularly as they became larger and more complex, could offer no clear answers. TQM's focus on the customer seemed simple enough, but in practice many groups inside and outside the organization were customers, and they often had different needs. Not only were there many different internal and external customers, but as Keller said, "There is so much ambiguity about which customers colleges should aim to please: students, professors, taxpayers, parents, or their graduates' prospective employers" (Nicklin, 1995, p. A34). To add to the complexity, one of the most important groups—students—were not only customers but also producers and products. "So what exactly is a student from the Total Quality perspective? On the one hand, lack of a straightforward answer suggests that TQM concepts don't fit well" (Ewell, 1993, p. 55). TQM/ CQI also proved difficult to implement because of its comprehensive nature. The objective is nothing less than "the transformation of the modern corporate enterprise" (Marchese, 1993, p. 11), and "moving towards total quality management requires the design and implementation of an entire set of changes that affect virtually all components of an organization" (Heilpern and Nadler, 1992, p. 143).

But even if TQM/CQI could improve every aspect of institutional functioning, there was no agreement on what the process itself really was. On one extreme was the statistical control perspective of TQM's founders that required check sheets, Pareto charts, Ishikawa fish-bone diagrams, histograms, run charts, scattergrams, and control charts (Schmidt and Finnigan, 1992). This perspective was not too congenial with traditional academic practices, but then none of TQM's eminent gurus "ever imagined that statistical quality controls or reliability engineering could be employed at colleges and universities, or tried to adapt TQM for higher education" (Keller, 1992, p. 50). At the other extreme were those who argued that higher education should soften the rigor of statistical control. It should take an eclectic approach emphasizing customer focus, continuous improvement, management by fact, benchmarking, strategic planning, and better communications rather than formulas or tools (Marchese, 1993; Seymour, 1992). The eclectic view made sense, but removing the statistical elements of TQM in the university version meant it was not TQM at all, but TQM-Lite or SLI (Something Like It). Given the differences in opinion and the variations and contradictions in methodologies (Melan, 1995), "there exists today no single, commonly accepted definition of quality management" (Marchese, 1997, p. 503), and it is impossible to specify what it is (Harari, 1993b). Perhaps TQM is nothing more than common sense, but then "this makes it difficult to pinpoint a given institution's definition and application of TQM and it also allows almost any institutional advance to be credited to TQM" (Entin, 1993, p. 30).

More challenging than the difficulties of organizational change and the confusions of definition was finding a fit between TQM/CQI and the traditions, values, and purposes of academic institutions. Some thought TQM led to centralization and strengthening the powers of management. Others believed it stressed participative processes that would reduce the social distance between leaders and followers, and inevitably weaken the influence of presidential leadership (Fisher, 1993). And some aspects of TQM raised serious social and educational issues. Using statistical processes to improve quality might appear innocuous, but embedded in that concept was the need to reduce unnecessary variation and train teachers to be managers who could apply statistical analysis to educational processes (Hittman, 1993). The ultimate purpose of TQM, at least as classically defined, was to "create a uniform production process by reducing variation in the raw inputs to the production process and by removing variation from the process itself" (Pallas and Neumann, 1993). Combining cultural stereotypes in defining "customer," simplistic definitions of "quality," and the consequences of reducing variation in an increasingly pluralistic society, TQM could be viewed not as an objective process for improvement but as a conservative ideological instrument for strengthening established forms of authority (Bensimon, 1995). At its extremes, critics argued that TQM was "a blatantly econometric and ethnocentric discourse where human variability is a 'virus' to be 'eliminated' under a war metaphor" and whose purpose is "to absorb and homogenize dissent and difference." For those opposed to TQM/CQI, "nothing less than the future of independent intellectual work is at stake" (Dennis, 1995).

TQM/CQI was perhaps the first management fad in higher education that provoked a serious discussion not only of its technical merits, but also of its educational and social implications. And when examined from those perspectives, the disconnect between the philosophy of the management process and the purposes of the institution for which it was being proposed became more evident. "When bringing TQM to campus, one brings a language developed in the realm of commodity production into the community of specialized academic discourse. . . . It is not useful to compare the acquisition of knowledge in a college classroom with purchasing chicken nuggets at a fast-food establishment, or even purchasing a car, unless one is attempting to illustrate absurdity" (Sloan, 1994, p. 459). Marchese, one of CQI's most articulate and sensible proponents, as well as one of its most insightful critics, summarized the

reasons that only a small number of campuses have truly implemented CQI: "It's too great a change, the time and effort are great,
the reason and reward for this are unclear, the language is off-
putting, the president doesn't buy in, nor does the faculty, and
maybe it's a fad" (Marchese, 1997, pp. 512–513).

Business Process Reengineering: Starting from Scratch (1990–1996)

Business Process Reengineering (BPR) was the consultant's answer
to the failure of TQM to solve the problems of corporate America.
TQM/CQI attempted to *improve* the status quo in an incremental
way; the value of BPR was that it would *challenge* the status quo
(Casey, 1995) through a revolutionary approach that would lead to
"breakthrough change" (Dougherty, 1994, p. 6). Using information
technology (IT) to identify new strategic and competitive advantages (Penrod and Dolence, 1991), the object of reengineering was
nothing less than organizational transformation. "Reengineering
needs to go far beyond writing new operational parameters or pro-
tocols. For transformation to be effective, it must begin with a strategic assessment of fundamental organizational goals" (Penrod and
Dolence, 1991, p. 13).

Of course, BPR was not the first management innovation to suggest the need to reevaluate and reorganize. Even TQM, which some
saw as a strategy for incremental improvement, was defined by others as "radical surgery" (Seymour, 1992, p. viii) that challenged the
basic assumptions of academic management. What distinguished
BPR from its predecessors was the centrality it gave to IT in the transformation. "The possibilities opened up by the new technology permit the dismantling or obliteration of . . . well-embedded, apparently
perpetual activities and processes. . . . The organization has not only
to rethink its use of IT; it has also to rethink its entire operational
structure given the potential afforded by advances in IT" (Bryant,
1998, p. 25). Because information systems *are* the organization, con-

trol of information is also a means of controlling the entire organization and influencing its culture, structure, and practices.

Development of BPR

In their 1993 best-seller *Reengineering the Corporation*, Hammer and Champy laid out the somewhat immodest claim that "reengineering is the only thing that stands between many U.S. corporations— indeed, the U.S. economy—and disaster" (p. xii). Reengineering was not a fad or "another quick fix that American managers can apply to their organizations" (p. 2). Instead, it meant "starting all over, starting from scratch. In business reengineering, old job titles and old organizational arrangements—departments, divisions, groups, and so on—cease to matter. They are artifacts of another age" (pp. 2–3). Organizations should look beyond functional departments and focus instead on processes and activities that produce value for a customer. Hammer and Champy based their ideas on an analysis of companies with which they had been consulting. Offering a number of vignettes and several case studies, but no data, they argued that in the future, "the only successful companies will be those that have drastically changed—reengineered—their business processes" (p. 5).

The formal definition of reengineering is "the fundamental rethinking and radical redesign of business processes to achieve dramatic improvements in critical contemporary measures of performance, such as cost, quality, service and speed" (Hammer and Champy, 1993, p. 32). Each of the four major words in the definition—*fundamental, radical, dramatic,* and *processes*—is significant. BPR calls for "disregarding all existing structures and procedures and inventing completely new ways of accomplishing work" when "a need exists for heavy blasting" (p. 33). It sounded revolutionary, although some called it "a contemporary repackaging of tried-and-true industrial engineering methods . . . now being administered in large doses to business enterprises that to survive must instantly show improved profits. . . . This extremism offers seemingly instant relief from the pressure on corporate executives to show immediate improvement" (Strassmann, 1994).

Previous expectations in the business world that investing in information systems would pay off had not been realized, but the reason for the disappointing performance was now clear: it was not enough to automate processes. Instead, new processes and structures would have to be created through reengineering and "a critical examination of *all* basic assumptions about the way things are done" (Penrod and Dolence, 1992, p. 8). Reengineering promised managers "certainty and control. Here, at last, is a clear-cut, nononsense guide to rebuilding their business and beating the competition" (Micklethwait and Wooldridge, 1996, p. 28).

BPR combined institutional strategy, work processes, people and technology to improve performance and sustain competitive advantage, and was "customer-driven, data-intensive, and results-oriented" (Dougherty, 1994, p. 4). The power of IT gave organizations the opportunity to "re-evaluate many of the assumptions governing their overall and everyday operations. . . . The outcome of such re-evaluation would be leaner, more efficient, more profitable enterprise" (Bryant, 1998). Reengineering rejects TQM's developmental, team-based approach to improving processes. Instead, "SWAT teams of top managers and outside consultants descend on a process; take it apart, try to wring steps, time, and costs out of it; and put in a new plan of work" (Marchese, 1997, p. 509).

The reengineering battle cry was, "Don't automate, obliterate" (Hammer, 1990). The basic ideas behind reengineering were simple, but "implementing them is a major undertaking by any existing organization" (Penrod and Dolence, 1992, p. 9). And indeed the list of ten required elements—including changing leadership styles, redefining organizational culture, redefining organizational structure, and creating a strategic plan—was somewhat daunting. With restructuring, positions would be integrated so individuals engaged in complex tasks would be connected through simple processes and teamwork, workers would make decisions, the steps in the process would be determined by natural precedence rather than previous rules, processes would exist in multiple versions rather than be standardized, work would be performed where it made sense, and checks and controls would be reduced. "When a process is reengineered, jobs evolve from narrow and task-oriented to multidimensional. People who once did as they were instructed now make choices and decisions on their own instead. Assembly-line work disappears. Functional departments lose their reasons for being. Managers stop acting like supervisors and behave more like coaches. Workers focus more on the customer's needs and less on their bosses" (Hammer and Champy, 1993, p. 65).

Although there was not full agreement on what BPR was or the extent to which it differed from TQM, the rhetoric was seductive. A 1994 survey indicated that 69 percent of large American corporations were engaged in one or more BPR projects. And half of the remainder were considering doing so (O'Neill and Sohal, 1999). How could something become so popular so fast? Well, it turned out that one of the attractive managerial outcomes of combining jobs to make them multidimensional was that fewer people were needed to do more work. No wonder it seemed that "corporate America has embraced reengineering strategies, turning organizations on their sides by placing customers at the center and flattening organizational hierarchies" (Dougherty, 1994, p. 3). It seemed too good to be true, and so the question was asked, "Is it a fad which will pass, or does it have the qualities to endure once the initial interest fades?" (M. Thomas, 1994, p. 28).

The answer came very quickly. Despite its grand pronouncements and unassailable logic, BPR did not work as promised. This assessment was not made by BPR's detractors, but by its major advocates. "Sadly, we must report that . . . many companies that begin reengineering don't succeed at it," acknowledged Hammer and Champy. "They end their efforts precisely where they began, making no significant changes, achieving no major performance improvement, and fueling employee cynicism with yet another ineffective business improvement program. Our unscientific estimate is that as many as 50 percent to 70 percent of the organizations that undertake a re-engineering effort do not achieve the dramatic results they intended" (1993, p. 200). A study in 1994 by a major BPR consultant firm found that of ninety-nine organizations using BPR, 33 percent reported strong results, 42 percent mediocre results, and 25 percent no positive results (Shapiro, 1995). Others (Keller, 1997) agreed with Hammer and Champy's estimate of a 50 to 70 percent failure rate. In the final analysis, "Hundreds of companies have tried the Hammer and Champy formula, often with unhappy results. For a variety of reasons, a reported 70 percent of such interventions fail; the 'outsiders' never understood the work well enough, technology wasn't the whole answer, the costs in employee morale outweighed the gains" (Marchese, 1997, p. 509).

In a 1994 survey of business executives, BPR received higher ratings than any other management technique in four of five outcome categories. In a comparable survey in 1996, reengineering did not score above average in any of them (White, 1996, p. 1). Was BPR too radical? Perhaps, but some argued it had to be because "compromise and incrementalism would doom the effort to failure." Nevertheless, the threat that BPR would brutally demolish existing organizations, and the confusion between BPR and downsizing and other cost-cutting strategies, was believed to be a main reason corporations and their workers frequently rejected the idea ("Repositioning Reengineering," n. d.). By 1996, the radical view of BPR in the business world was replaced by a more moderate and incremental view of organizational change (Malhotra, 1996).

Although Champy was still insisting that demand for reengineering remained high in 1996, others said that interest in the concept was fading, and reengineering as a consulting style was passé (Pham, 1996). Three years after launching "this decade's hottest management fad," Michael Hammer agreed that reengineering contained a flaw: it forgot about people. "I wasn't smart enough about that. I was reflecting my engineering background and was insufficiently appreciative of the human dimensions. I've learned that's critical." Not only had Hammer learned a lot, but "so have a lot of businesses, disillusioned by the backlash against layoffs, overwork and constant upheaval stemming from their efforts to adopt Dr. Hammer's model" (White, 1996, p. 1). Downsizing as a consequence of reengineering created hollow companies less able to compete, and cutting costs did not lead to productivity gains (Roach, 1996). As a consequence, "the term re-engineering has fallen from grace in corporate board rooms—associated with the downsizing of United States companies in the last six years" (Rifkin, 1996), and "some commentators have now consigned BPR to the long list of management fads and gimmicks that briefly flourish and then are rapidly forgotten" (Bryant, 1998). As the reengineering revisionists assess the negative consequences of the fad, they begin instead "preaching the virtues of 'growth,' 'trust,' and 'loyalty.' In time, there will doubtless be reengineering re-revisionists reaffirming the faith" (Micklethwait and Wooldridge, 1996, p. 5).

BPR in Higher Education

The forces confronting American business in the early 1990s were affecting higher education as well, leading to an "acute cost crisis, an increasingly demanding customer base, and an erosion of public confidence" (Dougherty, 1994, p. 3). BPR offered the means for finding quick and enduring solutions and for creating the foundation for "a process for transforming higher education" (Penrod and Dolence, 1992). What was called for was a rethinking of the basic structure of the academic enterprise, and "the first obstacle to reforming the way institutions of higher education set their goals and spend their funds is just this sense that colleges and universities are different—that they are not like other enterprises and hence should be exempt from the restructuring that is reshaping how America does business" ("A Call to Meeting," 1993, p. 3A). So what is preventing restructuring? Recalcitrant faculty, self-serving bureaucrats, and spineless presidents. And what has to be done? Transform the culture, get faculty support for a unified vision, simplify the curriculum, and outsource (including instruction) among other things. "Given strong leadership and a sustained commitment to the retraining of current staff, we believe that a five-to-seven-year process designed to re-engineer operations can yield a 25 percent reduction in the number of full-time employees an institution needs. Fundamentally, however, restructuring will strengthen an institution because the process itself will force a sustained reexamination of functions and procedures that have grown haphazardly over the last three decades" ("A Call to Meeting," 1993, p. 7A). The need for change transcended the economic benefits, however. "Higher education needs to reinvent itself and redefine its relations to various communities." Rather than respond slowly to social change, "how much more fitting it would be for higher education leaders to rise above the tumult to chart a new course and to craft new communities, not only for their institutions but also for society" (Doucette, 1993, p. 50).

In a refreshing if understated reality check, even BPR's proponents reluctantly appeared to agree that "putting institutional mission before divisional or disciplinary priorities, eliminating unnecessary programs and redistributing scarce resources, reexamining and redefining long held assumptions, finding new ways to measure what we do, changing the parameters for the way leaders are selected, and redefining the internal reward structure of the institution might prove to be very difficult to accomplish in any college or university" (Penrod and Dolence, 1992, p. 33).

The difficulties began with trying to define what a process was in higher education. Hammer and Champy (1993) said that "processes are what companies do" (p. 117) to convert input into output, so presumably the processes of higher education should be defined in terms of teaching, research, and service. On the other hand, reengineering always comes from the top down, and "if a company operates from consensus, its people will find the top-down nature of reengineering an affront to their sensibilities" (Hammer and Champy, 1993, p. 207). Almost by definition, reengineering would seem in conflict with notions of shared authority. Nevertheless, there were those who saw BPR in higher education as leading to increased performance and quality, satisfied customers, and reduced costs, as well as helping administrators reorient their thinking about mission and core competencies (Dougherty, 1994).

Reengineering originally was conceived to be applicable to the business practices of the university. Early advocates also suggested how technology could be used to improve student services, such as registration, that were initially developed to meet the needs of a pre-IT world (Penrod and Dolence, 1991). Others thought that to be successful, reengineering in higher education should start with teaching and learning rather than administration. To focus on administration would distort the mission of the institution: the goals and evaluation measures would address administrative rather than academic values, and attention would be paid to the management of resources, faculty, and students rather than to teaching, learning, and research. For reengineering to be effective in higher education, "the process must be driven by academic goals; issues such as appropriateness and effectiveness of teaching, learning and research must count for more than administrative measures like efficiency and profit" (Stahlke and Nyce, 1996, p. 51).

In 1993, a book published by CAUSE and funded by DEC (Heterick, 1993) helped to legitimate the use of BPR by presenting arguments both for and against the use of reengineering in the teaching and learning process. CAUSE is a professional association of information technology professionals in higher education, and DEC was at that time a prominent supplier of computer equipment used by many institutions. The book's Foreword declared that higher education is in financial crisis and on a collision course with its clients. Reengineering is the answer: "Like the corporate sector, our only responsible alternative is to 'do more with less' by restructuring the enterprise. This means, rethinking our assumptions about delivery systems, curriculum, organizational structures. And the mix of technology and personnel. It means virtually turning the enterprise on its head to find a better, cheaper, more effective way to deliver education, service, and research products" (Mingle, 1993, p. iii). Authors writing from different institutional perspectives offered views ranging from endorsement to rejection about the need for reengineering in research universities (Katz, 1993), liberal arts colleges (Smallen, 1993), community colleges (Bleed, 1993), and comprehensive universities (West and Daigle, 1993).

Even those who took the restricted administrative view did not necessarily believe reengineering would be useful. The primary activities of business and university were so different that if a university was not in serious trouble, "we are probably wasting our time to propose business reengineering. True administrative process redesign will be difficult to achieve in a university due to lack of support, opposition by vested interests, and limited demonstrated realizable benefits" (Porter, 1993, p. 49). Moreover, while universities may claim to have implemented reengineering processes, the examples described in the literature or at conferences turned out to have been incremental changes in process and not redesign at all. There were many reports of success prepared by consulting firms, but at least as of 1993, "there are no examples in the literature of business reengineering, as defined in this paper, being applied within higher education" (Porter, 1993, p. 49).

McClure (1993) thought that while administrative processes might be engineered to reduce cost or improve quality, instructional processes could not be because of lack of clear and measurable outcomes, and the fact that "you cannot reengineer a process that you do not control" (p. 47). Moreover, "while there are some cases in which we can document an improved educational output as a result of the technology intervention, in a brief survey of the literature I could find no studies documenting improved educational output per unit of cost. The educational gains from information technology typically have been at huge cost, in terms of the investment in both equipment and software, but more significantly, in faculty and support staff time" (p. 48).

Nevertheless, by 1994 some thought that reengineering had made significant inroads. "The latest management technique to migrate from the corporate world to the world of higher education is reengineering. This business redesign process has been cropping up on American college and university campuses from California to New York" (Pritchett, 1994–1995, p. 7). Clearly, "reengineering is more than a fad or the management technique of the month" (p. 8). By 1996, "reengineering has begun at perhaps several dozen U.S. colleges and universities" (Chabotar and Knutel, 1996–1997, p. 11). Whether it was effective was still up in the air, and exactly what was meant by reengineering was even more confused. Reengineering was called many things: process design concept, work process design, continuous quality improvement, restructuring, and organizational redesign, among others (Penrod and Dolence, 1992; Chabotar and Knutel, 1996–97). A course that incorporated technology was said to be "reengineered." An institution changing its structure was identified as being "reengineered." It was as if *reengineering* and *change* were synonyms, and that prior to reengineering, higher education never changed.

There were some university success stories attributed to reengineering. One institution reported significant savings from a reengineering project that transformed a time-consuming and expensive purchasing preaudit system to a more effective postaudit system (Harel and Partipilo, 1995). However, "if we take 'reengineering' to mean a substantial, deliberate, planned shift in a process or system, then it may not be appropriate to call what is likely to happen in teaching and learning a reengineering. The change process will be partially planned and partially accidental, probably with a trail of failed experiments" (Twigg, 1993, p. 38). Both the system of American higher education and categories of institutions within the system, noted Twigg, have historically reengineered themselves.

Restructuring was a fact of academic life and had been for a long time. A survey of institutions in 1994 indicated that most of them were making, and had been making, changes in their structures, curricula, and administrative processes. Although they were part of the process of incremental change and reflected "continuing actions over a number of years," they were numerous and extensive enough to influence fundamental institutional processes (El-Khawas, 1994, p. 11). Administrative offices were being reorganized, administrative layers reduced, administrative activity redesigned, programs eliminated. But was it reengineering? Restructuring (including plans to increase efficiency, changes in administration, and modifications in organizational structure) was going on in higher education, as it had previously in business. But academic economists were warning that 90 percent of corporate restructuring fails, primarily because of failure to cope with the human resource issues, and that successful change in higher education depended on the willing involvement of faculty (Horn and Jerome, 1996). Such willing involvement might be in short supply if the concepts of reengineering were applied to changing teaching and the educational delivery system in order to improve learning and student satisfaction at lower cost (Davis, 1995).

In the end, reengineering in higher education produced a lot of rhetoric and few examples. "Some colleges are merely claiming to be reengineering because it seems to be the fashionable thing to do. Others . . . are using reengineering as a public relations gimmick to justify wide-spread layoffs, while still others just haven't had much success reengineering because professors and administrators are resisting it" (Nicklin, 1995, p. A33). In the brave new world of management fads, almost any change in process could be called BPR by those who wanted to appear au courant.

Whatever Happened to BPR?

Davenport (1995) explained how older ideas of technology, business processes, and redesign were unintentionally merged to create the concept of reengineering in 1989 and became a $51 billion industry by 1995. The growth was caused by the burgeoning consultant industry, the sales interests of the computer industry, and the desire of top managers in big corporations to look good. Consultants developed program modification after modification, and their fees skyrocketed. They began to rely on downsizing and layoffs to produce quick bottom-line results that justified their fees. And the resultant bloodshed tore the social fabric of the organizations that had initially embraced it. When the dust settled around 1994, more critical assessments indicated some of the prominent "success stories" that had created the great interest in the first place had not really been engineering efforts but had been repackaged on a post hoc basis to appear as if they were. Other early success stories (including some described by Hammer and Champy) did not follow up to include their later disasters. In late 1995, reported Davenport (p. 4), although "reengineering isn't dead, it is effectively over." Although reengineering in industry was already under attack in 1996, advocates were arguing that its use in higher education "requires recognizing the broad principles of reengineering that have been applied effectively in business and industry" (Stahlke and Nyce, 1996, p. 50). BPR "offers a thoroughly researched and well-crafted prescriptive punch list for evaluating how well a college or university runs its business-related departments" (Casey, 1995, p. 8).

Many reasons were offered for the failure of BPR ventures. They failed because they were "short-term, near-sighted" answers to complex problems, and were ultimately seen as "euphemisms for paying fewer people less money, offering them lower benefits and reduced security but expecting higher performance" (Bryant, 1998). They were thwarted by the inertia of long-standing structures, the vested interests of organizational managers, the restrictions of traditional budgeting systems, the scarcity of appropriate data (Dougherty, 1994), "failures of intellect or courage" (Bleakley, 1993, p. A6), and the reactions of "staff workers and professors who are resistant to change" (Nicklin, 1995, p. A34). They did not work because, even more than TQM, BPR emphasized process while ignoring the substantive issues related to the purposes of the business (Shapiro, 1995). As with other fads before it, advocates claimed there was nothing inherently wrong with BPR, but most people implementing it had a misperception about what it really was and were not "doing it right" (Micklethwait and Wooldridge, 1996, p. 35). Instead of providing a framework for improving work processes, BPR was often promoted as a strategy for reducing staffing.

Since reengineering was hot and there was no accepted definition of what it was, "anyone who wanted to gain attention for a project of any sort was best advised to term it 'reengineering'" (Bryant, 1998). While acknowledging that reengineering has not been successful, "few concede that the technique itself may be at fault. The problems are with poor implementation, usually resulting from an uncommitted chief executive and top team. The main implementation problems are thinking too small, getting caught up in fixing subprocesses from the bottom up rather than seeing the big picture without constraints, and refusing to demand very significant improvements" (Hilmer and Donaldson, 1996, p. 104). But perhaps the most critical barrier was the one mentioned by Hammer (1990) in his original *Harvard Business Review* article: "No one in an organization wants reengineering. It is confusing and disruptive and affects everything people have grown accustomed to. Only if top-level managers back the effort and outlast the company cynics will people take reengineering seriously" (p. 112).

BPR was even more unsuited for higher education than for the business corporations for which it was originally prescribed. Even its creators acknowledged that BPR "must focus on redesigning a fundamental business process, not on departments or other organization units" (Hammer and Champy, 1993, p. 40). But the "work" that universities did *was* their departments. And the academic culture of higher education meant it would be necessary to dismantle higher education completely as we know it if BPR was adopted; the redesign would have to ignore the foundation of over four hundred years of tradition and start "with a clean sheet of paper" (Hammer and Champy, 1993, p. 49).

Ultimately, BPR failed, as so many other attempts to impose radical change on unwilling groups do. "Reengineering fits neatly into patterns of past revolutionary movements: In each case, the leaders call for uncompromising destruction of existing institutions. Only through this kind of attack on customs, habits, and relationships can newcomers gain influence with little opposition. The common characteristics of the elite that agitates destructively for positions of leadership is an arrogance that they are the only ones with superior insight, the only ones deserving of trust. Versions of 'throw history into the dustbin and start anew' have been attributed to every failed radical movement of the last 200 years" (Strassmann, 1994).

Part II

Understanding Academic Management Fads

5

The Life Cycle of Academic
Management Fads

We have now reviewed seven higher education management fads. Each began outside higher education and then diffused into academia. After being hailed for its great promise, each was eventually abandoned, only to be replaced shortly thereafter by another fad. These are not novel observations. They are consistent with the informal and anecdotal comments noted by higher education scholars in the past. In this chapter I will use the forty years of evidence already presented about these seven innovations to develop a more formal model of management fads from the time they enter into the higher education system until the time of their eventual abandonment, reinvention, or partial incorporation. I hope the model might improve our understanding of the effects of management innovations of the past and give both institutional and political policymakers a context in which to understand the possible trajectories of academic management techniques that may be introduced in the future. I have over simplified reality by referring to two systems—academic and nonacademic—although the management of some nonacademic professional institutions, such as churches, hospitals, and research laboratories, may more closely resemble the university than the business corporation.

I treated each of the seven fads in Chapters Two through Four as a separate case study. I then reviewed the cases iteratively using a process of explanation building (Yin, 1984) to see if there were patterns that could best integrate and explain the general process. My analysis proposes the stages in the life cycle of management fads within organizational sectors, suggests the lagged phases through which fads move between the nonacademic and the academic sectors, and discusses some similarities and differences in the fad adoption process in academic and nonacademic systems. If you have already read the previous three chapters, some of the phrases I use here (without attribution) to illustrate my generalizations will sound familiar to you. You can refer to earlier chapters to find the original statements and their citations.

Stages of the Fad Process

I believe there is a consistent and predictable five-stage cycle that describes the trajectory of management fads: creation, narrative evolution, time lag, narrative devolution, and dissonance resolution. The stage process is depicted in Figure 5.1. The fad trajectory appears to be similar in both the nonacademic and academic organizational sectors.

Stage 1: Creation

A crisis is claimed to exist in an organizational sector, usually related to a major change in the larger social system (for example, the cold war, recession) or an organizational subsystem within it (for example, lack of international competitiveness in business or lack of attention to customer needs in higher education). A new era of massive and widespread social, economic, demographic, and technical change is declared in which, it is argued, past operating assumptions no longer apply. The adoption of a new management technique is proposed to solve the problem. The new technique is supported by advocates (often, paid consultants whose livelihood depends on creating and disseminating this new management technique), dramatic but unverified narratives of success by external champions, and enthusiastic statements of early organizational adopters announcing the importance of what is called a proven concept that is already in wide use.

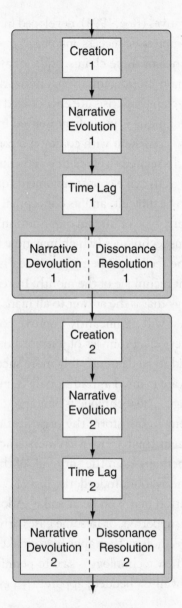

Figure 5.1. Life Cycle Stages of the Fads Process

The stories, or narratives (Roe, 1994), developed in this creation stage include claims of impressive success and dazzling results.

As a consequence of these claims, additional institutions participating in common interorganizational networks (Rogers, 1995) and accepting the claims of crisis are encouraged to adopt the new technique. The technique is initially presented in simplified terms that appear to be so consistent with common sense and rationalized organizational myths related to efficiency and effectiveness (Meyer and Rowan, 1992) as to make counterarguments difficult. The technique is said not to be difficult, and its conceptual simplicity can be applied to nearly any type of human organization. Advocates state that unlike previous techniques (which may now be explicitly denigrated as fads), the technique being promoted is more than a fad or the management technique of the month. Instead, it is presented as a winning strategy that is the answer to all managerial problems—a breakthrough that will significantly improve core organizational processes and functions. Promises of extraordinary outcomes are made, users are said to be demonstrably more successful than non-users, and resisters are painted as traditionalists unwilling or unable to respond to change. The technique is often presented as both necessary and sufficient to transform the organizational sector. True believers may present their views with messianic zeal and suggest that the success, perhaps even the survival, of the sector depends on adopting this innovation. Indeed, the loss of our status as a leading world-class nation may well be at stake. Adoption of the new technique may be supported, or in some cases driven, by the availability of a new technology that appears to make its implementation feasible. This new technology is said to permit the dismantling or obliteration of well-embedded, apparently perpetual activities and processes.

Stage 2: Narrative Evolution

Narratives begun in the Creation stage become elaborated and more widely disseminated. The innovation may be identified as the single most successful concept ever to have been picked up and put into practice in all of management history. Stories of successful implementation are increasingly distributed and the innovation hailed as highly effective. The narrative focuses on claimed benefits; little attention is given to potential costs. There are few counternarratives, and those that attempt to relate traditional counternarratives containing concepts such as shared authority or academic freedom are labeled as apologists out of touch with contemporary needs. It is asserted that the new technique has been widely adopted, if not throughout the system then at least by the higher-status members of the system—for example, 80 percent of the Fortune 500. These allegations of widespread adoption persuade even more institutions to adopt the technique through imitation or to maintain legitimacy (Meyer and Rowan, 1992). Consultants, champions, purveyors of the technology, and adopters increasingly circulate within the organizational system, declaring this the most popular reform of the decade, making presentations at professional meetings, and writing articles for professional journals that contribute to the diffusion of the innovation. These presentations serve to certify and reinforce the status of the person making them, the progressiveness of the institutions that are mentioned, and the quality of organizational leadership in those institutions. As some have said, these presentations tend to be rich in principles, slogans, and invocations and short on specifics, cost, and candor. The stories of success prove to be attractive to newspapers, news magazines, and other agents of mass media eager to spot new trends, so the name or acronym of the innovation, and simplistic statements of its foundational ideas, become popularized. As Meyer (1992, p. 252) explained it, "Knowledge and innovation claimants need to move quickly from technical communication networks into the public media, to get the attention of the public in general. To this end, successful demonstrations are important, as are exaggerated citations of allegedly successful demonstrations. Newness and newsworthiness are virtues." Organizations adopting the innovation are applauded for acknowledging the existence of serious problems, engaging in efforts to improve and reform, and conceding that system and social benefits should outweigh selfish interests of organizational participants. Managers not accepting the innovation may be castigated as bureaucrats who thrive on confusion or special interests who prefer to work in the dark. Opponents are identified as resistant to change, conservative, wasteful, and self-interested.

Stage 3: Time Lag

There is a lag between the time the new technique is created and disseminated and the time at which user reactions and independent analyses become widely available. Stories of successful adoption continue to be disseminated during this period. These stories are usually written by or about organizational members with vested interests in being seen as being associated with a successful program and whose leadership is thereby given visibility and praise. The unavailability of data makes it possible to exaggerate claims, advocate implementation based on theoretical grounds, and substitute "virtuous examples for data" (Meyer, 1992, p. 253). At the same time, revisionist and cautionary stories begin to surface, some reminding organizations of the unfulfilled promises of previous innovations and others suggesting that not all those adopting the innovation have been successful with it. Scholars and others (who may themselves have vested interests different from the promoters of the innovation) begin to disseminate analyses of new data that were not previously available. During this time lag period, the acceptance of the innovation peaks, and the pace of new adopters slows because those most likely to adopt have already done so.

Stage 4: Narrative Devolution

As the more recent revisionist analyses are disseminated, overly optimistic claims of success are replaced by overly pessimistic claims that the signs of disappointment are everywhere and that noticeable disenchantment has set in. The power of the original creation narrative is challenged by a new narrative of skepticism. Enthusiasm for the new technique based on initial reports of success becomes tempered by countervailing reports of failure as outcomes fall short of unrealistic expectations. Data collected by scholars and other observers studying the new technique indicate that it failed to produce its promised results. The original claims of success are now seen as either overstated or not sustained, organizational performance was not improved in the predicted manner, and claims of the extent of adoption had been wildly inflated. Finally, some call the fad a public relations gimmick with little or no impact on the organization itself. Surveys of users reflect increased dissatisfaction. Analysts report that "the success rate of any of these approaches is pretty low," state that they "know of no empirical evidence that any of these things increase productivity" (Bleakley, 1993, p. A1), and comment on how scant the documented evidence for its best practice remains. Acceptance of the new technique diminishes; journal and newspaper commentaries report on the reversal of fortune and declare the new technique to be effectively over, or dead as a pet rock. Each fad turns out to be based on old ideas and empty platitudes: "Each and every one of the paths, no matter what they say, are all based on the same principles, they all say the same thing. We love to remarket things, but there is nothing new. We are destined to make great time with each new 'management fad' but we will remain lost" (p. 7). The fad is declared a fraud that has failed everywhere it has been tried. No new institutions adopt the fad, although previous adopters may continue the fad as they discount new information that is in conflict with their previous beliefs. For believers, conflicting evidence—even completely discrediting evidence—may increase rather than decrease levels of commitment (Nisbett and Ross, 1980).

Stage 5: Resolution of Dissonance

There is significant overlap in time between stages 4 and 5, but I separate them here for purposes of analysis because they appear to have different dynamic properties. As champions and adopters see the demise of the innovation that only recently they had vigorously advocated, there is a need to account for its failure in ways that protect both their status and their ideological credibility. "A man with conviction is a hard man to change" (Festinger, Riecken, and Schachter, 1956), so it should not be unexpected that those who support the premises of a fad are not dissuaded from their views merely because it has not been successful.

Analyses of these seven fads reveal many of the rationalizations used, the most frequent of which are the poor quality of leadership, intransigence of followers, improper implementation, and lack of resources. Fads failed to work because the right methods of structure and process were not followed or the fad had not been properly implemented. Failure may also be attributed to foolishly implementing a "bad" version of the innovation, whereas success would have been ensured if only the "good" version had been implemented and done properly. The least frequent response to failure is to consider the possibility that the new technique itself may have been based on invalid premises, so that successful implementation was either highly improbable or even impossible. Identifying failure as resulting from the weaknesses of specific individuals, unforeseeable external forces, or correctable flaws in implementation sets the stage for reinventing the innovation and recycling it with minor modifications and a major change of name (Rogers, 1995), or for proposing a better innovation (clearly labeled as "not a fad"). This "better" innovation is claimed as both necessary and sufficient for organizational improvement and as having corrected the unfortunate problems leading to the abandonment of the earlier innovation. As an example, "whenever TQM methods are implemented as a quick fix to an immediate problem (as is often the case), participants expect to see quick results. When these results do not become immediately noticeable, TQM is dropped" (Sims and Sims, 1995, p. 19). The Creation stage begins anew, and the stages of the cycle are repeated.

Movement of Fads Between Organizational Sectors

Each of the management fads considered in this book was implemented initially in either business or governmental organizations before being diffused into higher education. There is relatively little overlap between the interorganizational networks of the innovation source groups in government and business and the higher education systems in which they were later applied. Members of both academic and nonacademic organizations have more association and communication with those inside their own sector than with those outside. For the most part, people in different sectors read different journals, attend different meetings, share different values and perspectives, and live in different organizational cultures. This discontinuity produces a culture lag, so events that are disseminated and generally known in one sector may not be immediately known in another. So how does the transmission between sectors take place? Here is one proposal.

As the apparently successful implementation of a management innovation in the original sector becomes conventional wisdom as part of its Narrative Evolution stage, groups or individuals concerned with issues of organizational efficiency and effectiveness suggest that the innovation may be suitable for adoption in new settings such as higher education. Exactly how the transition between sectors is accomplished is unclear. It may be related to the increasing availability of stories in the popular press, but research on the adoption of innovation (Rogers, 1995) suggests that interpersonal communications are more effective than mass communications in disseminating innovations. Moreover, interpersonal communications about innovations are more effective when they occur between individuals who are similar, while members of different sectors are more likely to be dissimilar. This suggests that a major vector of management innovation in higher education may be boundary-spanning individuals who have identities in both the nonacademic and academic sectors. These intersector carriers might include business leaders or legislators serving on higher education boards of trustees, college presidents appointed to business boards of directors, professional associations formed at least in part to maintain linkages between higher education and external groups, academics who read journals in multidisciplinary areas such as business or human resource management, and consultants who solicit clients in both the education and noneducation sectors.

As a consequence of culture lag, champions in academic institutions become familiar with innovations in the nonacademic sector at that time in the nonacademic sector's Narrative Evolution stage in which expectations are high and increased levels of adoption are claimed. Unaware of the revisionist analyses taking place during the latter part of the Time Lag and early part of the Narrative Devolution stages in the nonacademic sector, but persuaded by the enthusiastic reports developed during the earlier Narrative Evolution stage, champions in higher education begin the Creation stage in their sector. These fads may "arrive at higher education's doorstep five years after their trial in business, often just as corporations are discarding them" (Marchese, 1991, p. 7). The higher education sector then recapitulates the cycle of the nonacademic sector, but in academic procession–like fashion, always one to two stages behind. This relationship is depicted in Figure 5.2.

Similarities and Differences Between Sectors

Innovations are ideas or practices perceived as new by the adopting organization (Rogers, 1995), regardless of whether they are objectively new, so it is not surprising that the process of fad adoption in academic settings is similar to that followed by the same innovation in nonacademic settings. In both sectors, initial decisions to adopt management innovations appear to be based on subjective judgments disseminated by peers within a social system rather than analyses of empirical data, and in both sectors the momentum of innovators and early adopters is accelerated during the Narrative Evolution stage. When 10 to 20 percent of a population has adopted an innovation, it has reached the take-off point (Rogers, 1995). At this time, the fate of an innovation is in the hands of a group that Rogers refers to as the "Early Majority." Compared with innovators and early adopters, the Early Majority is more deliberative and has a longer decision time. Acceptance by the Early Majority sets the

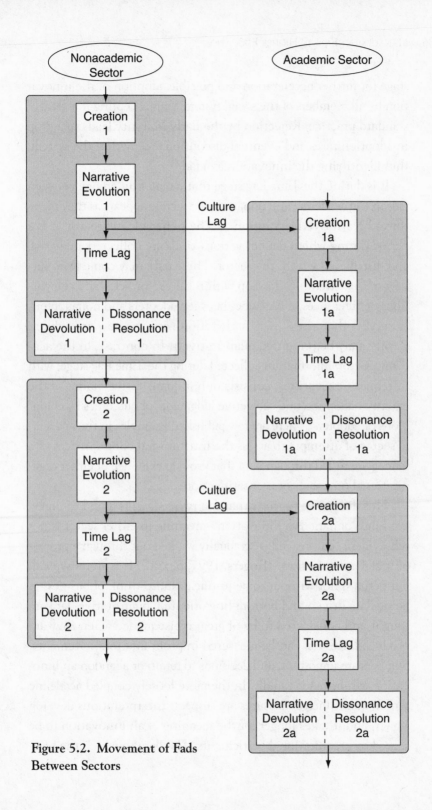

Figure 5.2. Movement of Fads Between Sectors

stage for further acceleration and possible adoption of the innovation by all members of the social system, thus accepting it as part of
standard practice. Rejection by the Early Majority leads to a drop
in adoption rates and eventual discontinuance within the system,
thus identifying the innovation as a fad.

It is during the Time Lag stage that a major difference between
fads in the academic and nonacademic sectors appears as they move
toward Narrative Devolution. In the nonacademic sector, it is a
period during which data of various kinds are collected, analyzed,
and distributed within the sector. These data may come from surveys of the extent of adoption within the sector, scholarly comparisons of differences in outcomes between adopters and nonadopters,
or surveys that assess users' satisfaction with the new procedures.
Results may be presented quantitatively. In contrast, in the academic sector, information collected during the Time Lag stage, with
infrequent exceptions, consists of nonquantitative claims of the
extent of adoption and subjective judgments of outcomes by champions or adopters. There are few published examples in the academic sector of attempts to assess the institutional consequences of a
management fad through data that provide evidence of either organizational outcomes or user satisfaction.

This difference suggests that the two sectors respond to different kinds of data. An innovation's meaning in either sector is not
self-evident, but instead is "gradually worked out through a process
of social construction" (Rogers, 1995, p. xvii). It is stereotypical,
but perhaps not without some justification, to think of business as
being data driven and bottom line oriented; quantitative data are
sought and considered to be of great consequence when they are
produced. Results can be measured in profit and loss statements,
numbers are important, and decisions to retain or abandon an innovation can be made rapidly. In the more loosely coupled academic
sector, quantitative measures are suspect. Interpretations develop
slowly, and it takes longer for the meaning of an innovation to be
shared by organizational participants. The data to which the busi-

ness sector responds may move more slowly in the academic sector as counternarratives of shared authority and other myths begin to respond to the original narrative of efficiency. The Narrative Devolution stage may be initiated by quantitative data in the nonacademic sector and interpretive data in the academic sector.

In addition to responding to different kinds of data, the meaning of "adoption" may differ between the sectors. In both the academic and nonacademic sectors, organizations may claim to have adopted an innovation without truly having done so. A large number of corporations adopt CEO incentive plans, for example, but only half actually use them (Scott, 1995). However, the hierarchical structures and legal authority systems of the nonacademic sector make it more likely that senior management can impose management innovations that may affect the institution's technical core. In contrast, the unique dual governance structure and loosely coupled processes of academic institutions buffer educational from administrative procedures and permit subgroups to operate with significant autonomy. This makes it easier in higher education for an innovation to be publicly "adopted" but not actually implemented in a way that affects core institutional processes. In this way, academic institutions may have greater opportunities than nonacademic ones to engage in what I call the "virtual adoption" of fads.

TQM/CQI, for example, which entered higher education through business, was identified by senior academic administrators in a 1993 survey as being used by 70 percent of all colleges and universities (El-Khawas, 1993). But by 1997, even TQM/CQI's avid advocates acknowledged that fewer than a dozen institutions had implemented it as a central component of their program (Marchese, 1997). More recent data suggest that fewer than 15 percent of all higher education institutions ever experimented with any aspect of TQM/CQI except in the most superficial way, and perhaps no more than a hundred seriously attempted to implement TQM/CQI techniques in portions of their institutional management (Birnbaum and Deshotels, 1999).

Academic institutions may have the ability to respond to fads as they respond to educational reforms: publicly adopt them as policy but never implement them (Cuban, 1990). "The act of supporting a policy with appropriate symbolic meaning can be more important to decision makers than its adoption, and its adoption can be more important than its implementation. Decision makers interested in building viable coalitions are likely to seek and find allies who will be vigorous in supporting symbolic decisions and lax in implementing them" (March, 1994, p. 196). Because business and government can more easily impose fad processes that influence what people actually do, they may be more sensitive to data that may confirm or deny the validity of the fad practice. In contrast, because the "adoption" of fads at academic institutions may be primarily symbolic and have little effect on what most people do, there may be less incentive to collect and analyze quantitative data that can validate or invalidate the innovation. Moreover, board members or legislators who may have pressured an institution to adopt an innovation are often transitory. They may have little opportunity or interest to follow up on outcomes of an implementation decision. Virtual adoption permits an external advocate to claim victory, even as it serves as a stalling technique for a manager (Dickeson, 1999).

Virtual adoption is essentially superficial, although at some institutions where adoption initiatives of senior administrators have been particularly intense, it may lead to some localized and undue disruption and discomfort. However, for the most part, it is unlikely to have any significant impact on the institutional core. Virtual adoption means that academic institutions may find it easier than other organizations both to adopt management fads and abandon them. Because the fad has been embraced only by the senior administration and not the technical core, neither adoption nor abandonment requires significant attention or effort from most of the organization's members or has a major impact on their daily lives.

Americans in general have a pro-innovation bias. We believe change is good. If adoption of innovations is slower in higher education than in manufacturing organizations, as asserted by Getz, Siegfried, and Anderson (1997), then higher education institutions will appear to be less rational and less technically efficient than other organizations. In the absence of compelling evidence (or, indeed, almost any probative data at all) that the adoption of a management fad can make colleges and universities more efficient or effective, the institutional strategy of overt acceptance and virtual adoption may be quite functional. Virtual adoption of fads allows an institution to have its cake and eat it too. Public claims of adopting an externally hailed innovation certify an institution's progressive attitude and concern for efficiency and improved management. Private isolation of the fad protects the institution from the disruptive effects it would have if it were really adopted.

Accounting for Management Fads

Suggestions by previous analysts of the existence of regularities in the management fad adoption process in higher education are supported by the patterns in this cross-case analysis of data describing the life cycle of seven management innovations. Management fads in higher education originate in nonacademic sectors, are disseminated in colleges and universities through the development of powerful narratives even as the fad is being challenged in its original sector, are virtually adopted in ways that recognize its symbolic importance while minimizing its potential disruption, and are eventually abandoned. This pattern is common but not universal; there are isolated exceptions. On a small number of campuses, a new management practice or process may take hold and be maintained long after most other institutions have rejected it. Occasionally a process considered to be a fad by most institutions may be integrated into an individual institution's culture and become a means by which the institution differentiates itself from others. These exceptional successes provide true believers with evidence they may use to argue that the innovation is sound and that its generalized failure is due to faulty implementation rather than an inadequate conceptual base. But perhaps a more realistic lesson to be learned is that in the context of the great diversity of colleges and universities in the United States, an idea may find fertile soil in some microclimates, even as it proves to be sterile in most others. If the success of management fads over the past forty years is measured mainly by the extent to which they have been adopted and maintained in recognizable form by institutions of higher education, it can be said with confidence that these particular innovations have uniformly failed.

Still, management fads in the academic sector continue to be created or reinvented despite the absence of data suggesting that they have been successful and in the face of the failure of most of them to be widely adopted by the sector. Why does this happen? Those who develop the fads, as well as those who support them, appear to view academic organizations through the lens of an organizational paradigm that emphasizes the importance of goals, rationality, and causality. The acceptance of this paradigm leads those who believe it to choose problems "that while the paradigm is taken for granted, can be assumed to have solutions" (Kuhn, 1970, p. 37). Fads therefore may be thought of as proposed solutions to puzzles seen as problems because of the paradigm being used. Management fads may sometimes be explicitly claimed by their creators to reflect a new paradigm, but in reality they reflect the old paradigms of rationality.

Although fads fail, the paradigm supporting them remains. As Kuhn pointed out, failure of a paradigm to solve problems does not by itself negate the paradigm; it merely suggests to its adherents that the puzzle has not yet been solved and that further work is necessary. For example, after acknowledging that TQM/CQI has been ignored or rejected by most potential users, advocates still point to a small number of limited but presumably successful programs to claim that the system does work; it just is not being implemented properly (Marchese, 1997). It is typical to deny the failure of a fad by arguing that others have used it successfully, it takes time to overcome past practices, and results will be achieved in the future (Nohria and Berkley, 1994). Because of these arguments, there are no data that can convince a true believer that a fad is not effective, and the positive value of a fad therefore cannot be disproved. Narratives cannot be overturned by countervailing evidence, but only by a different paradigm or "an equally straightforward narrative that tells a better story" (Roe, 1994, p. 40). Unless and until higher education is able to tell its story with a narrative more compelling than market-oriented economic utility, it is safe to assume that another fad, similar in many ways to the ones we have seen over the past forty years, is around the corner, and it will go through the stages within sectors and the phases between sectors described here.

Fads develop outside higher education and then are imported. I can think of no example in which a management innovation developed in higher education has been explicitly exported to business. Why is business in the lead? Some may say it is because business is more concerned with management than is education. A more cynical suggestion is that businesses have more consultants than education who make money by proposing and marketing fads. Why do consultants give priority to marketing fads to business over education? As Willie Sutton reasoned when asked why he robbed banks, "Because that's where the money is."

Although management fads in higher education have not had the positive outcomes promised by their proponents, it is also true that the loose coupling of academic organizations has prevented the dire consequences predicted by fad opponents. At the same time, it would be a mistake to believe that fads have no consequences at all for the organizations or systems that adopt them, either in reality or virtually. Some of these consequences may be negative: people become cynical and resistant to new ideas, the judgment of leaders is questioned, and funds and energy are seen as being diverted from more important institutional activities. But there may be positive consequences as well if fads "are kept in the proper perspective and incorporated into the collective wisdom of a company" (Rifkin, 1994,

p. 11). As we shall see in Chapter Eight, fads may have important latent functions in cuing attention, promoting action, and increasing variety. And even after the fad itself has faded from view, its residual legacy, like the smile of the Cheshire Cat, may remain and indirectly influence institutional structure and values (Bohl and Luthans, 1996). Even when fads fail, they are important; the more we understand them, the greater the opportunity there is to increase their potential for institutional improvement and decrease their potential for institutional disruption.

In the next chapters we extend our view of fads by using data from the seven case studies to answer four questions: Why do academic institutions adopt fads? How do managers make sense of fads? What are the residual effects of fads? And how can institutions best manage the fad process to make it more constructive?

6

Organizations and Fads

We have seen how colleges and universities adopt fads and then either isolate them from the core activities of the institution or fail to implement them at all. The adoption of fads continues despite research in business showing that management fads usually don't deliver what they promise (Nohria and Berkley, 1994). In this chapter we examine how characteristics of the environment, academic institutions, institutional participants, and the fad itself might encourage the adoption of management fads, limit their apparent effectiveness, and explain their failure. Both here and in Chapter Seven, I have used some important ideas drawn from the social sciences to illuminate the fad phenomenon. The ideas in these chapters should be read as speculations or hypotheses rather than conclusions. Their purpose is not to provide answers but to provoke thought and encourage further research.

The Environment

Higher education is in crisis. Indeed, higher education crises have been claimed for so long that crisis now appears to be its natural state. Hundreds of claims of crisis have been documented during just the past twenty-five years (Birnbaum and Shushok, forthcoming) ranging from the pandemic (the crisis of finance) and transcendental (the crisis of confidence) to the logistical (the crisis of parking). The world is filled with problems, and we "tend to turn perceived national problems into educational crises and reforms" (Meyer, 1986, p. 47).

Claims of crisis are used both inside and outside institutions to support ideologies and gain attention, power, and control of organizational and symbolic processes in a noisy policy environment. Some claim we live in a time of unusual turbulence and higher education is responding too slowly. These claims are used to justify bold experiments with new management techniques. But is the pace of change in the present really so different from the past? College presidents during the post–GI Bill period of the 1940s or the student demonstrations of the 1960s and 1970s would have been surprised to be told they were living in placid times. Allegations of turbulence are coupled with claims of institutional stagnation and lack of improvement. These claims are made not only by higher education's critics but also inadvertently by its supporters. The widely cited generalization that "teaching remains one of the few human activities that does not get demonstrably better from one generation to the next" (Bok, 1992, p. 18) ignores a host of other professions— legislator, judge, symphony conductor, minister, poet, novelist, magazine editor, and college president, among many others—that similarly can make no claim of generational improvement. Rather than challenging the claim, other academic leaders may use it as the basis for saying that "the state of teaching and learning in American higher education seems not better than it was 20 years ago" (Marchese, 1993, p. 12). And so the cycle of self-inflicted wounds continues.

Institutions that uncritically accept these claims of crisis or stagnation become receptive to management innovations. A belief that turbulence is of a different order of magnitude than in the past makes institutions vulnerable to fads that claim to be able to predict or control the environment. Although there is general agreement that American colleges have been superbly adaptive in the past, it is alleged that current threats mean the muddling through and piecemeal adaptation of the past must now be replaced by "strategic planning and a new management style" (Keller, 1983, p. 38). Claims of crisis and institutional stagnation lead to moralistic calls for reform. This, in turn, supports attacks on the educational community "as archaic and corrupt, to be cleansed by the application of a wider rationality" (Meyer, 1992, p. 253). Institutions may adopt new management techniques to satisfy critics and symbolize their intention to reform. As a result, "the quest for new organizational practices—for new words, new structures, new designs, new systems, and new strategies—has become a rather frenzied pursuit. . . . The constant talk about 'new practices for a new age' is shortsighted and may lead us both to misunderstand the past and ignore what is really important in organizations" (Eccles and Nohria, 1992, p. 4).

Is it really true that higher education changes less and is less innovative than business, as some claim (Getz, Siegfried, and Anderson, 1997), or are analysts looking at higher education in the wrong way? Perhaps change in higher education should be measured not from the top of the organization as it is in business, but from the bottom. Innovation is not institutionalized in the hierarchical structure of colleges and universities as much as in the work of academic departments. "Such change is widely overlooked since it is not announced in master plans or ministerial bulletins and not introduced on a global scale. . . . In a bottom-heavy knowledge institution, grass-roots innovation is a crucial form of change" (Clark, 1983, pp. 234–235).

We do not know how fads are introduced to higher education, but the complexity of their organizational networks suggests multiple vectors. In our analysis of fads, we have seen how diffusion may be related to the actions of legislators, boards of trustees, or institutional presidents. But where do *they* get infected by the fad bug? How does the technology transfer actually take place? Do institutions copy the presumably superior practices of their aspirational peers? Do mobile individuals carry fads with them from their previous employment? Do institutions learn from other institutions with which they have contact (cohesion)? From similar institutions (structural equivalence)? If so, what marks their similarity (Scott, 1995)?

Organizational Networks

We often assume that institutional leaders independently are able to decide whether to adopt a management innovation. But because of the influence of other organizations, this assumption is often false. As colleges and universities attempt to coordinate their activities, gain access to resources, and negotiate continuing relationships with external agencies, they become integrated into a *network* of organizations (Håkansson and Snehota, 1995). These networks include regulatory bodies such as trustee boards or legislatures; professional groups such as accrediting agencies; foundations; other organizations such as businesses; associations of similar institutions; consultants; and others. Although all of these external agents may sincerely believe they are acting in the best interests of higher education, they have other agendas as well. As a consequence, some external agencies may pressure institutions to adopt an inefficient administrative technology or to reject a technically efficient one (Abrahamson, 1991, p. 594).

Fads, like other forms of organizational learning, can be diffused through coercive, mimetic, and normative processes. Coercive processes include rules established by government, professional associations, accrediting bodies, or other authoritative groups. Mimetic processes are seen when organizations copy routines they learn about through institutional contact, consultants, or the movement of people between institutions. Normative processes involve dissemination through publications, experts, and educational activities.

Government

We have already seen how PPBS, MBO, and ZBB were adopted first by the federal government and then by the states, where they were often imposed on all public agencies, including higher education.

Although these coercive processes were applied directly only to public colleges and universities, some private institutions then copied what were publicly identified as more effective management processes. Even in the absence of federal directives, some state governments required public institutions to participate in strategic planning, TQM/CQI, and benchmarking exercises. Some performance indicator programs were mandated by law; in several states, educational systems themselves preemptively initiated such programs as a way of averting state legislative action (Gaither, Nedwek, and Neal, 1994). The motivation for imposed programs was largely constabulary, and state agencies often did not understand how the social meaning of these fads would be constructed on the campus, "especially the negative consequences that accrue when an apparently desirable innovation is used under different conditions. Change agents are especially likely to make this mistake when they do not empathize with the innovation's users" (Rogers, 1995, p. 423). Governments do not always empathize with higher education, and indeed their directives often spring from a basic distrust of academic institutions (Schmidtlein and Milton, 1988–1989).

Business

Business is the avatar of "proper" organizational structure and process. Businesses often are urged to adopt new management techniques on the grounds that "'leading-edge companies have embraced it and benefitted from it.' The implication, of course, is if a firm wants to be leading edge, it will have to adopt this new language" (Eccles and Nohria, 1992, p. 89). Institutions of higher education, wishing to appear to be on the leading edge, are under pressure to do the same. Higher education management becomes susceptible to fads as institutions come under pressure to be more rational and businesslike (Allen and Chaffee, 1981, p. 27), and so educators borrow from business in their drive to appear more efficient (Cuban, 1990).

Institutions of higher education are networked with businesses both directly and indirectly. Colleges and universities have continual contact with, and therefore are influenced by, businesses from which they purchase supplies and services and to which they send their graduates. Businesspeople are disproportionately represented on boards of trustees and are more likely than are academics to think that running a college is like running a business. The attitude of business frequently is, "If we can make these decisions in the business world (cutting costs, downsizing, introducing technology) why can't it be done in higher education?" (Trombley and Sevener, 1998, p. 14).

Associations

Colleges and universities are members of many associations, often voluntary in nature, that have powerful mimetic (and sometimes even coercive) influence: accrediting organizations that assess institutional conformance to educational and managerial standards, national associations that encourage certain institutional roles or activities, and associations of institutions in specific educational sectors whose members influence each other through personal contact and the development of formal policy positions. Professional associations in higher education have played a particularly influential role in championing and disseminating fads. NACUBO's support of benchmarking and AAHE's support of TQM/CQI are two visible and recent examples, but others are seen in each of the fads described in earlier chapters. The support of such official and semi-official groups helps to legitimate the fad (March, 1994), thus making its adoption even more likely. And institutions are more likely to adopt a fad if they see other institutions similar to themselves adopting it. Those who believe in a fad can have their belief reinforced by continual contact with others who share it, even when confronted with evidence that does not support it (Festinger, Riecken, and Schachter, 1956).

Consultants

American firms spend an estimated $15 billion a year on outside management advice (Micklethwait and Wooldridge, 1996), and consultants are one vector of fad adoption. Frequent adoption of fads in higher education may reflect both an institution's interest in being seen as on the cutting edge of management excellence and a deep-seated management insecurity and "implicit admission of ineptitude in management" (O'Shea and Madigan, 1997, p. 5). Business consultants write books so they can get into the lucrative lecture circuit, which then leads to consulting opportunities and the marketing of videos and newsletters. "Get an article into *Harvard Business Review*, pump it up for a book, pray for a best-seller, then market the idea for all it is worth through a consulting company. There have been many variations on the theme, but most fad consultant efforts fit the same pattern" (O'Shea and Madigan, 1997, p. 189). An article in *Fortune* titled "In Search of Suckers" notes that "in recent years [consultants'] advice has loosed a plague of fads—upsizings, right-sizing, downsizing—precipitating layoffs in the tens of thousands. Meantime, gurus themselves never have looked happier or better fed. Their pelts are sleek" (Farnham, 1996, p. 119). Little is known about the effects of consulting in business, although there is growing concern that consultants often may serve their own interests rather than those of their clients (O'Shea and Madigan, 1997).

Higher education does not have the deep pockets of big business, and for that reason among others it makes less intensive use of consultants. Nevertheless, consultants have played an active role in creating and disseminating each of the seven fads in their original settings and in transferring the technology to higher education. Consultants may be one of the sources from which management innovations in the business sector penetrate higher education. For a beleaguered institution, appointing a well-known consultant may not improve productivity but may nevertheless be a valuable way for the institution to maintain legitimacy (Meyer and Rowan, 1992) by giving a public appearance of facing up to its problems.

Organizational Characteristics

Colleges and universities are not organized like business firms. Unfortunately, "the vast majority of everything that has been written

about management and organization over the course of this century
. . . has had as its model, usually implicitly, the machine form of
organization," which is bureaucratized, formalized, hierarchical, and
tightly coupled (Mintzberg, 1994, p. 399). In contrast, colleges and
universities are professional organizations—loosely coupled systems
in which managers with limited authority provide support for relatively autonomous specialists performing complex tasks within relatively stable structures. Much of the criticism of change in higher
education arises out of the failure to appreciate the importance of
the differences in organizational structures and processes.

Structure

The relatively tight coupling of business organizations permits control through hierarchical directives. Higher education is more
loosely coupled (Weick, 1976); what happens in one part of a university often has little direct or immediate effect on other parts of
the institution. Control through managerial coordination is therefore more difficult; instead, controls are provided by the routines
and culture of the institution and the professional training and socialization of the participants. The reality that actions of those at
the top of educational organizations are not tightly connected to
behaviors by those further down means "many reforms seldom go
beyond getting adopted as policy. Most get implemented in word
rather than deed" and without altering other cultural aspects of deep
structure (Cuban, 1990, p. 9).

Some innovations are desired by managers because they help to
certify the institution's social legitimacy; many of these same innovations would decrease organizational effectiveness if they were
implemented. Institutions respond to this irony by adopting the innovation ceremoniously; they protect their technical activities by
separating their formal structures from their work activities (Meyer
and Rowan, 1992). Separation of structure from work does not
mean that there is no innovation but rather that innovation is often
not necessarily initiated by, or even related to, the desires of top

managers. Even though major innovations proposed at higher levels of centralization in colleges and universities may never be implemented, the initiatives of individuals and small groups may lead to constant innovation and change. Academic institutions are criticized for both resisting change and being too faddish; loose coupling makes it possible for both positions to be supported (Meyer, 1992).

The metaphorical depiction of colleges and universities as organized anarchies (Cohen and March, 1974) has led some critics to see academic management as a pathological process that needs to be remedied by increased doses of rationality. From an organizational perspective, however, I believe the anarchical properties of higher education institutions are effective accommodations to the particular nature of their multiple goals, technologies, and decision processes.

Management

Managers in many organizational settings, including business, are expected to provide "leadership." American culture is likely to depict good leaders, particularly in business, as acting in a decisive and directive manner. College presidents, deans, department chairs, and others are under external pressure to behave in the same way, and implementing a new management innovation is one way to demonstrate authoritative leadership. Some managers, uncomfortable with not having a reliable technology that more clearly links college processes to college outcomes, find fads attractive. However, there is evidence that academic leaders may be more likely to fail than succeed if they adopt new procedures that violate academic norms or make adoption decisions outside accepted governance frameworks (Birnbaum, 1992).

Academic managers are frequently admonished to be more innovative and assertive. However, there is no evidence that doing so would strengthen our colleges and universities, and some believe it would be unwise for colleges and universities to try to emulate the change-driven cultures of many for-profit corporations. Within higher education, constancy is not weakness but strength. Many of society's needs remain relatively constant, suggesting the value of a similar level of consistency on the part of nonprofit organizations that serve those needs. Because of the importance of society's demands for reliable, accountable performance, nonprofits should greatly value continuity. "Potential organizational change should be approached cautiously, with a strong regard for traditionality as a mechanism of continuity" (Salipante and Golden-Biddle, 1995, p. 3).

The assumption that higher education is poorly managed is frequently accepted as a matter of faith. The claim is that faculty fail to recognize modern realities and administrators "often refuse to introduce the operating styles and procedures from the best organization theory and practice, management and planning, partly out of fear of faculty criticism but partly because they usually share the biases and naiveté of the faculties, despite the need to make their complex enterprises function better" (Keller, 1983, p. 34). These are serious charges. If there was evidence that following the management precepts of business would improve higher education, the failure of academic managers to do so would be unconscionable. However, the rhetoric of criticism is not supported by evidence.

Imitation

If an organization has clear goals and understands its management technology, it might be able to predict whether an innovation would improve its efficiency. But when goals are uncertain and the effects of various management technologies are unclear, it is difficult or impossible to assess the technical efficiency of any new proposal in advance. Unable to design their management system based on rationality, institutions faced with uncertainty are likely instead to imitate what similar institutions are doing (Abrahamson, 1991, p. 591). That is why scholars of business firms can ask, "Isn't it odd that, once ten companies announced they have met some success by overhauling their business processes, another 1,000 follow suit almost immediately? . . . Businesses are led to change not by the inherent merits of the case but because everyone else is doing it" (Robbins and Finley, 1996, p. 35).

The history of academic management fads suggests this same pattern of imitation between entire state systems or between in-stitutions. When one state adopts an innovation, it may spread to other states as part of a process of imitation, even in the absence of credible evidence that the innovation is instrumentally effective. For example, the adoption of PPBS in California or strategic plan-ning in Ohio made it likely that other states would also do so. Adop-tion by prestigious research universities of TQM/CQI made it likely that other research universities would follow their lead, and lack of adoption by major liberal arts colleges made it even less likely that others like them would do so. Institutions will tend to imitate other institutions when the environment, goals, and technology are uncertain. Similar institutions might tend to adopt similar fads, both because they might be facing similar performance gaps and because they are more likely to be influenced by institutions like themselves.

Institutional Legitimacy

Organizations survive only if they are considered legitimate by both external and internal audiences. When an organization has clear goals, understood technologies, and a well-defined product, it is relatively easy to measure its efficiency and effectiveness. Because output can be assessed, such organizations can use efficiency or effectiveness criteria as a legitimate basis for requesting the support necessary for their continued survival. But when it is not possible to agree on purposes or to assess outcomes, an organization cannot use efficiency or effectiveness as the basis for garnering support. Instead, it achieves credibility and legitimacy by conforming to cer-tain social expectations about how that particular kind of institu-tion is supposed to look, how it is structured, and how it should conduct its business. The success of some institutions may depend more on being perceived by important constituencies as adhering to organizational myths than on their actual efficiency or effectiveness. The value of new management systems is one such myth, and this need to appear legitimate makes institutions vulnerable to management fads.

External Legitimacy

If a college or university is to be considered a legitimate organization, it must be seen as adhering to the myth of rationality. Institutions of higher education cannot satisfactorily demonstrate their technical success by measuring their outputs; they do so by incorporating rational elements, such as innovative management techniques, into their structures and processes. Institutions that adopt technologies that are seen as innovative "establish an organization as appropriate, rational, and modern" (Meyer and Rowan, 1992, p. 25), and improve their chances for survival. Fads may not have much to do with how a campus really works, but they may help an institution "manage the impression that outsiders have about it. The image of quantitative rationality is used to discharge a university's obligations to the state without immediately affecting internal patterns of decision making" (Rourke and Brooks, 1966, p. 103).

The adoption of fads can serve other symbolic purposes as well. When external observers criticize higher education for lack of change, the adoption of a new management technique can signal innovativeness. The institution that adopts strategic planning may improve its image by developing "a reputation for innovation and progressive thinking that is attractive to potential students and benefactors" (Shirley, 1988, p. 12). PPBS, for example, was seen as a way of enabling a university "to make effective appeals for large donations . . . by presenting the image of a well-managed institution" (Peterson, 1971, p. 18). Budget requests created by ZBB had an added dimension of credibility and suggested that the proposal had been thoroughly reviewed from the ground up, so no fat remained (Wildavsky and Hammond, 1965).

Internal Legitimacy

Outsiders may have their concerns for legitimacy assuaged when an institution conforms to the myth of rationality. The further an outsider is from the internal workings of the institution, the greater is the power of the myth. But the same myth cannot satisfy insiders who know, from their own experience, that rationality is only a facade. Insiders instead find organizational legitimacy in the illusion of certainty. Sometimes certainty can be provided through institutional superstitions (Gimpl and Dakin, 1984). Engaging in the rituals of fads, such as forecasting and planning, relieves anxiety by suggesting that predictability is possible. And sometimes satisfaction can be provided through magic.

Management consultants have been called "the witch doctors of our age, preying on business people's anxiety in order to sell snake oil. Modern management theory is no more reliable than tribal medicine" (Micklethwait and Wooldridge, 1996, p. 12). Adopting a fad substitutes the problem of fad implementation for the management problem itself, and "concern for the latest fire will supplant concern for still smoldering blazes—an essential magical process" (Dirsmith, Jablonsky, and Luzi, 1980, p. 324). Substituting a technical problem for a social one may provide practitioners with an increased sense of security by explaining awkward facts without disrupting fundamental organization beliefs, as magic also tries to do. Fads thus become ritualistic devices for increasing a sense of certainty in an uncertain world, even though they are not instrumentally used because they contradict institutional myths about how decisions are made (Masland, 1983).

Fads can also be used to contain political conflict by establishing procedures that appear to be rational, and therefore fair. Benchmarking, for example, is presented as based not on "opinions" but on "facts" (Alstete, 1995, p. 9). Answers that are arbitrary and useless can nevertheless be acceptable and comforting if the procedure used to generate them has an air of rationality (Dresch, 1975, p. 247) and may make the decision more acceptable (Chaffee, 1983). The process of some fads may give the impression that the institution is interested in sharing responsibility for decisions and give people a sense of security about the future of the institution (Tan, 1990).

The Nature of Fads

Innovations are social technologies that promise to affect relationships between actions and outcomes, help the adopter more successfully achieve desired objectives, and reduce uncertainty. But at the same time, innovations have uncertainties of their own. In the beginning, it is difficult to decide if an innovation is something in which an organization should be interested. Even after the innovation has been implemented, its outcomes are often not clear until the meaning of the innovation is socially constructed by organizational participants (Rogers, 1995, p. xvii).

Research has shown that innovations are more likely to be adopted when they exhibit five characteristics: relative advantage (more economical, more prestigious, more satisfying); compatibility (consistent with current values and past experiences); complexity (easy to understand and use); trialability (can be experimented with on a limited basis); and observability (the results can be seen) (Rogers, 1995). However, the adoption of a technology by an organization is not necessarily a sign the technology is superior to other technologies. Regardless of the nature of the technology or the adopting group, "the best technology doesn't always win" (Pool, 1997, p. 151). Whether a technology is adopted depends also on political forces, the nature of previously adopted technologies, historical coincidences, and other random factors. It is difficult to convince people already committed to a technology to switch their allegiance to a new one.

The rate of adoption of successful innovations has been shown (Rogers, 1995) to take the shape of an S-shaped curve. The part of the curve where 10 to 20 percent of the population has adopted an innovation is the critical point at which the future of an innovation is determined. When the adoption rate goes beyond that level, it is frequently impossible to stop it from spreading throughout the population. In the case of an unsuccessful innovation, rejection begins somewhere before this critical point as adoption rates level off, diminish through discontinuance, and eventually disappear. It is this process of initial adoption, leveling off, and discontinuance that defines a fad. Discontinuation of a fad suggests it was never institutionalized and made part of accepted practice (Rogers, 1995, p. 183). It may also be evidence that the fad has not conferred relative advantage on the institution. Institutions may discontinue a fad because they discover it is ineffective, its faddish appeal dwindles, or the competitive advantage it gave to early adapters dissipates as a greater number of institutions adopt it (Abrahamson, 1991). Discontinuance is also related to compatibility. The original adoption of an innovation may be made by managers who may see it as compatible with their own beliefs and values, but in an academic institution, the success of an innovation depends on the acceptance of faculty and nonmanagerial administrators who must implement it. Compatibility can be affected by even such simple things as an innovation's name. TQM, for example, was renamed CQI in higher education to avoid being contaminated by the words *total* and *management*.

Previous chapters indicated that many institutions adopt managerial fads only virtually, while others adopt them in reality, only to later discontinue them. Institutional interest has already been related to the nature of the environment, or of organizations. But there may be characteristics of academic management fads themselves that facilitate their initial adoption and permit their consideration by others even though they have not been successful in their original setting. Fads may spread through a system of institutions in a process of thought contagion analogous to the spread of a virus in a host population. Fads may originally be adopted because they appear to be reasonable; once initiated, they may continue and spread even in the absence of evidence they work because they are undefinable, complex, nonfalsifiable, and idealized.

Contagion

Ideas can be disseminated within a population of institutions through the transmission of memes—ideas that are capable of self-propagation through repetition. The more an idea is repeated, the more likely it is that others will hear it and repeat it in turn. A core idea—the fad essence—can be a meme through which individuals or institutions "infected" by a fad can transmit that fad to others. A number of modes of meme transmission have been identified (Lynch, 1996), of which several appear particularly relevant to higher education management fads. Memes are most likely to be contagious when they have built-in mechanisms for sabotaging competing ideas (for example, declaring traditional management processes ineffective), offer a cognitive advantage (the idea seems plausible to people when they hear about it), and offer a motivational advantage (the belief that adopting or maintaining a fad will lead them to be better off). The fastest mode of meme transmission is proselytizing by hosts who support the idea and disseminate it to others as a potential cure for problems plaguing the population (for example, associations that have advocated specific management systems to their members).

Instead of considering how people adopt ideas, mimetics (the study of memes) asks how ideas adopt people. In higher education, those who see universities primarily from structural perspectives are more vulnerable to "contagion" from ideas developed in other settings that promise efficiency. Those who see universities primarily from cultural and interpretive perspectives are less vulnerable. Memes can spread widely, even when they do not confer any economic advantage on believers, by manipulating a host institution's communication system. Just as biological viruses spread more rapidly as opportunities for contact increase, so memes can spread more rapidly as communication density increases. And if the memes are embedded in vivid stories of success, they may overwhelm (at least for a time) the older ideas that they are trying to replace.

A meme, like a fashion style, may spread by self-advertising because the novelty that makes it stand out and be memorable also encourages imitation. As it becomes increasingly noticed, it "makes adopting the style more enticing to attention seekers, and better noticed by many others. Once the style achieves prevalence, it grabs less attention, setting the stage for the next style to capture attention and spread" (Lynch, 1996, p. 33) as part of the fad adoption cycle.

The idea that words can circulate through a social system looking for hosts to which they can become attached may at first sound whimsical, if not absurd. But we can all recall examples. Those of us who were professionally active in the 1960s and early 1970s will doubtless remember "relevance," a great meme: easy to remember, difficult to argue against, and impossible to define clearly. This previously invisible word was quickly applied to all facets of higher education, and it influenced the reform rhetoric of the day. The 1990s saw the creation of equally powerful memes, such as reengineering, reinvention, quality, reform, accountability, and K–16, among others—ideas to which all institutions were exposed, for good or ill, and which led to infection in some. Memes are words that fall trippingly on the tongue. Almost everyone is "for" them in principle; it is when we try to implement them that we discover there is no agreement on what they mean. When a management innovation is transformed into a meme, it serves as a solution seeking a problem to which it might be the answer (Cohen and March, 1974).

Reasonable

Fads sound reasonable. Most of us have so thoroughly internalized the notions of managerialism and rationality that undergird academic fads that the ideas behind them are accepted without question. Systematic is better than random, efficiency better than waste, coordination better than helter-skelter, consistency better than contradictory, rational better than unreasonable (Wildavsky, 1973, p. 141). When fads seem reasonable, reasonable people must be in favor of them, just as reasonable people must be for quality, planning, and "best practice." The more reasonable something sounds, the less the need is to subject it to critical analysis and think through its implications. And even if fads fail to do what they originally claimed, they can still be justified by their claimed secondary benefits, such as increasing communications, motivation, or interaction (Gimpl and Dakin, 1984).

Undefinable

What really *was* TQM or any of the other management fads we have considered? There was no standard definition. As Entin (1993, p. 30) put it, at different institutions one was likely to find "a swirl and confusion of ideas about TQM. The TQM advocate stated, or acknowledged when asked, that TQM had much in common with good sense management techniques; they were not invested in a rigid menu of techniques but were quite flexible and pragmatic in approaching the implementation. This makes it difficult to pinpoint a given institution's definition and application of TQM and it also allows almost any institutional advance to be credited to TQM." At the same time, it is impossible to know whether the same kinds of changes might have been seen in institutions without TQM. Innovations are reinvented (Rogers, 1995) by users who adapt them to their specific situation or decide to implement some parts of the innovation but not others.

Reinvention is more likely to take place when an innovation is complex, abstract, and claimed to solve a wide range of problems, all elements of fads. Tailoring an innovation to specific institutional needs is highly desirable; at the same time, if a fad cannot be clearly defined and it cannot be stated with certainty whether a fad has been adopted, then it is not possible to study its effects reliably. When the core elements of a fad are unstable or imprecise, apparent replications among organizations may lack fidelity (Tornatzky and Fleischer, 1990), so a fad may appear to "work" in one setting and not in another that it may superficially resemble.

One consequence of reinvention is that two organizations may claim to be using an innovation when they have in fact adopted the same name but two quite different processes. This permits advocates to argue that companies that have successfully used TQM are "doing something right, something we call TQM." On the other hand, "those who fail are doing something wrong. Are the failures TQM programs that do not work, or do they just call them that?" (Becker, 1993, p. 30). Without a clear definition, "real" TQM can never fail; only "ill advised efforts made under a falsely claimed TQM banner" fail (Becker, 1993, p. 33). Since there are more "bad" TQM programs than "good" TQM programs, TQM was believed by some to have been relegated to fad status (Secor, 1995, p. 85). But since TQM was offered in almost a thousand variations, how could the True Grail be identified amid the host of false ones? These questions about TQM could be applied with equal validity to each of the other fads we have considered.

Complex

When an innovation such as TQM "claims to operate on all parts of the system simultaneously" (Ewell, 1993, p. 50), it is by definition so complex that its implementation cannot be fully documented or its consequences clearly discerned. Managers are told that TQM or BPR, for example, cannot be implemented on a fragmentary basis, but must be part of a total institutional commitment (McGuinness and Ewell, 1994, p. 9). The requirements for successfully implementing such comprehensive management changes are so demanding, numerous, and internally inconsistent that it is virtually impossible to meet them and therefore always an excuse for why they fail. For example, Hammer and Champy (1993) suggest that if you follow the rules, reengineering will almost always succeed. The rules? Change processes rather than fix them; do not focus on business processes; do not neglect people's values and beliefs; do not settle for minor results; do not quit too early; do not place prior constraints on the process; do not allow culture and management attitudes to subvert the process; do not try to do it from the bottom up; do not skimp on resources; do not have someone who does not understand reengineering lead the effort; do not bury it in the middle of the corporate agenda; do not drag the process out. Just to make sure there is always an out, "undoubtedly, there are more paths that lead to reengineering failure than those we have just listed. People are remarkably resourceful in finding new ways to drop the ball" (Hammer and Champy, 1993, p. 213). Of course if you do not succeed, then by definition you will have violated one of the stated (or unstated rules) that will account for the failure.

Nonfalsifiable

Rationality suggests that fads would be adopted only if there was evidence they were effective. Yet because of their reasonableness and undefinability, adoption may continue to be urged by the faithful for a related but completely nonrational reason: the effectiveness of fads cannot be disproved. When fad implementation is followed by institutional success, a causative relationship can be claimed. Failures are usually ignored or explained away on an ad hoc basis. A fad may not work because it was a "false" version, but many other explanations are offered as well. Failure of a fad can indicate "the practitioner was unskilled, broke a taboo, used the wrong material, or that the mystical forces have changed" (Gimpl and Dakin, 1984, p. 130), just as the failure of the witch doctor "is usually attributed to an imperfection in execution or the unanticipated intervention of some hostile forces. The analysis is never discredited; the appearance of rationality is preserved" (Morgan, 1986, p. 134). True believers resolve failure by rationalization: "They denied the problem, falling back on faith; they acknowledged some superficial difficulties, but promoted the process anyway; they accepted the failures to date, but insisted that more planning would resolve them; and finally they projected the difficulties onto others, notably 'unsupportive' managers and 'uncongenial' climates, under the labels of the 'pitfalls' of planning" (Mintzberg, 1994, p. 135). Their faith is thus confirmed regardless of the outcomes.

It is easy to retrospectively rationalize the failure of a fad. It was too ambitious or not ambitious enough; it gave too much attention to political and cultural elements or not enough. It would have worked had there been greater effort, more commitment, more dedication, or if people had tried harder (Wildavsky, 1973). Fads are said to fail because senior management was not committed to the fad, or the organizational climate was not congenial to it (Mintzberg, 1994). Fads fail because "individual campuses may have a weak and unsupportive president, limited planning or institutional research capacity, a traditional administrative climate, a timorous faculty, or other hindering factors" (Meredith, 1993, p. 30) such as "failures of intellect or courage" (Bleakley, 1993, p. A6). After a spate of surveys reported negative results from TQM programs in industry, the conclusion was not that there was something wrong with the TQM philosophy, but that the *implementation* of TQM was deficient or erroneous (Brigham, 1993). The potential explanations for failure are legion; one explanation seldom considered is that perhaps it was not such a good idea in the first place. When one fad fails to serve as the ultimate single solution to organizational ills, another takes its place. We seem not to learn the lesson that single solutions do not work. And we fail to see the dangers in adopting them.

In the final analysis, the theoretical benefits of organizational fads are easy to proclaim but difficult to demonstrate in practice in a manner that empirically confirms the theory. Fad proponents emphasize outcomes (such as effectiveness) that are not measurable and whose magnitude cannot be specified in advance. The fad would work, it is claimed, if the assumptions that the fad advocate makes were followed. In this way, fads are like other theories of rational choice that have been criticized for not specifying in advance the outcomes to be achieved, selecting confirming evidence, ignoring alternative explanations, disregarding anomalies or outcomes inconsistent with the theory, and developing elaborate post hoc explanations for failure (Green and Shapiro, 1994).

Because institutions function in the real world rather than the ideal world of the fad advocate, an institution or its participants rather than the fad itself can be blamed for the failure. The cause-and-effect assumptions of the fad can be maintained despite failure by invoking "disturbing causes," so that "rational choice assumptions are both self-evidently true and unfalsifiable" (Friedman, 1995, p. 12). The more complex the system is, the easier it is to create plausible explanations for failure that permit the system's advocates to maintain the faith. In the same way, apologists for management innovations "explain" the failures of each new technique and search for the next best way that will finally overcome the defects of its predecessors. The theories behind fads work as long as the uncertainties, vagaries, and complexities of the real world can be ignored. "The plain fact of life is that when it comes to TQM, theory doesn't usually match reality, hence all the depressing empirical findings about TQM outcomes" (Harari, 1993b, p. 34).

Idealized

We have many descriptions of fads that presumably succeeded, at least in their early stages; we have far fewer analyses of fads that failed. Initiation is applauded; failure often leads to strategic silence (Tyack and Cuban, 1995, p. 113). Reports of successful management innovations may bring favorable publicity to an institution and its managers. Advocates may promote the success through case studies in books and professional journals; institutions can be cited as exemplars and managers as visionary leaders. Other institutions, seeing these reports and eager for the same approbation, may attempt to copy the innovations. Once these institutions come to believe in the desirability of the innovation, they tend to process information in ways that help perpetuate their beliefs. They seek out and recall confirming data, ignore or rationalize disconfirming data, and act in a way that creates self-fulfilling prophesies (Nisbett and Ross, 1980).

There are a relatively large number of early stories of success, because it is in the interest of the institutions and the fad advocates to sponsor such stories. There are relatively few public acknowledgments of failure because institutions and fad advocates have no vested interest in having this information disseminated. Moreover, the media have little interest in publishing stories about such non-events. It should not be surprising that institutions are not eager to discuss failed activities. Institutions are exceptionally sensitive to their public image. Acknowledgment of failure may cast doubt on the performance of managers and publicize (perhaps in exaggerated form) the existence of institutional problems that may capture the unwelcome attention of politicians and the general public (Schmidt-lein, 1990).

The Nature of People

Fad advocates generally take the value of fads as rationally self-evident. When fads fail, they provide explanations that protect their belief in the value of the fad while assigning blame to others. Often these explanations are tautologies, such as "institutional inertia" or "staff workers and professors who are resistant to change" (Nicklin, 1995, p. A34), that offer answers without meaning. It is easy to paint different role groups as the villains of the piece. "Resistance from the old guard and 'not-invented-here' attitudes" (Seymour, 1991, p. 12), presidents' and deans' beliefs that "management certainly was a matter of experience and 'feel,' not careful analysis and quantification" (Keller, 1983, p. 105), and higher education participants who "are seemingly incapable of understanding the need to communicate" (Seymour, 1992, p. 169) are among the culprits.

Another problem was "the thick, deep adherence by campus department chairmen, deans, vice presidents and presidents to incrementalism" (Keller, 1983, p. 106). "Incrementalism" is often cited and given the aura of a religion with specific theologies and rites to which people are committed. But incrementalism is not a matter of faith; it is instead a matter of experience and common sense. People may espouse the values of vision, anticipatory action, and change, but when they have the responsibility of management, they usually engage in the eminently sensible behavior of taking one step at a time.

On some campuses, fad implementation procedures reflect a lack of faith in people. This diminishes levels of trust among faculty, administrators, and trustees, which in turn reduces the possibility of successful implementation (Schmidtlein and Milton, 1988–1989, p. 12). Controls are necessary because people—particularly people whose training and socialization led them to expect to be guided more by their professional authority than by management structures—are ornery. If they do not see the value of a management innovation, they are unlikely to support it. "Employees' commitment to the use of an innovation is a function of the perceived fit of the innovation to the employees' values" (Klein and Sorra, 1996, pp. 1062–1063). Employees can respond to an innovation with enthusiasm, indifference, or resistance. "In the face of a poor innovation-values fit, a strong implementation climate results only in compliant innovation use and/or resistance. Further, innovation-values fit may vary across the groups of an organization, engendering intraorganizational conflict and lessening implementation effectiveness" (Klein and Sorra, 1996, p. 1073). Those trying to implement the fad often blame failure on the resistance of those below and proclaim, "'If only you dumbbells had appreciated our brilliant strategies, all would be well.' But the clever dumbbells might well respond, 'If you are so smart, why didn't you formulate strategies that we dumbbells could implement? You knew who we are: why didn't you factor our incompetence into your thinking?'" (Mintzberg, 1994, pp. 284–285).

Advocates of innovation and change are often acclaimed as heroes, and those who oppose them as villains—"non-believers who do not see the potential benefits (to individuals, organizations and society) of innovative change and whose motives are felt to be self-interested and narrow. Their responses and actions are cast as irrational barriers to the ultimate good which the innovation promises" (Frost and Egri, 1991, p. 271).

The Bottom Line

Neither successes nor failures may influence the true believer. "The occasional success, however rare, will . . . be attributed to the choice of tactics, and its effectiveness will seem to be an unassailable fact of the person's own experiences. Because no single failure serves to disconfirm the strategy's effectiveness (after all, nothing works all the time), the only way it can be shown to be ineffective is by discovering that the rate of success is lower with this strategy than with others" (Gilovich, 1991, p. 153). The only way this rate can be discovered is through comparative research, and no such research has been done. So we keep trying, "each time claiming that the last failure revealed the true problems, which would be solved next time. Never put into question were the premises that underlay the whole exercise: that planners, or at least their systems, can be smart enough to figure out centrally . . . the comprehensive future of an entire enterprise" (Mintzberg, 1994, p. 140). As one BPR advocate said after observing its ultimate rejection by business, "I hope there comes to be some skepticism about the next big thing. The next big thing will get us into trouble" (White, 1996, p. 1).

7

Managers and Fads

A nalysts of the failure of a past fad have asked "why chief executives persist in adopting ZBB, and, for that matter, why do users down in the bureaucracies sometimes also seem to like ZBB?" (Hammond and Knott, 1980, p. 2). The same question could be asked about each management fad we have considered. Good managers want to make their organizations better, but there is little empirical evidence to suggest that any of the seven management innovations considered in the previous chapters were technically efficient or made the organizations that adopted them any more effective.

And yet some managers embrace these new ideas. Most business CEOs have tried at least three innovative management programs, and believe they have to try more if they are going to increase corporate productivity (Bleakley, 1993). By 1998, the average business was using over fourteen different management techniques, although 77 percent of managers agreed that such techniques promised more than they delivered (Rigby, 1998). Trying and failing does not seem to moderate the "feverish search for new management methods" (Njoku, 1977, p. 201) even among the most rational of managers. Jimmy Carter, a nuclear engineer as well as a policy wonk, championed ZBB in Georgia (where it failed), and then transported it to the federal government (where it also failed). History suggests that managers who adopt management systems to improve institutional effectiveness often do not assess the effectiveness of the management systems they adopt (Hammond and Knott, 1980).

Most administrative and faculty managers in higher education are thoughtful, experienced, and accomplished people. If they were rational decision makers, they would adopt an innovation when it was shown to be technically efficient and conferred a competitive advantage on those who used it (Abrahamson, 1991). Yet managers adopt fads even in the absence of such advantage, and they may remain committed to them even when faced with empirical evidence they are not working. How can this be explained?

One answer to the question of why managers adopt fads is obvious: legislative or gubernatorial mandates, particularly for public institutions, may leave them no choice. Even when managers believe that a new technology is questionable or worse, they may accept it because of overwhelming political pressure or as a preferred alternative to further external intervention. That might help explain why TQM/CQI was claimed to have been adopted by 22 percent of all public institutions but only 6 percent of all private institutions (Birnbaum and Deshotels, 1999).

But the adoption of fads also may be encouraged because of the ways managers think about their roles and themselves and the ways they make decisions under conditions of uncertainty. This chapter emphasizes the ways in which managers can sometimes be misled into believing things that are not so. This is not an indictment of the frailty of managers but a recognition that managers, like all of us, are subject to cognitive biases that may lead them to see patterns where none exist, to become increasingly confident even as accuracy diminishes, and to seek advice from friends who are likely to share their own opinions (Plous, 1993). In this chapter we discuss six different but interrelated biases that may influence a manager to adopt and continue to support a fad in the absence of evidence it will have the desired effect.

Role Biases: Managers Take Charge

Managerial roles carry with them expectations of leadership, effective action, and the making of good decisions. Managers want to improve their institutions. They want to make a difference and leave a mark. They are selected for their roles in part because of their success in previous managerial positions. Faced with a problem, their roles tell them they must "do something," and their previous successes lead them to believe that when they act they are unusually effective. People in general are often overly confident about their knowledge and the certainty of their judgments (Nisbett and Ross, 1980). This certainty may be even greater when individuals fill managerial roles in which they are expected to have expertise. College presidents, for example, generally believe they are more effective than the "average" president and that their institution has significantly improved during their tenure (Birnbaum, 1986). But even though presidents may have great confidence in their ability, "the inferences they have made from experience are likely to be wrong. Their confidence in their learning is likely to have been reinforced by the social support they receive from the people around them and by social expectations about the presidential role" (Cohen and March, 1974, p. 201). In lieu of using empirical data, managers may engage in symbolic, role-related behavior, such as implementing management innovation, to demonstrate their influence.

Academic managers operate in organizations whose ambiguous and conflicting goals, responsiveness to multiple internal and external forces, and problematic technologies make it difficult to ascertain relationships between managerial cause and institutional effect. Adopting a new managerial technique is one way of fulfilling the role's requirements for effective action. "Management is a fertile field for fads and quick fixes because the problems are intractable, yet the pressure to be seen as 'doing something' is intense. A manager who is using the latest technique supported by an eminent expert or who is following the widely applauded prescriptions of a best-selling book can hardly be criticized, while those who ignore the latest trend risk being judged old-fashioned and unprofessional" (Hilmer and Donaldson, 1996, p. 8).

Adopting a new managerial system fulfills other role-related expectations as well. When managers begin their tenures, they go through an initial period of heightened activity, communication, and sense making. During this period, they learn more about the nature of their new position and take symbolic actions to signify that they are "taking charge" (Bensimon, 1987; Birnbaum, 1992). The need to initiate new management processes for symbolic purposes may be particularly great in organizations, such as colleges and universities, in which leaders may have relatively little instrumental effect.

Managers in bureaucratic organizations expect to exert influence since their experience and intrainstitutional networks make them more knowledgeable about their organizations than those they manage. When managers begin their new jobs, however, they often find their discretion is limited by existing structures, communication patterns, and routines; their subordinates know more about the way things get done than do the managers. One way managers can realign influence with structure is by learning the intricacies of the current system, a time-consuming process. Alternatively, they can achieve the same effect by invalidating existing knowledge and processes. By restructuring the system so subordinates no longer understand it, organizational coordination will require managerial expertise and initiative. Implementing a new management technique is one way that newly appointed top executives gain control of their organizations (Hammond and Knott, 1980, p. 70).

If the new technique can be presented as rational, it may generate less of a negative response than if it is seen solely as a political ploy. "The credence given to 'rational' procedures plus the scramble to master the intricate details of the new techniques may hold the bureaucracy at bay while the newcomers learn something about their jobs" (Hammond and Knott, 1980, p. 71). PPBS or MBO can serve the purpose as well as TQM/CQI, benchmarking, or any other fad that is rational, complex, and comprehensive.

For example, a new president may use an inaugural speech to "take charge" by calling for a complete transformation of the institution's culture and systems through "a comprehensive application of total quality principles" (Johnson and Smith, 1995, p. 308). Or a new president might announce a program of responsibility-centered budgeting to signal the view that higher education is a business (Binzen, 1996, p. C3). New managers may be as likely to adopt a fad to send a signal as to influence any specific outcome. One study, for example, found that while new presidents often began their tenure by supporting new planning processes, they were often unable to specify their reasons for doing so (Schmidtlein and Milton, 1988–1989, p. 8).

When a new technique has been identified as the mark of a new administrative order and central to institutional renewal, the manager's commitment to maintain the new process and avoid objective assessment of its effectiveness may intensify. Invitations to tout the innovation at national higher education meetings fan the ego and may make reconsideration even more difficult (Trombley, 1998, p. 16). Publicly speaking about an issue leads managers to believe that they really understand it and may increase their commitment to take action (Mintzberg, 1994, p. 390).

We are taught to believe that good managers make tough decisions, stand firm in the face of opposition, and steadfastly pursue the vision. Even a manager who initially questioned the value of a fad may come to support it after it has been adopted. If managers are required publicly to defend fad-related behavior that they might have originally questioned, "the performer can be fully taken in by his own act; he can be sincerely convinced that the impression of reality which he stages is the real reality" (Goffman, 1959, p. 17). It is difficult for managers to maintain over time a duplicity between what they say and what they really believe; managers can seduce themselves with their own rhetoric.

The manager's role may thus encourage the implementation of a management fad in order to symbolize a new order of things. Managers must dismantle existing systems to disrupt established organizational patterns that they may be less able to influence and substitute a new system that strengthens managerial control and in which the manager has superior expertise. If there is validity to the proposition that fads may be related to management succession, it might be expected not only that fads are more likely to be initiated by new managers, but also that they are more likely to be terminated when the management champion departs (Ross and Staw, 1993). This then opens the door for the implementation of a still newer system that will mark the contribution of the successor.

Role biases may also influence the adoption of fads by more experienced managers as a means of escaping the boredom of routine and satisfying the role expectation that good managers are innovators. Change causes disruption, and some managers derive "personal satisfaction from the turmoil. To them it's an adventure, or a military campaign, a break from the routine of monitoring accounts receivable and inventory turns" (Robbins and Finley, 1996, p. 37).

Cognitive Biases: Managers as Intuitive Scientists

Academic managers are smart people. If they followed the procedures of scientific inquiry, after hearing about a new management technique they would collect data that would help them sensibly decide whether to adopt it. If they decided to adopt, they would study whether it was making the institution more effective or whether it was having undesirable consequences. They would then use this analysis to decide if the technique should be continued or terminated. But managers are unlikely to collect and analyze data as formal scientists. Instead, they act as intuitive scientists (Nisbett and

Ross, 1980; Birnbaum, 1986), relying on experience more than data. As they make decisions, their perceptions and thought processes are likely to be influenced by a number of factors that may compromise "scientific" rationality. Their expectations may lead them to perceive and believe in relationships that exist only in their imaginations and ignore relationships that empirically exist. These cognitive biases could lead managers to believe incorrectly that the implementation of a fad has improved, or will improve, institutional success, or fail to see that a fad has undesirable outcomes.

Adopting a New Management Technique

Although the processes by which managers in higher education learn of new management techniques are yet to be empirically determined, it is likely that sources include the mass media, professional journals and associations, contact with colleagues at other institutions, and formal and informal consultants. In the early stages of fad adoption, each of these sources is likely to present only positive assessments. As managers seek a new way to deal with intractable problems, they may find their decision processes influenced by two cognitive errors, which I call the "A Box" Fallacy and the Cat on the Toilet Seat Fallacy.

The "A Box" Fallacy

How might a manager scientifically decide whether to adopt a fad? One way would be to separate institutions into two groups—those that had adopted the fad and those that had not—and then determine how many institutions in each group were successful or unsuccessful. Neither "adoption" nor "success" would be easy to assess, but almost any criterion would do as long as it is determined before the assessments are made rather than afterward and as long as it is uniformly applied across institutions. The manager would then complete a 2 x 2 table similar to the one shown in Figure 7.1.

With the numbers of institutions entered in each of the four boxes, the manager could now make reasonable inferences about

The institution was:

The institution:	Successful	Unsuccessful
Adopted a fad	A	C
Did not adopt a fad	B	D

Figure 7.1. The "A Box" Fallacy

possible associations between fads and success and decide if adopting a fad might pay off. Unfortunately, no one in higher education has collected data like these for any management technique, so that this kind of analysis is not possible. Instead, most of the writing about academic management fads consists of the stories of institutions that adopted a fad whose consequences were claimed to be successful—that is, only institutions in box A. People in general often use box A data to judge the strength of relationships (Einhorn, 1982; Gilovich, 1991), and box A stories are the most common basis for claiming that fads and success are related. We seldom hear about institutions that were similarly successful without adopting the fad (box B) or fad adopters who were unsuccessful (box C). And other than the horror stories told by true believers or consultants about the failed institution that could have been saved had they only adopted a specific managerial product, we *never* hear about box D, although it is a key component of the inferential process. I call this tendency to consider only examples of positive outcomes the "A Box" Fallacy. It leads people to make unsupportable generalizations about the value of fads, even though legitimate judgments cannot be made without comparing data in all four boxes (Nisbett and Ross, 1980). Considering only the A box (which contains the predicted "event") also means giving less attention to the other boxes (which contain nonevents) (Gilovich, 1991). Managers seduced by the "A Box" Fallacy to see the fad as potentially valuable are now set up for the Cat on the Toilet Seat Fallacy.

The Cat on the Toilet Seat Fallacy

You may have heard about someone who trained a cat to balance itself on a toilet seat instead of using a litter box. Very few cat owners would accept this as a good argument that they can train their cat to do the same feat. They would be quite right to reject generalizations based on extreme cases or unusual events. It violates the statistical principle that small samples should not be taken as representative of the population from which it is drawn, because it leads people to make logically unsupportable generalizations (Kahneman and Tversky, 1982).

But the Cat on the Toilet Seat Fallacy is a staple of the fad adoption process. Stories of claimed successful use of fads often appear as single-case presentations in book chapters or journal articles, to convince others of the value of the fad. These "institution-which" statistics ("let me tell you about an institution which . . .") are presented as probative evidence even though they should be given no inferential weight (Nisbett and Ross, 1980, p. 6). In studying the wide range of management tools used by business, for example, every one of them—including those with the lowest average ratings—had some extremely satisfied users (Rigby, 1998). Managers who become excited by an innovation can easily find someone who can attest to its validity. A rational decision maker would insist on reviewing the experiences of a large number of institutions before making a judgment. But managers, like most intuitive scientists, "tend to be insensitive to sample size, accepting small samples of information as being no less useful in their estimates than large samples. They place greater emphasis on assessing the quality of data drawn from experience than on the size of the sample" (March, 1994, p. 86).

People tend to believe what others believe, exaggerate the degree to which others believe it, and believe their own views are shared by others. The cognitive logic appears to be that the more people who believe something, the more likely it is to be true and the more reasonable it is for us to do the same. This is why fad adoption can be influenced by consultants and champions of fads who allege that the fad of the moment has been implemented by a huge proportion of some normatively excellent group such as the Fortune 500. The often-erroneous belief that something enjoys wide social support makes managers more resistant to considering the possibility that their own adoption decision may be a mistake (Gilovich, 1991, p. 112).

Assessing a New Management Technique

Deciding whether to adopt an innovation is difficult because of the paucity of valid data. It might be thought that, by comparison, assessing the consequences of a new technique, once adopted, would be relatively easy because the manager would be able to collect evidence and observe outcomes personally. But valid assessment can be as cognitively tricky as the adoption decision itself. Having been instrumental in making the decision, managers may be more likely than others to overestimate its benefits. For example, surveys in the early 1990s indicate that satisfaction levels among executives who had initiated any of a dozen management fads ranged from 35 to 60 percent. At the same time, employees and customers rated the effectiveness of these fads at between 10 and 20 percent (Bleakley, 1993).

Managers may feel the dissonance of decision maker's remorse after deciding to implement a new management technique. To reduce dissonance and justify their choice, they tend to accentuate the positive aspects of the alternative they have chosen as well as the negative aspects of the alternative they have not chosen. The cognitive biases of managers who adopt innovations lead them to give more attention to outcomes that are desirable, direct, or anticipated than to outcomes that are undesirable, indirect, or unanticipated. Once managers are committed to an innovation, they tend to gather information to support, rather than challenge, their decisions so that their beliefs are made consistent with their actions (March, 1994, p. 39). The implementation of a fad on a campus often occupies a great deal of the time and attention of the managers responsible for them. We have already noted that expectations of success are likely to overwhelm evidence of failure. These two factors of attention and expectation may lead managers to make faulty judgments because of a common cognitive bias known as the availability heuristic (Nisbett and Ross, 1980). The availability heuristic suggests that potential causes of a phenomenon that are most salient, or most easily brought to mind, are also more likely to be considered the causes of outcomes (Ross and Anderson, 1982). Because managers expect a fad to have positive outcomes and because fads are salient in that they take up a disproportionate amount of managerial time, managers are more likely to see evidence of success than of failure and more likely to attribute success to the fad. As Gilovich (1991, p. 50) has observed, "When examining evidence relevant to a given belief, people are inclined to see what they expect to see, and conclude what they expect to conclude. Information that is consistent with our pre-existing beliefs is often accepted at face value, whereas evidence that contradicts them is critically scrutinized and discounted."

We search for, discover, or invent reasons that the decision we made was a good one. We come to think the decision is important because of the time we spend on it, and that alternatives we rejected are less important because we spend less time on them (Weick, 1995, p. 159). Studies that confirm one's position are praised as well as conducted; those that oppose one's position are seen as flawed and invalid. Studies of both kinds are likely to strengthen one's original conviction. Once managers have made up their minds, it is difficult to persuade them otherwise, regardless of the evidence that may be presented (Gilovich, 1991).

Perceptions are affected by both what people expect to see and what people want to see (Plous, 1993). Because expectations are so powerful and outcomes so equivocal, managers are particularly likely to see positive results from a new management technique during the earlier stages of its implementation. Receiving positive feedback about outcomes may lead managers to assume erroneously that they were caused by a fad, to see no need to seek more task knowledge about the fad, and therefore to remain ignorant of the real consequences of implementing the fad (Einhorn, 1982). Later in the process, negative evidence may accumulate to the point at which it can no longer be ignored even by a committed advocate. However, managers may turn over more quickly than fads, so "by the time a fad has run its course and disillusionment might be expected to set in, those who have participated in it have assumed new responsibilities. As they do, the institution loses the opportunity to learn what has worked, as well as what does not work" (Hammond and Knott, 1980). This means that "we may never institutionalize what we have learned—both pro and con—about the innovation itself or about the risks and benefits of adopting exciting innovations for a short period of time" (Allen and Chaffee, 1981, p. 5).

Normative Biases: Managers Act Appropriately

The public rhetoric of fad adopters may be cloaked in the language of rationality, using concepts of accountability and efficiency in order to build legitimacy for their actions. "The objective, unbiased, impersonal and logical nature of rational reasoning makes it more palatable to others and more persuasive. Since managers must inevitably persuade others to act collectively to get things done, a great deal of their rhetoric has a rational character" (Eccles and Nohria, 1992, p. 52). But while managers say what good managers are expected to say, their behavior may be based more on copying what good managers are supposed to do. If others are adopting ZBB or TQM, a manager who faces problems that seem to have no obvious answers may adopt them as well. The logic is simple: "I am a good manager, in a certain kind of institution, and I do not know how to cope with a specific problem. Good managers are expected to cope with problems. To confirm my status as a good manager, I will do what I see other good managers doing in institutions like my own." The more managers do the same thing, the more legitimate the adoption becomes.

A manager's decision to adopt or not adopt a fad is usually made logically, not arbitrarily or capriciously. At the same time, there is little evidence that adoption decisions involve generating alternatives, comparing them to preferences, and making choices that are the hallmark of the logic of rational choice. Instead, they appear to follow what March (1994) has called the logic of appropriateness. "A logic of appropriateness is different from a logic of consequence, but both logics are logics of reason. . . . [The logic of consequence] makes great demands on the abilities of individuals and institutions to anticipate the future and to form useful preferences. The [logic of appropriateness] makes great demands on the abilities of individuals and institutions to learn from the past and to form useful identities" (p. 101).

Managers may adopt a fad when there is a normative standard to do so and when they do not know what else to do. Fad advocates contribute to the development of that normative standard and therefore increase the likelihood that managers, faced with uncertainty, may respond by adopting a fad in order "to behave in a normatively praiseworthy way" (March, 1984, p. 30). Most people do not adopt an innovation because they have been exposed to empirical evidence about it, but because of subjective evaluations provided by people seen as being like themselves who attest to its value or have already adopted it. Adoption is a process in which uncertainty is reduced through modeling and imitating the behavior of network partners, or by adopting the conceptual orientations espoused by trustworthy consultants, friends, and professional associations (Rogers, 1995; March, 1994; Scott, 1995).

Managers protect themselves by justifying their actions as based on practices adopted by others or recommended by prestigious professional groups. As Callahan (1962) pointed out, following the publication of an influential report on school reform, "any superin-tendent who could say that he was adopting [the report's] recom-mendations, or better yet, that his school system had already been following them for years, was almost impregnable" (p. ii).

Managers may make a public show of adopting a fad as a way of presenting themselves to others and influencing the impressions others have of them (Goffman, 1959). They may support innova-tive practices as a means of building their professional reputations. This may in part explain what we have already seen: public claims of fad adoption need not necessarily lead to fad implementation. Managers learn that the benefits of symbolic adoption are not nec-essarily augmented by actually trying to put a fad in practice. It may also be that the pace of change is too rapid to do anything even if they wanted to. Managers go with the flow.

Self-Efficacy Biases: The Illusion of Control

When senior American managers were asked what they would least want subordinates to know about them, 95 percent replied they would not want them to know how inadequate they felt in their jobs (Micklethwait and Wooldridge, 1996). If managerial efficacy is problematic in business, it is even more so in higher education. College and university managers live in a world in which others expect them to do things that make a difference, yet at the same time they find their discretion to act constrained by existing struc-tures, ongoing routines, the professional prerogatives of others, the lack of slack resources, and the loose coupling that characterizes academic governance.

Academic managers, like the rest of us, need to believe they are effective and have influence. If they are to maintain that belief, they must also believe they have some control over institutional life. If they cannot exercise real control, it is important at least that there be the illusion of control. Fads are like the idea-of-the-month man-agement books that "hold out the chimera of control. The fact that they do not deliver may not diminish their appeal: If you're con-fused, it's reassuring to know that everyone else is, too" (Samuel-son, 1999, p. A21). Managers may implement fads because they do not know what else to do. They initiate fads as part of the pro-cess through which they look for work (Cohen and March, 1974) and buy management books because they offer a sense of security (Micklethwait and Wooldridge, 1996).

Fads help simplify the world and make it more sensible. By iden-tifying processes and sequential steps within processes and provid-ing a plausible rationale for them, managers can act as if they are doing their jobs when they otherwise would not know what their jobs were. Managers use the rationalization and rhetoric of fads not "just to impress others, but also to convince themselves that all is well and that they have the ability to cope" (Morgan, 1986, p. 90). Fads provide an illusion of control in a world that otherwise seems uncontrollable. Most fads must be initiated by the managers, and their initiation allows managers to establish structures and pro-cedures, ask for reports, and give orders. Most fads generate large amounts of data that administrators can examine and analyze to strengthen the illusion that the data reflect some innate organi-zational properties or processes. One of the reasons the outcomes of fad implementation are not usually seriously assessed may be that the real purpose of fads may not be to improve education but to at-test to the influence of management, and nothing does that like adopting a system that requires people to modify their activities.

Analyses of ZBB, for example, suggested some reasons that man-agers could continue to endorse it even though it did not do what it claimed. ZBB permitted budgeters to maintain the rationality of comprehensive budgeting even as they practiced incremental bud-geting. It led to increased attention to the budgeting process so they could feel more important and useful, and did not require change (thus confirming they had been making rational decisions all along). Some ZBB practitioners thought they were learning something new, although these turned out usually to be newcomers who were indeed learning about their department's programs and processes. President Carter, for example, said the first year of ZBB budgeting in the federal government had taught him a lot—but then, probably everything he did in his first year taught him a lot. Even when people did not believe they themselves had learned a lot from ZBB, they were likely to believe that either those above them or those below them had done so (Wildavsky and Hammond, 1965; Hammond and Knott, 1980).

Managers may endorse fads, on one hand, because they appear so simple and intuitive. For example, "Many managers are attracted to TQM, not tqm, and hence make ready customers for an appealing product. TQM is clear and tangible; you know exactly what you're buying and for how much. In contrast, tqm is simply sound management, which is anything but tangible, finite, or straightforward" (Harari, 1993b, p. 35). On the other hand, there may also be advantages to endorsing a fad because it is so complex. "There is nothing more empowering than believing you know a complicated secret" (O'Shea and Madigan, 1997, p. 197). Claims that an institution has successfully adopted a fad can confirm both a manager's status as an innovator and an institution's position of leadership among its peers. For a manager, being the champion of a fad has other benefits as well: it "suggests that a manager is open to change, willing to take risks, in touch with the latest thinking. The chance to put the fad into practice gives him much higher visibility throughout the company, tests his mettle as an agent of change and not a stooge of the status quo" (Micklethwait and Wooldridge, 1996, p. 59). A senior manager may embrace a management fad in order to demonstrate fitness for higher office (Marcus, 1999).

Autocratic managers may find top-down fads to be a confirmation of their management style. Chief information officers may find some fads appealing because they highlight their organizational importance (Strassmann, 1994). Chief financial officers may endorse them as consistent with their belief in rationality, even in the absence of proof they work ("What You Really Think About Reengineering," 1995). New managers might support fads because they require others to learn a new language and procedures "which the newcomers know (or act like they know) better than the bureaucrats do. Thus the rationalistic appearance of the reforms may give the new administration opportunity to accomplish changes that might not otherwise be possible" (Hammond and Knott, 1980, p. 103).

The need to see themselves as in control is not unique to managers. It is also shared by those to whom managers are responsible who are more likely to "alleviate their anxieties about lack of knowledge by ensuring that managers engage in formal planning" (Mintzberg, 1994, p. 213) or whatever the fad of the moment happens to be. The further removed trustees, legislatures, or community interest groups are from the organization itself, the more likely they are to believe in the effectiveness of the fad in controlling the organization.

Commitment Biases: The Trapped Manager

The old adage says, "You got to know when to hold 'em and know when to fold 'em," but managers often find it difficult to acknowledge that a program for which they are responsible does not work. One study of institutions that adopted MBO and MIS programs (Baldridge, 1979) found that only 18 percent of the managers of projects judged by the researcher to be unsuccessful agreed that the project outcomes were disappointing. Although it might be thought that a manager might reduce or completely remove support of a fad that appeared not to be working, failure may lead to increased, rather than decreased, dedication. This phenomenon, referred to as the escalation of commitment, has been studied frequently over the past quarter-century in both laboratory and natural settings. Although never specifically applied to higher education, a significant body of research has suggested a number of ideas that may apply to decisions to maintain an academic management fad even in the face of evidence it does not work.

Escalation of commitment typically begins with "the bright prospect of future outcomes through a given course of action" (Ross and Staw, 1993, p. 703), a characteristic of the initiation stage of the life cycle process described in Chapter Five. Because universities have ambiguous goals and outcomes that are difficult to measure, it is exceptionally difficult to estimate costs and benefits of a new project. Organizations in general are likely to be influenced by negative results when they are clear-cut and obvious during a project's early stages (Ross and Staw, 1993); the tendency of universities to delay judgment means that ending a project at its earliest and most vulnerable stage may be less likely than in other organizations. When a program is implemented but after a time the organization does not improve, the manager may be ensnared. "He has wasted a large part of his credibility by committing to a so far fruitless change program. But his only choice is to go on, trying to pick up the pace, in spite of growing skepticism. To do so, he must further commit his personal credibility in the new wave of initiative, exposing himself more and more to backlash. Like the squirrel in a rotating cage, all he can do now is run faster and faster" (Gouillart, 1994, p. 59).

Managers who find themselves in a situation in which they are assessed by the success of their programs, and thus have to justify continuing or even expanding a program that is ineffective, are trapped. The benefits they see for continuing may be illusory, since the application of more resources may not salvage the program as they hope but only increase the ultimate loss. This tendency to escalate failing programs is exacerbated when a manager implements a policy that is unpopular in the organization, since he knows he will have even greater need to protect himself (Fox and Staw, 1979).

Management commitment to a failing program may continue or increase for various reasons. Projects are likely to persist if setbacks can be blamed on temporary rather than permanent causes, if ending the project would be expensive, if it is believed the project can be turned around with additional investments, or if the project has been built into the structure and management of the organization. Psychological determinants may also play a role. People (particularly successful people) tend to overestimate the chances of success and underestimate the chances of failure, try to self-justify decisions they have been instrumental in making, take risks in situations to avoid loss (as opposed to avoiding risk in order to preserve gains), and be influenced by sunk costs already expended. Managers may continue to support failing projects to avoid appearing incompetent and losing face to others, to protect their reputations, and to conform to leadership norms suggesting that good leaders persevere through adversity. Even when faced with compelling evidence that something has not worked, someone who begins with a deep commitment "will frequently emerge, not only unshaken, but even more convinced than ever before. Indeed, he may even show a new fervor about convincing and converting other people to his view" (Festinger, Riecken, and Schachter, 1956, p. 3). Zealots are people who increase their commitment as they lose sight of their goals.

Organizational factors may also be important. In complex social systems, it is often hard to start things and just as hard to stop them. New staffs and structures are created, the fad gets embedded into aspects of the system, including relationships between people, and there may be political support to continue the fad from groups inside the organization (Staw, 1981, 1997; Ross and Staw, 1986).

Expectancy Biases: The Placebo Effect

Every fad has been seen by some people as having some positive outcomes for some institution at some time. Sometimes the value of fads may be seen only by their managers; at other times, both managers and others provide testimony of improvement. It is possible that in some cases, the implementation of a new management technique really has improved institutional effectiveness. But it is also possible that in other cases, fads function in organizations as placebos function in medicine: they do not affect the "disease" (an abnormal state of the organization), although they may temporarily improve the "illness" (the perceived suffering that accompanies disease) (Brown, 1998).

Ill people may feel better for any of three reasons. The body may naturally cure itself of the underlying disease over time with no treatment at all (for example, the common cold). Or a treatment with active components such as drugs or surgery may lead to specific effects (for example, antibiotics curing infection). Or a treatment with inactive components may lead to nonspecific effects, an outcome commonly referred to as the placebo effect (Turner and others, 1994). A placebo (Latin for "I will please") is most likely to be effective when a patient expects a treatment to work. In general, 30 percent of people receiving as placebo in a drug trial will experience improvement (Wade, 1996), and improvement rates as high as 70 percent have been documented in specific trials. Placebo effects result from the symbolic importance of a treatment rather than its ability to cure disease. Part of the symbolic power comes from the presentation of the placebo as new and as a breakthrough in modern science. The placebo effect has been recognized for a long time. As one physician urged years ago, "Hurry, hurry—use the new drugs while they still work" (Goleman, 1993, p. C3).

Placebos in medicine can be sugar pills, surgical interventions, words—anything that leads a patient to have an expectation of success even though the treatment itself has no active components. Patients can improve after a consultation even if not followed by treatment (K. B. Thomas, 1994). The placebo effect can be exceptionally robust; it can last over extended periods and have apparent outcomes superior to a proven treatment with active components. In medicine, placebos are more effective when responding to subjective sensations; when the placebo treatments are in conformity with the patient's stereotypes of what treatments look like; when the physician is optimistic and enthusiastic; when the physician shows signs of being a respected healer; when successes are publicized and failures ignored; when the provider is seen as interested, warm, friendly, and prestigious; and when the treatment is impressive, expensive, and involves a ritual that promises relief (deSaintonge and Herxheimer, 1994; Turner and others, 1994; Brown,

1997). Organizational analogues are present for all of these ingredients as institutions go through the fad cycle. When fads function as placebos, institutional change can be ascribed to MBO, TQM, or whatever nostrum is in use at the time.

Just as placebos can lead to a relief of symptoms for those who believe, so symptoms can increase in severity when patients who believe are given a nocebo ("I will harm"), which leads them to expect distress ("What Is a Nocebo?" 1997). Educational "experts," consultants, and others who are seen as authoritative sources of organizational knowledge therefore can create organizational illness by incorrectly diagnosing it, just as they can appear to cure it by incorrectly prescribing a fad. When the institution does not get "better," the fad itself can be absolved from failure through the same processes of rationalization used in medicine to explain why the operation was successful but the patient died: the dosage was too small, the patient waited too long before seeking help, the physician was not competent, it was the wrong kind of patient. In earlier days, it was God's will, or the patient did not have sufficient faith (Gilovich, 1991). Such explanations may be even more difficult to refute when the definition of "better" is unclear. For true believers, placebos can be seen as effective because of the tendency of people to search for confirming evidence (Gilovich, 1991), bias the data generated, give greater weight to confirming than to disconfirming cases, remember confirming evidence more clearly, and thus be more likely to recall it (Nisbett and Ross, 1980). In the calculus of fad advocates, one success can confirm a strategy's effectiveness, while multiple failures may do little to disconfirm it.

Part III

Working with Academic
Management Fads

8

The Legacy of Fads

We do not know much about management fads. The literature consists largely of advocacy and stories of presumably successful implementation at one or another institution. There are few empirical studies of academic management fads, and none that looks at them from a holistic perspective, including their indirect, as well as their direct, effects. We know that changes in management systems have some impact on the technical core of an organization, but we do not really know how this happens. There are a number of reasons we may never know enough about management fads to reach some unequivocal judgment about their effects on individual institutions, much less the higher education system as a whole.

First, fads seldom exist in pure form. PPBS, for example, may have looked similar in the states that adopted it because they also were likely to have copied the form used by the federal government. But there was no clear understanding of exactly how program budgeting was to be done, and it was generally recommended that not all features of the new system should replace the old system immediately. The actual process in many states therefore came to be a mixture of some aspects of the new PPBS with some of the aspects of Ur-Management as practiced in that state. The budgeting system was thus hybridized, incorporating some of the new processes into the existing ones (Schick, 1971). Institutions alter whatever system they adopt for their own purposes. This adaptation and evolution is useful, but one consequence is that the same name or acronym may be used to identify processes that may not closely resemble either each other or the original innovation. Fads mutate and evolve over time as consultants develop their own proprietary products, as they did for MBO, TQM/CQI, and strategic planning.

In addition, there is no agreement on the desired outcomes of fads, the consequences of fads are difficult to measure, and fads may have disparate effects in different parts of the institution. Fads promise to make things better, but do not provide a priori criteria that would make it possible later to determine if they "worked." The problem is that "implicit in each fad is a cause-effect statement that is rarely made explicit and never properly supported" (Donaldson and Hilmer, 1998, p. 17). Unless the implicit is made explicit, the assessment of fads will continue to be compromised by the cognitive biases of the assessors and the ease with which events occurring at the same time erroneously can be interpreted as causally connected. Academic institutions are complex, nonlinear systems, and their responses to changes in one part can have counterintuitive and surprising effects in another. The implementation of a social technology, just like a physical technology, can bite back with unintended consequences as it "introduces more subtle and insidious problems to replace acute ones. Nor are the acute ones ever completely eliminated; in fact, unless we exercise constant care and alertness, they have a way of coming back with new strength" (Tenner, 1996, p. xi). These unintended consequences are often difficult to uncover, much less predict, in physical systems where measurement is less problematic. Consider how much more challenging it is in social systems to determine, much less predict, the outcomes when "new structures, devices, and organisms meet with real people in real situations we could not foresee" (p. 9).

Despite our inability to understand fully the consequences of academic fads, we can make two statements with some degree of confidence. The first is that all academic management fads fail on their own terms. The second, and much more important, is that all academic management fads leave legacies that remain in higher education long after the fad has disappeared.

The Failure of Academic Management Fads

The management literature, in both business and higher education, sounds the consistent theme that fads have failed to have the direct effects they claimed. Consider a partial litany of criticism: PPBS was "a failure as a system" (Harvey, 1977, p. 39); "planning fails everywhere it has been tried" (Wildavsky, 1973, p. 128); "zero-base budgeting is a fraud" (Anthony, 1977, p. 26); "the management fads of the last fifteen years rarely produced the promised results" (Nohria and Berkley, 1994, p. 129); "total quality management, benchmarking, reengineering, empowerment of the individual, and other current remedies are being proposed to unshackle U.S. workers and allow their creative juices to flow, although no empirical evidence [shows] that any of these things [increase] productivity" (Bleakley, 1993, p. A1).

Not only do fads fail, but their failure gives rise to still further fads that criticize their predecessors and claim to have corrected their errors. Fad advocates are likely to note that "none of the management fads of the last twenty years—not management by objectives, diversification, Theory Z, zero-based budgeting, value chain analysis, decentralization, quality circles, 'excellence,' restructuring, portfolio management, management by walking around, matrix management, intrapreneuring, or one-minute managing—has reversed the deterioration of America's corporate competitive task. They have only distracted managers from the real task at hand" (Hammer and Champy, 1993, p. 25). These critics then use the failure of past fads as the basis for claiming their own proposal will finally solve the problem. To these critics, the difference between a management innovation and a fad is clear. My proposal for change is a creative innovation that will change the course of management. *Your* proposal is a fad, and more of the same old thing. My innovation offers the road to salvation; your fad is a false god. But the most interesting aspect of fads is not that they fail, but that even in failure, they have important consequences. When fads die, they leave something behind.

The Fad Residual

After a management innovation is adopted, it may take one of several paths. It may be institutionalized and become an accepted and unremarkable part of organizational routine. It may become hybridized, merging with existing practices to produce a modest change in procedure. It may disappear without a trace. But if it is a fad, "The process of implementing it is followed by the dissipation of its 'hard' statement of intentions and the adsorption of its personnel and institutions into the climate around it" (Rose, 1980, p. 109). In this way, as Chaffee (1985) points out, "The effects of a borrowed system will probably be more residual than direct. When a higher education institution adopts a system, or even is just exposed to its concepts and practices, the institution is likely to discover subtle changes in its management processes" (p. 133). Even as the fad product is seen as not having lived up to its promise, the "good ideas do not go away. Tempered against the realities of the marketplace, they become part of the way a company does business, as well as the breeding ground for even more effective ways of managing" (Bohl and Luthans, 1996, p. 2).

Fads almost always are based on a good idea containing "a kernel of truth" (Davenport, 1995), which is part of the reason that even in the face of failure, advocates can claim its concepts are sound. Even though PPBS, for example, was a failure, it was said to have left "a positive residue of thought and action" (Harvey, 1977, p. 39). Of course, if a fad can have a positive residual effect, it can have a negative one as well. Marchese (1991, p. 9) reminds us that the Chinese expression for *fad* translates as "a gust of wind," and gusts of wind can have harmful as well as beneficial outcomes. Sometimes, depending on their ideology, different observers can characterize the same effect in quite different ways.

In this chapter we turn our attention to some of the residuals that fads leave behind as they evaporate and diffuse into a sector's, or an institution's, policy environment. We begin with the negative consequences of fads, which are the most obvious and observable and serve as the basis for many criticisms about them. We then turn to the positive consequences of fads, which are more subtle but perhaps more profound, and which suggest that fads may be critical elements of institutional evolution. From this perspective, the process of adopting and then abandoning fads may be seen as essential to the survival of the higher education system.

Negative Residuals of Fads

What is the harm of a little fad? Based on the results of annual surveys of business use of new management techniques, Rigby (1998, p. 42) answers that question by noting that, among other things, fads may lead to imbalances in strategic resources, internal divisiveness, unrealistic expectations, and loss of employee responsibility; they destroy strategy by encouraging institutions to do what others do. Some of the negative residuals of fads are seen in many types of organizations; others may be particularly troublesome to higher education.

Tyranny of Numbers

Most academic management fads emphasize quantification; some go to the extreme of claiming that if something cannot be measured, it cannot be of value. Measurement mania can be particularly disruptive to educational organizations. Superficial aspects of institutional output are often more easily measured than more substantive ones (Etzioni, 1964), and things that can be quantified are usually considered to be more important than things that cannot

(Cheit, 1977). But an educational philosopher might claim that those things of greatest value are precisely those things that *cannot* be measured and, indeed, the purpose of education is to turn tangible resources into intangible resources (Bowen, 1977). If we cannot measure what is valuable, we will come to value what is measurable, so that passion for measurement can distort organizational efforts by prizing and overproducing what can be measured and neglecting what cannot.

Obsessive measurement can also reduce the social legitimacy of, and therefore the social support for, higher education. One of the characteristics of institutionalized organizations is that confidence and good faith (of those inside as well as outside the organization) are supported by adherence to ceremony and ritual rather than by evaluation and inspection. Society has confidence in the good faith of colleges and universities to the extent that these institutions are believed to do what they are supposed to, even when these activities are inconsistent with perceptions of technical efficiency. Confidence is essential to institutional viability when technical effectiveness cannot be measured. Increasing the evaluation and inspection of an institution undermines its social legitimacy (Meyer and Rowan, 1992). The irony of quantification is that the more we are committed to measuring the effectiveness of colleges and universities, the less effective we are likely to believe them to be. And in the final analysis, numbers and object data are less important as determinants of institutional change than are the relationships created by working together to construct a shared sense of reality (Lueddeke, 1999).

Illusion of Certainty

Attempts to quantify the unmeasurable often give managers a false sense of certainty. Making decisions under conditions of certainty is much different from making decisions under conditions of uncertainty; the worst error of all is to make uncertain decisions under the illusion of certainty. Some fads purport to represent complex and indeterminate situations through series of elaborate tables and charts processed by computers using sophisticated models. The ephemeral is made to seem concrete. As Boulding (1978, pp. 46–47) said, "We have to be particularly careful not to be misled by numerical measurements of efficiency, especially where the numbers do not represent the significant reality, as in general they do not. Everything indeed that is presented to the decision maker in terms of numbers is evidence, not truth. To believe that evidence is truth is a sure recipe for making bad decisions. In universities this could be catastrophic."

"Rational" decision processes based on measurement may often lead to irrational decisions that, because they appear to have been derived scientifically, are difficult to refute. For example, the benchmarking process in South Carolina included exactly thirty-seven measurements of quality. The reason? That is what the law stipulates! Although there was no rational basis for selecting thirty-seven or subdividing them in one way or another, the arbitrary number gave an appearance of rationality that satisfied the legislature. The process led to irrational results, comparable to "the ancient practice of spilling the entrails of goats on the ground and reading messages from the patterns" (Trombley, 1998, p. 15). The reading of goat entrails was an ancient, messy, low-tech, and low-cost precursor to environmental scanning. It was tough on the goat, but in the hands of a skilled shaman probably no less accurate or useful than many current practices based on today's technologies. One administrator acknowledged that benchmarking "may enable higher education to regain some of the credibility it has lost, not only in South Carolina but nationwide. But do I think it will affect, in the near future, what goes on in the learning experience of a single student in this state? No, I don't think so" (Trombley, 1998, p. 16). After considerable turmoil, South Carolina has now decided to use the benchmarks to allocate only 5 percent of institutional budgets.

Simplicity, Complexity, and Change

Fads distort reality, as they simultaneously simplify and complicate. They simplify by substituting formal procedures for the heuristic understandings of experienced managers. But they complicate as well because the sequences of analysis and behavior required by the fad may be quite complex. One might think, following the law of parsimony, that simpler processes and explanations would drive out complex ones. But just the opposite may occur. People who have simple (and objectively accurate) explanations for phenomena they have just observed are often impressed by the complex, sophisticated (and objectively inaccurate) explanations given by others. As a consequence, they may change their own explanations to be more complex as well, and in doing so become less accurate and reduce their own effectiveness (Weick, 1995, p. 84). It is easy retrospectively to construct elaborate interpretations of why fads did not work and ignore the simpler explanation that it may be due to a mismatch between a fad's premises and the institution's core technology.

The rationalizations used to explain why the previous fad did not work provide the basis for believing the next fad will finally have it right. But aside from the distorting possibilities of fads themselves, there is also the question of the effects of change induced by fads. The continual adoption of innovations, done in the name of organizational survival, may in fact have precisely the opposite effect. Constant change may inhibit reliable performance as it diminishes an organization's sense of its competencies, history, and commitment to continuity (Salipante and Golden-Biddle, 1995). Institutions require a considerable degree of stability to carry out their functions effectively.

Reducing Managerial Competence

Effective managers make sense of institutional problems through experience and the knowledge they have developed over time. Management is more an art than a science; it involves "intuition, creativity, discernment, an appreciation of the interaction of form and function" (Enarson, 1975, p. 174). When fads are based on received formulas, numbers, or procedures, they may limit managerial discretion, and therefore managerial competence. Fads may look rational but be technically inefficient. Adopting technically inefficient fads interferes with management's use of techniques that may appear to be less rational but in fact are technically superior in the context of the academic environment. In giving precedence to process over judgment, fads may trivialize or denigrate "the very thing that is in so much need of improvement, namely the management of large, complex organizations. . . . Fads are symptoms of a more fundamental problem—the loss of respect for management and for professional managers" (Hilmer and Donaldson, 1996, p. x).

Implementing the techniques and tools that accompany most fads is time-consuming and often a distraction from directly confronting problems (Enarson, 1975). Management fads thus can provide and legitimate opportunities to *avoid* work rather than to *do* work (Heifetz, 1994). Before we do something, we must have a plan, and to plan we need data, and so we must develop data definitions and collection systems, which requires the development of computer programs. And on it goes. A fad can distract managers from dealing with current situations. "It requires that they divide their attention, putting aside their normal work to organize and conduct a new and unfamiliar task. That usually involves generating data and managing some kind of consensus-building process. All this takes time and energy" (Leslie and Fretwell, 1996, p. 240)—and, as managers well know, lots of money.

As a consequence, fads can weaken rather than improve institutional performance as they "devalue human resources in organizations, destroying managerial competencies and organizational capabilities. . . . Many of the current trends propagated in the popular business press undermine the status and relevance of managerial work critical to the success of large, complex, global corporations" (Donaldson and Hilmer, 1998, p. 7).

Increasing Cynicism About Management

Does this business situation sound familiar to colleges and universities? "Every few months, our senior managers find a new religion. One time it was quality, another it was customer service, another it was flattening the organization. We just hold our breath until they get over it, and things get back to normal" (Hammer, 1990, p. 112). The culture of higher education is not kind to managers. Presidents, deans, department chairs, faculty committee heads, and others quickly learn the limits of their authority and realize that their influence depends on the grudging acceptance of others. The experienced academic manager who told the faculty, "I know I'm an evil; the question is whether I'm a *necessary* evil," neatly captured the ambivalence of academic managers and those whom they presume to manage.

Managers who successfully pursue a project build up constituent support that facilitates their future efforts; managers whose project is conspicuously unsuccessful may find it difficult to recover their credibility. Because fads promise much and deliver little, they may set up for failure the managers who support them. Failure affects not only constituents but eventually managers themselves, "who are disillusioned by the fact that a lot of extra work has not resulted in any significant reallocation of resources [and who] will undoubtedly develop negative attitudes towards the system" (Suver and Brown, 1977, p. 81). Managers can become less enthusiastic and less likely to innovate. The most enthusiastic advocates of campus planning, for example, tend to be those who have never done it, while people who have experienced two or more planning cycles tend to be cynical about the benefits of planning (Schmidtlein, 1990).

As management innovations fail, managers shift from one fad to the next, and "employees wise up to this syndrome rather quickly. Experience teaches them not to become overly enthusiastic about any new idea. They learn to shrug it off, reasoning that 'if we wait until Monday, this too shall pass'" (Nohria and Berkley, 1994, p. 131). Adoption of fads exposes organizational participants to contradictions because the essential notions of successive fads are often mutually incompatible. An institution that moves from the supposedly incremental processes of TQM to the revolutionary process claimed for BPR, for example, encourages organizational instability "by abandoning one nostrum for its opposite or by preaching completely contradictory things. . . . Such fad surfing has an effect on companies' culture" (Micklethwait and Wooldridge, 1996, p. 326). Those who have worked in good faith on implementing the latest fad now have confirmed their suspicions that managers really will not implement them or support them (Keller, 1997).

Managers may learn little from the failure of management fads. The political benefits are symbolic and immediate; the real costs of time, effort, and frustration come later (Hammond and Knott, 1980). By then, the managers have moved on to other positions, leaving behind messes that their successors can attribute to the uncooperative nature of followers. But there is some justice in the world: in their new position, these managers may inherit a similar mess, which, of course, can be corrected only by implementing a new management innovation.

Centralizing Bureaucracy

Academic management fads, including those such as MBO or strategic planning that claim to increase lower-level participation in decision making, instead usually lead to increased centralization of power. The implementation of fads, particularly those resisted by significant institutional actors, requires coordinating management systems and making executive decisions. The recognition that "reengineering never, ever happens from the bottom up" (Hammer and Champy, 1993, p. 207) applies to other fads as well, and a fad that encourages centralization discourages "the very commitment it claims so earnestly to require" (Mintzberg, 1994, p. 166). Regardless of policy intentions, the implementation of a fad—performance funding, for example—usually "involved a strengthening of central administrative functions" (El-Khawas, 1998, p. 323).

Given the changes in structure, process, and resource allocation required by fads, how could it be otherwise?

Fad implementation strengthens the core at the expense of the periphery in other ways as well. Fads are often predicated on increasing the number of specialized personnel or the creation of additional managerial officers (or both). PPBS and BPR, for example, required a commitment to MIS technology as well as staff; strategic planning and TQM/CQI presume the establishment of offices and individuals charged with developing and monitoring the program. This means that fads are expensive. Almost all management fads have extensive data collection, analysis, and interpretation needs. As an example, critics discussing performance indicators have commented on the "large amounts of meaningless data [that] are being compiled that, in the end, will make little difference. . . . 'This is costing the state a fortune,' said one administrator. 'We have a number of people who are dedicating a significant part of each day to this, and when all the numbers fall out, what are they going to mean?'" (Trombley, 1998, p. 16). Hiring statisticians to analyze the data, as some institutions did for benchmarking, was of no real value, since the numbers did not meaningfully represent anything of real importance to the managers. Particularly in public systems, demands for campus data from a central coordinating office often are not accompanied by the allocation of resources required to manage them. At the same time, the central office may add personnel to monitor institutional compliance.

Weakening of Commitment to Education

The adoption in higher education of language developed in other organizational settings can have an effect on how people view the academic enterprise. Words and phrases such as *personal growth, intellectual development, the scholarly community, humanism, improving society,* and *liberal education* give way to discussions of accountability, cost-benefit analysis, and reengineering. Institutions find that the corporate language of products, markets, customer service, and profits distorts views of their purposes and often leads to faculty opposition. The metaphor of faculty members committed to leading the younger generation into enlightenment gives way to the faculty member as a professionally or vocationally trained worker: "As the metaphoric model changes, so does the language and, ultimately, the reality" (Chiarelott, Reed, and Russell, 1991, p. 37).

Fads are not value free, and the values they espouse either implicitly or explicitly are frequently those of the marketplace of commerce rather than the marketplace of ideas. An institutional focus on "planning, goal setting, the designation of objectives, and quantitative evaluation can distort and even subvert the expressed humanistic goals" of higher education (Saurman and Nash, 1975, p. 179). Rationalists accept as a matter of faith that fads have worked in other organizations, and therefore that they can be made to work in higher education as well. The more thoughtful advocates for change temper their support with a note of caution: "I'm not sure that a headlong, externally driven rush into [TQM] makes sense for us. Too much of value could be left behind" (Marchese, 1993, p. 13). What could be left behind may be the very essence of the purposes of higher education.

Creating Self-Fulfilling Prophesies

There is almost universal agreement that colleges and universities are critical to society. But because their purposes are unclear and their outcomes cannot truly be measured, they are continually subject to criticism from external groups concerned that their interests are not being appropriately attended to. Different audiences may see colleges and universities as too selective or too open, too liberal or too conservative, too ivory tower or too captured by the marketplace. Continual claims of a crisis in higher education can generate such a crisis through repetition.

When accusations that higher education is faced with a crisis of public confidence are repeated often enough, they create a crisis of public confidence. Claims that institutions are inefficient and badly managed may lead to new management systems that make them even less efficient. Plans that identify some institutions or some units within institutions as of lesser quality or importance than others may lead them to "lose their most competent and thus more mobile staff, their recruitment opportunities, and their morale" (Schmidtlein, 1989–1990, p. 15), thus diminishing their quality or importance still further. When fads are implemented to respond to a crisis of any kind, they focus attention on examples of the crisis. The examples become increasingly visible, vivid, and thus more cognitively available. This confirms their importance and justifies increasing attention to resolve them.

Positive Residuals of Fads

If we were to look only at the negative outcomes of fads, the case could be made that they diminish organizational effectiveness, threaten colleges and universities as institutions, and harm managers and others. But there is another side to fads that suggests that despite their disadvantages, they serve critical organizational functions. For example, fads help institutions remain alert to their environment so they can consider the possibilities of change. As Bohl and Luthans put it (1996, p. 3), "Pity those organizations that have not gravitated toward the new and innovative, tested the latest fad, tempered it against economic realities, and emerged as stronger and more resilient." The implementation of a fad, with its promise of improvement, can play a positive role in institutional renewal because it is "an unusual event, during which a social organization changes . . . what it does and how it does it. The process of change remains uncertain, difficult, frequently painful, and fraught with new incarnations of old problems, at the same time that this process is stimulating, exhilarating and renewing" (Tornatzky and Fleischer, 1990, p. 11). Fads can be dangerous if accepted uncritically but beneficial "if they are kept in the proper perspective, and incorporated into the collective wisdom of the company" (Rifkin, 1994, p. 11).

Recognizing the Importance of Data

Judgment without data can be arbitrary; data without judgment can be sterile. Ur-Managers lived in an environment rich in the soft data of culture, politics, and interaction, but impoverished in the hard data of demographics, costs, and resources. Good management needs balanced attention to both, and the requirements of many fads encouraged the development and maintenance of systems for data collection and analysis. Hard data inform soft data and increase the effectiveness of management processes. The problems of fads are not created by giving managers access to more data but by the adoption of rational *systems* in which hard data, rather than soft data, are given primacy. Because this imbalance is not consistent with academic culture, "rational systems" turn out to be ineffective and therefore irrational.

Emphasizing Alternative Values

Organizations have multiple and conflicting goals, values, and processes, and they cannot simultaneously and equally attend to all of them. Attention to one goal often comes at the expense of attention to another, and there is no way any organization can optimize all its values. At the same time, an organization cannot give exclusive attention to only one of its goals and ignore the others.

Fads provide organizations with periodic, externally induced cues that activate attention to important organizational values to which appropriate attention had not previously been given. As a fad circulates through an organizational sector, it encourages long-term organizational balance by emphasizing a new goal and preventing overemphasis on the goal furthered by the previous fad. Institutions operate through self-correcting processes that direct attention to alternative values when any value is given too much, or too little, attention (Birnbaum, 1988).

Each of the values at the core of the seven fads presented in this book has merit. PPBS focused institutions on the need to see the relations among inputs, outputs, and the necessity of trade-offs. MBO reminded institutions of the role that subordinates can play in designing and implementing programs, and ZBB asked them to reconsider the current value of past decisions instead of accepting them as given. Strategic planning emphasized the need to act in response to a changing environment, benchmarking invited institutions to pay attention to the best practices of other organizations, TQM/CQI emphasized teamwork and quality, and BPR examined processes. Some fads looked internally at structures and processes; others focused externally, emphasizing the market and sensitizing institutions to costs and pricing. No organization could simultaneously give full consideration to inputs and outputs, employee participation, best practices, and all the other elements of each innovation, including the interactions among them. The adoption of fads allows institutions to attend to these matters sequentially. Even when the fad itself disappears, a residue of thought and action in the fad remains behind in the atmosphere of the organization.

The constant introduction of new techniques can also have more general effects on capturing the attention of managers and improving managerial effectiveness. Although ZBB failed on its own terms, managers in Georgia still believed it had improved both the quality and quantity of data available to managers, and it helped them to organize information. ZBB is not just a set of technical procedures but a state of mind. It helps budgeters get in the "habit of thinking about efficiency in on-going programs as well as alternative ways of thinking about program objectives" (Lauth, 1980, p. 128). ZBB also gave managers new ideas about program reviews, alternative costing, and the linking of cost benefits to broad institutional goals (Harvey, 1977, p. 39). The residual effects of strategic planning included "sensitivity to the environment, awareness of competition, and appropriate response" (Chaffee, 1985, p. 136). Performance indicators forced managers to "analyze their campuses more carefully and to do better planning" (Trombley, 1998, p. 16). Benchmarking led to "introspection, which forces participants to go inside their own institution, collect information, and raise questions" (Alstete, 1995, p. 44).

Producing Variety

Organizations in general, and institutions in particular, are conservative. They tend to do what they best know how to do (Pascale, 1991, p. 11). Over time, they develop routine ways of defining and then solving problems. These processes are stored in institutional memory because they have proven pragmatically to be effective. In a stable environment, it is functional for institutions to rely on their previously successful experiences to respond to familiar problems. As long as the environment remains unchanged, there is no compelling need for the institution to alter its tried and proven responses. But as environments evolve, institutions must evolve as well; if they do not, old responses may result in failure rather than success. They need to consider new responses. But how can they discover what alternative new responses might look like?

Darwinian evolution can be used as a metaphor for thinking about how organizations evolve. Genetic mutations in species create a variety of forms. Most mutations are harmful, but some provide organisms with a competitive advantage that makes them more likely to survive and reproduce because they best fit into environmental niches. Less fit organisms die out. It is this natural sequence of variety, selection, and retention that permits species to evolve over time.

The development and survival of organizations follows the same path (Weick, 1979). The key element of evolution, usually overlooked, is variety. Without variety, there are no alternative pathways open to either organisms or institutions. Over the long term, institutional forms, like the forms of organisms, must change or die. In biological species, variety is caused by genetic mutations; variety in organizations probably has many sources, but one of the most important may be fads. Fads introduce new ways of thinking about management processes, new procedures, new languages, and new ideologies. These may not be incorporated into the institution in their entirety, but elements of them remain in the ways some people think and act and in parts of some organizational routines. When situations change and thus call for novel responses, these elements are potentially available to managers to be considered as part of the solution. As managers expand their behavioral repertoires, they themselves become more cognitively complex (Birnbaum, 1988). This complexity may help them think about how new practices developed in one fad may be combined with some ideas suggested by another fad. Experience with fads may thus provide managers with alternative ways of framing problems and considering solutions.

Reinforcing Management Myths

The illusions of certainty and control may lead managers to make decisions that exacerbate rather than help solve an institution's problems. At the same time, if they are to make sense of their world, people in general must believe their institutions have some control over their own destiny, and managers in particular must believe in their own efficacy. Institutions live through the myths they create about how things happen, and part of that myth is that rationality is important and what managers do has influence. The adoption of a fad, and the activities of managers in implementing the fad, reinforce these myths. Belief in the myth encourages managers to initiate and persist in potentially effective behavior, even if the probabilities of success are low (Birnbaum, 1986). Myths provide additional leverage and confirm the authority of a manager who is the recipient of vast amounts of data not routinely available to others or who is authorized to establish processes for planning (Diran, 1978). "The stories, myths and rituals of management are not merely ways some people fool other people or a waste of time. They are fundamental to our lives. We embrace the mythologies and symbols of life and could not otherwise easily endure. Executive and management processes contribute to myths about management that become the reality of managerial life and reinforce a belief in a human destiny subject to intentional human control. Since managerial rituals are important to our faith, and our faith is important to the functioning of our organizations as well as to the broader social and political order, these symbolic activities of administration are central to its success" (March, 1984, p. 31).

Diversifying Interaction and Promoting Activity

Coherent cultures, values, and systems of communication are a product of continuing cycles of selection, repetition, and retention that become supported by institutional structures and rules. Managers and nonmanagers increasingly interact with each other in expected ways, often following ritualistic scenarios and scripts that have been found useful in the past. These patterns are self-reinforcing; the more they are followed, the greater their influence is in the future. While some communications networks within the institution, and between the institution and the external world, are strengthened, others remain unexploited. As some interactions become more likely, other interactions become less so. As interaction decreases, subsystems of the institution may become relatively isolated from each other over time, and important information available to one part of the institution may not be known to another.

The introduction of a fad often alters established institutional structures and processes. Fad processes may supplement or replace existing channels of communication, the people who participate in these channels, and the topics about which they communicate. A fad may create new groupings of people who otherwise might have never interacted in the institutional setting. Most strategic planning systems, for example, mandate committees and task forces of various kinds that bring together people from different offices and different organizational levels. TQM/CQI created cross-functional, problem-solving groups, while benchmarking called for teams to visit other institutions to study their processes. These new systems of interaction may create multiple pathways for the flow of information, increasing fidelity and ensuring essential redundancy in case the "regular" system fails. Planning and similar managerial activities may increase the cohesiveness of those who participate in it and help them to affirm their faith in the future (Gimpl and Dakin, 1984). And the outcomes of such fad-induced processes may enable an institution to act even in the face of ambiguity.

Managers may adopt fads in the belief they will improve the degree to which they can control outcomes. This belief is often illusory, although it is possible for managers to encounter evidence selectively that confirms the false belief. But although the effort to control may fail, it has the advantage of leading to action that might not otherwise be taken (March, 1984). When the world is confusing and uncontrollable, people often tend to do nothing. But sometimes it is better to "do something—anything—since activity may uncover elements of control which were previously unnoticed": (Gimpl and Dakin, 1984, p. 133). Although fads that give managers the illusion of control can have negative consequences, they may also benefit institutions by encouraging necessary activity. Fads like strategic planning "animate and orient people" (Weick, 1995, pp. 54–55). They can lead people to act and then to interpret their actions; the completion of these two processes (and in that order) can help people decide what should be done next. Organizations can make sense only from elapsed experiences; only after something has happened can it be interpreted and given meaning. "An organization would be in a better position to improve its efficiency if the elapsed experience were filled with action rather than inaction. Action, when viewed retrospectively, clarifies what the organization is doing, what business it is in, and what its projects may be. Inaction, viewed retrospectively, is more puzzling and more senseless. . . . Actions, in other words, provide tangible items that can be attended to" (Weick, 1979, p. 245).

Different fads propose different technologies for decision making and the exercise of management power. But much of what managers know is tacit, based on experience and intuition, and not capable of being accurately transmitted to others (Mintzberg, 1994). That does not mean that good managers are not logical, but rather that they are more likely to use "fuzzy logic" (Kosko, 1993) than the linear logic of positivism. Fuzzy logic is useful in situations in which alternatives are not necessarily black or white and answers right or wrong. It suggests how judgments under ambiguity can be made more effectively based on rules of thumb, or common sense, rather than on rigid prescriptions. Words like *quality*, *benefit*, and *educated* stand for fuzzy sets of things. Academic institutions are not either of high quality or not of high quality. They are at the same time both of high quality and its opposite, in various degrees. In the next chapter I place the fad phenomenon in a social context, and then suggest some ways that academic managers can respond to the need to be both rational, and its opposite, in varying degrees.

9

Managing Fads

I have two dogs and three cats. They all have fur, four legs, and tails. The physiology and biochemistry of both species are quite similar, and they share much of their genetic structure. But they behave differently. The dogs come when they are called, seek affection and attention, and warn when strangers approach. The cats come when they feel like it and hide under the bed when strangers lurk. Why can't a cat be more like a dog?

On the other hand, I have to walk the dogs even in freezing rain, while the cats use their sandbox in the warm, dry basement. And the dogs need to be washed, brushed, and clipped, while the cats groom themselves fastidiously. So why can't a dog be more like a cat?

I think about dogs and cats whenever someone says, "Why can't a university be more like a business?" Most business leaders think that colleges and universities would become more efficient and productive by adopting business practices. Most faculty members believe on the contrary that their missions are so different that higher education has little to learn from business (Immerwahr, 1999). It is not a new debate: "We have heard it all before: if we could just run our universities as General Motors is managed, most of our educational problems would vanish" (Bailey, 1973, p. 8). Thinking that what is good for one kind of organization is good for another is like thinking that what is good for dogs is also good for cats. Universities and businesses are different kinds of organizations.

Certainly institutions of higher education resemble businesses in some ways. They both sell goods and services, hire personnel and secure other resources, compete for customers, and depend on external support. "So if it walks like a firm and its talks like a firm, isn't it a firm? The answer, pretty clearly, is No" (Winston, 1997, p. 33). Institutions of higher education (except in the proprietary sector) have no owners and cannot distribute profits, so there is less pressure to operate efficiently. They function in a "trust market," in which people do not know exactly what they are buying and may not discover its value for years. Their participants and managers tend to be motivated by idealism rather than by profits. All "customers" are subsidized, the product is sold at less than the cost to produce it, and the value of the product is enhanced by the quality of the people who purchase it. Compared to business firms, colleges and universities have multiple and conflicting goals and intangible outcomes. "Employees" may be more committed to professional groups outside the corporation than to their own managers, may think of themselves more as principals than agents, and may themselves have roles in management (including selection of the chief executive), as well as permanent appointments over which managers have no discretion (Winston, 1997; Brock and Harvey, 1993; Marks, 1998). One former college president, who subsequently served as a corporate CEO, characterized some of the differences between the reactive world of business and the reflective world of the university in this way: "Business leaders do not speak of constituencies to be wooed, appeased or won over, as do college presidents; higher education leaders do not issue directives, orders, or edicts as do business CEOs. In all my years in higher education, I never once heard a dean, faculty member, or anyone else respond, 'Whatever you say, Chief'; in business it's common to hear it" (Iosue, 1997, p. 10).

The differences between cats and dogs can be explained by genetic structures developed over eons of time and modified by the intentional breeding practices of humans. Organizations, unlike animals, do not have genes; they have memes. The differences between universities and business firms can be explained by the cultural replication of successful social forms over time. Businesses look the way they do because firms with this form have proven to be more successful than firms with alternative forms. Universities look the way they do for the same reason: their form has proven to be superbly suited to what they do. The differences between firms and universities reflect the requirements of their different technologies, as well as the need to conform to the expectations of the social groups to which they are responsive.

But although the similarities between businesses and universities are superficial, the more we appear to be business enterprises, the more that business solutions are likely to be prescribed for our problems. Are weak leaders and intransigent faculty inhibiting change? The answer is restructuring and reinvention. Abolish tenure, hire outside contractors at lower cost, and get rid of unproductive programs. Establish an "Endowed Chair of the Junkyard Dog" to set concrete efficiency goals, reduce costs, and eliminate the unnecessary (Mahoney, 1997, p. B5). Never mind that "some of the redundancies and inefficiencies of universities are part of that ultimate product of human activity which is the reason for living at all. These redundancies are also an extremely important reserve of high-quality ability in time of crisis. To make universities narrowly efficient might well be the greatest disservice we offer society" (Boulding, 1978, p. 45).

Calls for business-related reform ignore a significant body of theory and research showing that management theories, control systems, strategies, and structures that are sensible for some kinds of organizations may be unthinkable and destructive in others (Sergiovanni, 1995; Scott, 1995). The strength of higher education comes precisely because of its perceived contrasts with the world of commerce, and treating academic institutions as if they were businesses would destroy their autonomy and their cultural cohesiveness (Bowen, 1993; Kennedy, 1996). If we model ourselves increasingly on business and are seen by society as using business techniques and exploiting business opportunities, we become just another voice among many in the marketplace. As we respond to diminished funding by seeking new sources of financial support, academic altruism gives way to academic capitalism (Slaughter and Leslie, 1997). "The more we're like other enterprises, the more easily trust is displaced by a familiar sense of 'caveat emptor'—let the buyer beware" (Winston, 1993, p. 407).

Summary and Trial Balance

Academic institutions are integrated into the social, economic, and political systems of our society, so it is not surprising to find that they have been significantly influenced by the triumphs of managerialism and rationality that have characterized much of twentieth-century America. In schools, the two revolutions had the effect of transforming administrators into business managers and executives, a capitulation to business ideology that Callahan described as the "American tragedy in education" (1962, p. 244).

Higher education, although not immune from the same pressures, fared better. Colleges and universities, with higher social status, political clout, and levels of professionalism, were much less socially vulnerable than the locally controlled schools. They could not escape the push toward managerialism and rationality, but they were better able to protect themselves from its worst excesses. They did this in part by publicly endorsing the language of reform even as they protected the technical core of the institution, evidence that managers often act more sensibly than they talk (March, 1984). They virtually adopted new management techniques that permitted them to maintain external credibility. They incrementally continued to modify and improve management processes, but usually they did not enact major management innovations in any serious way lest they lose the internal credibility on which their effectiveness ultimately depended.

This analysis is consistent with earlier predictions that "management innovations are unlikely to cause disaster in institutions. Colleges and universities tend to have a great deal of inertia in the system based on tradition, habits, and the general social feeling that they perform a worthy function" (Allen and Chaffee, 1981, p. 5). Still, higher education was not unscathed by the demands that it change, and attempts to impose inappropriate management systems have had several costs.

Some of these costs are organizational and technical in nature. Our national culture leads us to believe that change is good, even though "most new ideas are bad ones, most changes are detrimental, and most original inventions are not worth the effort devoted to producing them" (March, 1994, p. 238). The implementation of a fad typically involves major changes in the administrative and management processes of the institutions that adopt them. Fads often have significant fiscal implications, and they require expenditures of time and attention on the part of university personnel at both the operational and the policy levels. More important, management systems influence ends as well as means, and they can have insidious consequences for institutional programs, purposes, and values. What appear to be only technical and ideologically neutral approaches to cutting costs or improving efficiency may, if implemented, have profound educational and social consequences. Fads have not caused, but have contributed to, three major trends in higher education over the past half-century: the weakening of colleges and universities as institutions, the impairment of academic management, and the eroding of the higher education narrative.

Weakening Colleges and Universities as Institutions

Contemporary rhetoric sees colleges and universities as sources of technical advancement, engines of economic growth, instruments of social policy, and agencies for meeting customer demands. These instrumental views are not necessarily wrong, but they are misleading because they ignore the even more potent institutionalized aspects of colleges and universities that infuse them with value and develop their character and identity.

There are a large number of academic institutions, and their normative management and governance systems are widely shared. They collectively develop organizational grammars of structure, process, programs, habits, and technology that distinguish academic institutions from others. Both their numbers and their shared characteristics lend them legitimacy. Proper colleges or universities must look and act in expected ways if they are to "achieve standing as legitimately representing what they are" (March, 1994, p. 60). Businesses are primarily utilitarian organizations, managed by information, that attempt to maximize profit. Colleges and universities are primarily normative institutions, managed by ideology, that attempt to fulfill a mission (Albert and Whetten, 1985). Each organization form supports the organization's specific purpose. The fact that it may be institutionalized does not make a university "better" than a business, but it does make it different (Scott, 1995).

Adherence to their central traditions has made universities among the oldest and most successful institutions in Western civilization. Since it is difficult for the achievements of a university to be quantified, these institutions are dependent on gaining the respect of society "by their adherence to their central traditions in ethos, substance and procedure" (Shils, 1981, p. 183). Economic enterprises may require constant change to survive. But institutions survive and prosper because their consistent, mission-driven values have been internalized by their participants and confirmed as important by the culture in which they function. Constancy is more important than change because it is this very continuity of practice that leads to reliable mission-based performance (Salipante and Golden-Biddle, 1995, p. 4). Consider this: only one of the twelve largest business firms in 1900 still existed in 2000 (Thurow, 1999). But each one of the twelve largest public and private universities in 1900 ("Principal Universities and Colleges," 1901) exists and still thrives one hundred years later.

The power of institutionalization can be seen not only in the longevity of organizations, but also in the loyalty and affection of their participants. The most successful institutions are not those with the most money, but those that remain resilient "because their faculty, staff, students, and friends are committed to them" (Leslie and Fretwell, 1996, p. xvii). This record of commitment in higher education is impressive. Former students and employees continue to contribute time, money, and energy. Gift giving is at record highs. Graduates in increasing numbers are returning to the town of their alma mater to retire (Loose, 1998). Colleges are building or expanding campus cemeteries to accommodate alumni who want to be buried there, in coffins decorated with school colors (Oldenburg, 1996). There is little evidence that General Motors has been experiencing a surge of interest for similar services, and it is unlikely that virtual universities will either.

Advocates of change acknowledge that "a culture that has been ingrained by three centuries cannot be changed in three decades" (Wheatley, 1995, p. 62). But some view this not as a strength but as a problem to be overcome. The comment that "the ability of universities to withstand the rise and fall of governments, as well as countless wars and social movements, is the stuff of mythology" (Seymour, 1995, pp. xvii-xviii) was not meant as a compliment but as an explanation for their presumed inability to change. Instead of being the stuff of mythology, it could with even greater accuracy have been said to be the stuff of civilization. It is also the stuff of organizational culture—an organic and fundamental aspect of institutions, and one of the most difficult to change intentionally. Advocates for many fads agree that their nostrums can work only if higher education is willing to change its culture so it does not pose an obstacle to the fad (Sims and Sims, 1995). Fad proponents do not want just a change in management practice; they call for "an entirely new organization, one whose culture is quality driven, customer oriented, marked by team-work, and avid about improvement. . . . 'Corporate revolution' and 'paradigm shift' are the words one hears" (Marchese, 1991, p. 4). They call for "fundamental alterations of culture and structures" (Ewell, 1993, p. 50) that "will relentlessly create change in virtually every aspect of the institution" (Sims and Sims, 1995, p. 12) and reform the byzantine structure of higher education (Bruegman, 1995). I suggested to my cats that they could be more like dogs if they would only make a long-term commitment to cultural change, and they raised their tails in indignation and stalked away. I told them that unless they were willing to consider a new paradigm, they might become a relic in the twenty-first century, and they shredded my drapes. They knew I was exhorting them to do something impossible. The truth is that we do not know much more about how intentionally to change an institution's culture than about changing cats to dogs.

But for some, there *is* a way to effect change: impose it. "To create something new one must destroy something old. If academia is going to do what it is supposed to do, create an environment that will prepare students for the future, it is going to have to destroy part of its past" (Wheatley, 1995, p. 62). Burning institutionalized villages has never effectively captured the hearts and minds of their inhabitants. Management fads infused with corporate values do not fit well in academic environments (Kennedy, 1996). Universities have created their own cultural realities by learning how to act as they are supposed to. They can change only by forgetting what it is they already know (Pallas and Neumann, 1993). But artificially forcing "forgetting" through imposed and unwelcome change is ultimately a failing and destructive strategy that may cause an institution to change its character and identity and lose sight of its mission, core expertise, and long-term perspective—the basic competitive advantages conferred by continuity (Salipante and Golden-Biddle, 1995, p. 4). Proposing that universities strengthen themselves by replacing internal values, missions, and goals with those more consistent with the desires of outsiders is a recipe for institutional disaster. It is as difficult to change a university as to change a religion. Both are citadels of tradition, and both "provide relief from the fast-paced, often meaningless and haphazard, day to day activities. Religious and educational traditions, symbols and rituals provide members a much needed representation of stability and security in their otherwise chaotic, anomic life. They enable individuals to periodically reaffirm what they feel are society's core values" (Albert and Whetten, 1985, p. 283).

Impairing Academic Management

The academic managers' lot is not a happy one. Many serve at the sufferance of those they are presumed to manage, and the responsibility they bear for organizational performance is usually not matched by a comparable level of authority (Birnbaum, 1989). Many of the academic management fads of the past forty years attempted to rectify the disparity between responsibility and authority by providing managers with what appeared to be greater leverage and more effective tools. They emphasized hard data, calculation, rationality, order, and linear logic, and they tried to distance managers from the norms and values of the institutional core. But while hard data can be useful, academic managers must also have soft data, judgment, intuition, fuzzy logic, and tolerance for chaos if they are to be effective. Managers should not be distanced from an institution's culture but integrated into it. New techniques that are inconsistent with campus culture cannot strengthen academic management. Instead, they are likely to become substitutes for academic management "and positioned, in many cases, as panaceas that obviate the need to think as long as the formula is followed" (Shapiro, 1995, p. 205).

Ur-Managers might be thought of as practicing "normal management," in the same way that most scientists practice "ordinary science" (Kuhn, 1970). Most managers, most of the time, try to solve puzzles with which they are confronted. The Triumph of Rationality was an attempt to engage in revolutionary science—to challenge the existing paradigms. In management, however, there is no way of objectifying either the paradigms that drive managerial action or the nature of the actions themselves. Commitment to, and general acceptance of, the paradigm of Ur-Management does not necessarily mean that it is objectively right, but only that it is socially right and accepted. If one paradigm is to be replaced with another, it must be seen as being more successful in solving problems considered important by the field. New rational management paradigms not only do not solve the essential problems of the field better than Ur-Management, but in fact often create additional problems.

Fads establish frameworks that promise to find answers. But often there may be no answers at all other than those that a manager who has internalized an institution's history, culture, and political milieu crafts out of personal knowledge, experience, and instinct. That is why good managers give great weight to soft information gained through interaction. These soft data help "explain and resolve the problems that arise, provide the basis for the construction of their mental modes of the world, and facilitate an early response to unfolding events. While hard data may inform the intellect, it is largely soft data that generate wisdom" (Mintzberg, 1994, p. 266). If they are to be effective, managers cannot ignore either kind. Managers cannot place excessive reliance on summaries and surveys or on the products of structured processes. Hard data are important, but as Neustadt (1990) has said about the decision processes of U.S. presidents, it is "the odds and ends of tangible detail that, pieced together in his mind, illuminates the underside of issues before him. To help himself, he must reach out as widely as he can for every scrap of fact, opinion, gossip bearing on his interests and relationships" (p. 129).

Many fads suggest that managers must stand apart from the values and norms of the organization if they are to be able to reform it. But "people removed from the daily details of running an organization can never gain the requisite knowledge" (Mintzberg, 1994, p. 269). Nor can they manage the institution effectively through processes that try to make it orderly, because managerial work is what happens in the *middle* of chaos. Managers must be "active, involved, connected, committed, alert, stimulated. It is the 'calculated chaos' of their work that drives their thinking, enabling them to build reflection on action in an interactive process" (Mintzberg, 1994, p. 291).

Good managers are not insensitive to traditional notions of decision rationality, but they must temper this with the additional elements of administrative rationality—"the facts related to emotions, politics, power group dynamics, personality and mental health" (Pfiffner, 1960, p. 126). Managers who adopt more structured systems may, as a consequence, find their ability to manage symbols and meaning diminished and their institutional influence thereby constrained (Birnbaum, 1992). Effective management in the academic organization requires an understanding of institutional traditions and culture, which in turn comes "from a thorough immersion in the affairs of an institution, in its history and its life, and from a mastery of its institutional theories that bear on the future" (Wiseman, 1979, p. 735).

Sound management reduces uncertainty through the application of judgment to context-specific situations in order to define problems in ways that may lead to effective action. By prescribing a structure and a rhetoric through which problems may be viewed, fads may disconnect a problem from the context in which it occurs, and thus prematurely reduce uncertainty. In doing so, fads may restrict the pragmatism that is the heart of management (Donaldson and Hilmer, 1998; Eccles and Nohria, 1992). Fads do not strengthen management; they are an alternative to management.

Eroding the Higher Education Narrative

In the past, being a professional was ennobling. It presumed a calling—a vocation—and a dedication to service. A physician (one who healed) served the needs of a patient (one who suffered). A professor (one who professed) served the needs of a student (one who studied). Today we question whether concepts such as "student" and "teacher" are appropriate in the postmodern age. Do we have students, or are they customers, clients, stakeholders, constituents, or (indeed) products? Do faculty members profess, or do they manage, coordinate, or facilitate learning? While we engage in arcane debates about words, my local branch of a discount clothing chain no longer refers to salespeople as clerks, but as "educators" (because "an educated consumer is our best customer"). So in our brave new world, professors are coordinators, while clothing clerks are educators. New paradigms indeed!

Words are important because they are the building blocks of the stories that guide our lives. Neil Postman (1995) has said, "For schools to make sense, the young, their parents, and their teachers must have a god to serve or, even better, several gods. If they have none, school is pointless" (p. 4). The god to which he refers is a narrative—a compelling story of ideals, purpose, and continuity that provides participants with meaning. Every culture, and every institution in a culture, has its own narratives. In the United States, the educational narratives of the past have been stories of personal virtue, civic participation, democracy, and social justice. The narrative gods of the present appear to be economic utility, consumerism, and technology—a weak foundation on which to build a just social order or excite the imagination. The idea of higher education as a social institution has been displaced by higher education as an industry (Gumport, 2000).

The degradation of the narrative may be higher education's most critical problem. Our past narratives spoke of such ideals as a liberating education, the free person, critical thinking, personal growth, social justice, knowledge for its own sake, and improving society. What are the narratives that drive us now? Is meeting the needs of the customer, preparing students to strengthen the economy, or the presumed cost-effectiveness of virtual institutions the stuff from which great societies are built? The social construction of narratives is part of an interpretive process through which contending ideologies vie for supremacy. Dominant narratives cannot be displaced merely by presenting arguments or data refuting them, but only by providing a different narrative that tells a better and more compelling story (Roe, 1994). One way of making a story compelling is to exaggerate it, connect it to important social values and symbols, and propose solutions that "appear to be in the public interest, or natural, or necessary or morally correct" (Stone, 1988, p. 122).

Although they may not appear to have a political purpose, academic management fads are solutions that further specific ideologies. Academic management fads have not themselves degraded the narrative, but they are technical vehicles that contribute to the degradation. Fads help perpetuate a simple narrative. Business and industry are highly efficient and effective; higher education is not. Higher education could improve if it adopted the management techniques of business such as outsourcing, TQM/CQI, benchmarking, or reengineering. But intransigent faculty will not permit it because they are protecting their own selfish interests, and academic managers are too timid to stand against them. The solution to the problem is to free managers to be entrepreneurial and market driven. The simplicity of this narrative is its power, and the story of a small, privileged elite that benefits at the expense of the public is an evocative story that taps into the American psyche. So is the narrative of a fad that pledges to right the wrong and put the university in its place.

Interesting stories are more likely than accurate ones to be accepted. For those who doubt the power of the new higher education narrative or its consequences, consider the trustee boards that are increasingly intruding into academic affairs, the push to lower costs through adopting virtual processes that disengage students from professors and from each other, the disaggregation of the university through outsourcing, and the de facto degradation of a predominantly full-time professorate into a part-time workforce of replaceable and nontenurable parts. The professor, once a partner in shared authority, is now considered only one of a number of institutional "stakeholders" (Nelson, 1999). The problem is not that these changes are taking place as much as that they are taking place without empirical evidence supporting *any* of the claims that they

will make institutions more efficient or more effective. Just as advocates of CQI, benchmarking, or any of the myriad of other management fads must rely on anecdote because they have no data, so
most of the proposals to reform higher education are based on ideas
that appear sensible but whose consequences are unknown.

The outcomes of higher education are obvious and compelling
but impossible to measure directly. As Bowen (1977, p. 12) noted
in his exhaustive economic analysis of higher education, the chief
product of higher education is learning that results in changes in
people. "Production in higher education, then, is not the transformation of resources into tangible products; rather it is the transformation of resources into desired intangible qualities of human
beings." For this reason, "the call for accountability cannot be satisfied if all the results of higher education must be reduced to neat
qualitative terms, preferably with dollar signs" (p. 22). The major
purpose of higher education is to affirm the promise of human life,
not to improve managerial efficiency (Bailey, 1973). Unless and
until the current narratives are supplemented or replaced by new
ones that emphasize some transcendental intellectual, ethical,
moral, or humane purpose, fads will continue to reinforce the utilitarian norms that erode the essential nature of institutions that
have served us so well for so long.

Using Fads Constructively

There can never be a management system that supports in equal
measure all the goals to which higher education is committed. The
history of academic management fads indicates that the quest for a
better system will continue as long as the search for a better way
continues: "It is impossible to predict what the next fad will be. The
only safe prediction is that new fads will come and go just as management by objectives, zero-base budgeting, and a host of other
management innovations disappeared because they did not focus
on the kind of fundamental changes that organizations require in

order to become high performance organizations" (Lawler, 1996, p. 255). Thus, we have a double bind—the total overhauls that faddists call for are least likely to be adopted; the kind of culturally focused soft management that would be most effective is least likely to be politically protected.

So what rough fad, its hour come round at last, may even now be slouching toward higher education? How about "agility," in which opportunistic institutions use technology to create cooperative virtual relationships and "a wide array of temporary alliances with others in order to grasp specific market opportunities" (Godbey, 1993, p. 39)? Or consider "expeditionary strategy" to "position the learning enterprise for success in a new, turbulent environment . . . [involving] rapidly developed prototypes that anticipate learner needs, then continuously improve themselves in response to evaluative feedback" (Norris, 1998, p. 13). Will we recycle the old "accountability-center budgeting" (Balderston, 1974) fondly known as "every tub on its own bottom," or replace it with its newer siblings, responsibility center budgeting (RCB) (Brinkman and Morgan, 1997) or responsibility center management (RCM) (Slocum and Rooney, 1997), in which units are responsible for their income, their costs, and their pricing policies? Or should we consider performance-based appropriations (PBA) (Carnevale, Johnson, and Edwards, 1998), using performance measures either to reward institutions meeting specified objectives or punish those that do not? PBA is currently used in eleven states and being considered in many more. Outsourcing? Privatization? Permatemps? Balanced scorecards (BSC)? Dashboards? Management for results (MFR)? Knowledge management (KM)? Learning-centered colleges? Have they already come and gone, or are they the first indications of major trends? Of one thing we can be certain: "Somebody's writing a book right now that will come up with a more popular phrase, and we'll all be doing that" (Bleakley, 1993, p. A6). Tomorrow's managers will probably have an even greater variety of management innovations from which to choose than managers of the past as "management fashions seem to be growing even more fickle; the life cycle of an idea has now shrunk from a decade to a year or less" (Micklethwait and Wooldridge, 1996, p. 14). Each new idea offers opportunities, as well as threats. Here are some suggestions about how to get its benefits without its potential costs, by managing academic management fads constructively through the three phases of exploration, implementation, and evaluation.

Consider with Skeptical Interest

The history of managements fads suggests the truth of the admonition that "managers must be cautious when new concepts are proposed, particularly if these concepts suggest a 'quick fix'" (Hitt and Ireland, 1987). Simple answers to complex problems are enticing, but usually not effective over the long run. "Most administrators should approach any innovation which involves fundamental management functions and which is predicated on the rational model of decisionmaking with extreme skepticism and with a careful analysis of how the institution actually does or could make decisions" (Allen and Chaffee, 1981, p. 29). Although fads are retrospective social constructions, and so cannot be identified in advance with precision, managers can use the duck test: if it looks like a duck, swims like a duck, and quacks like a duck, it is probably a duck. You can construct a similar fad test by determining how many of the following statements are made in support of X, the next appealing management innovation you are urged to consider:

X is not a fad.

X is superior to a previous innovation, which *was* a fad.

X will solve the problems created by the previous fad.

X will lead to radical transformation of the institution.

X requires institution-wide implementation.

X will require a major change in institutional culture.

X will replace old ways of doing things.

X will significantly improve efficiency and effectiveness.

X is based on solid theory, objective data, and analysis.

Members of a prestigious group have adopted X.

Institutions adopting X have experienced high levels of success.

Adoption of X is necessary to ensure institutional survival.

X is opposed only by the ignorant or self-interested ideologues.

If it looks like a fad, sounds like a fad, and promises like a fad, then it almost certainly is a fad. A fad should never be adopted. But neither should it be rejected out of hand. Instead, a fad calls for skeptical curiosity. An incipient fad may have components or ideas of great value if given prudent consideration. As Ewell (1999) has pointed out, fads can be useful prisms through which institutions may examine their own practices from new perspectives. The metaphor of a prism suggests that an alien fad may shed a blinding light. But if it is decoupled from its sources or sponsors and disaggregated into its primary colors, analyses of its components may usefully illuminate institutional practices and conversations.

Invest in Knowledge

A good manager requires a thorough knowledge of the university as an institution and as an organization, experience in administration, and knowledge of management practices. Good managers need a base of knowledge if they are to determine which new ideas may be consistent with their technology and culture. They should keep current in the literature, particularly with journals that translate research into practice (Hitt and Ireland, 1987). They should search for good ideas that are "properly supported by the facts and whose logic can withstand the tough criticisms of peers. By these standards, much of what is touted as a pathway to better management is at best unproven and at worst misleading and dangerous" (Hilmer and Donaldson, 1996, p. xi). A prudent manager will insist on having as much information about a management innovation as possible before considering its experimental use. If the innovation is being practiced at an accessible location, a visit to that campus by a knowledgeable team of administrators and faculty to determine how it *actually* operates and how participants and others respond to it is of great technical as well as political value. Institutions or associations making general claims of an innovation's success should be asked to provide the data or other evidence on which such claims are based. If the innovation comes from a sector outside higher education, the literature of the innovation in that sector should be consulted to overcome the time lag that otherwise would precede its use in higher education. Insist on rigorous documentation rather than relying on self-promoting "case studies" or arguments by advocates. Study not just the innovation, but the theories or concepts that undergird the innovation. Are they sensible in the context of your institution?

Avoid the Bandwagon

Management fads are often promoted by institutional associations, foundations, peer institutions, consultants, and other parties at interest. Adopters are pictured as leaders, nonadopters as laggards, and institutions are urged to demonstrate their management responsiveness by being in the vanguard. But there is limited advantage to being an early adopter of an unproven innovation and significant advantages to waiting until evidence of its value is available. Innovations have costs, and early innovators have the additional costs of trying out alternative versions to see what might or might not work; later adopters can select from among prescreened alternatives. Studies of new products in over fifty different markets indicate that those who end up being market leaders tend to adopt more than a decade after the pioneers (Micklethwait and Wooldridge, 1996, p. 154). There is no need to be first; if the idea is a good one, it will be available for some time (and in a refined form). If the idea is not a good one, it may fade so quickly that you will be able to avoid any cost at all.

Anticipate Resistance

Almost any new idea, regardless of its quality, will be opposed by some campus constituencies. Managers should anticipate resistance and take steps to respond to it. It is as foolish to adopt a management innovation that constituents will not implement, and then blame it on them, as it is to propose a plan requiring a doubling of the budget and then blame the environment for not providing it. The level of constituent support, like the level of financial support, must be part of the effective manager's calculus. Taking steps to respond to resistance does *not* mean using managerial power to impose a management innovation on an unwilling campus. Such imposition is likely to increase, rather than decrease, resistance. Instead, managers should make constituents partners in the great experiment.

Before deciding to adopt an innovation, managers should consult widely with representative campus groups, including potential opponents. Following the idea of cross-functional teams developed by TQM/CQI and benchmarking, managers should form cross-role exploratory committees whose membership includes opponents as well as advocates. The committees should review documentation from other sites and conduct site visits to observe the innovation in situ. Opposition may be somewhat diminished if several of the other ideas in this section are followed, such as experimental adoption, limited scope, and integrated assessment. Including opponents may co-opt them as they interact with those who are strong supporters. Of equal importance, it ensures that supporters have to respond to the strong skepticism of opponents. The committee will thus have the benefits of being exposed to the strongest arguments both in favor of and opposed to the innovation. Participation in the review process may convince committee members, and through them the campus, of the desirability of trying out a new idea. Alternatively, thoughtful, data-driven, principled opposition may make the more persuasive case and save the institution from making a costly mistake. Assertive unilateral promotion is likely to be met by passive group resistance.

Start Small

Some proponents of management innovations insist that they must be implemented organization-wide in order to be successful. This is almost certainly a recipe for disaster. The larger and more widespread the change, the greater is the likely resistance and likelihood of unknowable but undesirable consequences, and the less will be known about how any specific aspect of the change affected any aspect of the institution. A tactic more likely to succeed is to support a subunit of the institution that expresses an interest in experimenting with the new idea. Pilot testing permits the innovation to function under the most favorable conditions, isolates it from the conservative tendencies of nonparticipating units, and permits an analysis of how well the innovation fits with the institution's culture (Hitt and Ireland, 1987).

Management innovations can be either sustaining (improving existing products and processes and relatively risk free) or disruptive (developing new products or processes, with a strong possibility of short-term failure) (Christensen, 1997). The importance of pilot testing new management technologies in a small subunit is particularly important when the new technology is likely to be disruptive. Failure is unlikely to lead to significant institutional problems. Success may make the institution stronger in the future and give it a competitive strategic edge.

It may be argued that when institutions are in serious difficulty, large-scale reforms are needed and changes in subunits are not going to have a major impact. This may be true, but innovative techniques should never be implemented as a means of last resort to improve a poorly managed institution. Innovative techniques should be implemented when institutional management is under control and modest experiments can be conducted. In other words, fads may be useful as a supplement to, but not as a substitute for, good management.

Do Not Overpromise

Because most innovations do not work as predicted, extravagant promises and heightened expectations are unlikely to be fulfilled, leading to cynicism and further erosion of confidence in management. External advocates of management innovations are often expert in publicizing the expected benefits of the proposal, but they rarely understand the culture of educational institutions or of the faculty, and how any innovation might be altered or reinvented in real-life applications (Tyack and Cuban, 1995). Overpromising can not only make even modest successes appear to be failures (as in using world-class benchmarks), but also increases the risk of creating trapped managers. If managers have irrevocably connected the success of the innovation to their own career performance, they may be more likely to increase their commitment to the innovation long after others are aware that it has failed.

Culturally Customize

Every innovation, whatever its source, must be tailored to the needs of each individual institution if it is to be successful. The manager's primary goal is not to implement the innovation; it is to help make the institution better. It is not to "seek out novelty; it is to make sure the company gets results. Pragmatism is the place to start" (Nohria and Berkley, 1994, p. 130). Pragmatic management requires sensitivity to the context provided by history, culture, past success and failures, and a willingness to make do with available resources. In the academic context, resources transcend the purely financial, and include morale, expectations of the participants, institutional purpose, and commitment to professional values.

Managers who know the heartbeat of the institution, have considered which components of an innovation are suited to it and which are not, and have earned the trust and support of constituents are in a position to lead and act. "Like everything else in management, robust action is about finding out what works in particular contexts and situations—it is about the pragmatic know-how gleaned from actual experience" (Eccles and Nohria, 1992, p. 11). It is incorrect to believe that higher education does not change; data show that change in structure, program, and management in higher education is constant (El-Khawas, 1994). But not all change is successful. Successful change is most likely when it is integrated into normal campus decision processes and involves broad-based committees (Schmidtlein and Milton, 1988–1989) that bring faculty and administrators together early in the process. It should be consistent with an institution's consensual, faculty-based culture (Swenk, 1999), hybridize new ideas into traditional practices (Schick, 1971), and function incrementally and conservatively while constructing a social consensus about what works and what does not (Presley and Leslie, 1998). Management techniques should not be blunderbusses, cutting a wide swath and replacing everything that came before it. Instead, they should be arrows in a quiver, available to the manager as circumstances, and the nature of the problem and the environment, permit. Effective managers "will use their intelligence and intuition to work out their own approaches, adapting the theories of other people as they go along" (Shapiro, 1997, p. 143). Managers should treat fads as sources of ideas rather than as rules. Institutions will not find value "by following a general rule and doing what everyone else does" (Donaldson and Hilmer, 1998, p. 17). They will find it by shaping ideas to their own cultures.

Adopt Experimentally

Managers must wear many hats and therefore must necessarily engage in inconsistent behavior. A manager working with constituents to determine whether and how a management innovation should be adopted is wearing a policymaker's hat. When acting as a policymaker, a manager becomes committed to a course of action. Once support is committed, withdrawal of it may be seen as an admission of error or a violation of a leadership stereotype that suggests that administrators should be resolute in pursuing their goals even in the face of negative feedback (Staw and Ross, 1980). Once managers decide to adopt an innovation, they should take off their policy-making hat and put on their policy scholar hat. This change in perspective means that they are no longer invested in proving the quality of their decision, but in conducting a sound experiment. In doing so, they serve as advocates of the institution rather than of the innovative process. Managers should approach the experiment with optimistic skepticism.

Adopting an innovation based on external proposals is often resisted; experimenting with new ideas recommended by colleagues may be more consistent with academic culture. Experimental adoption (Staw and Ross, 1980) reduces institutional risk and institutional resistance.

Do Not Relax Commitment or Support

Once there is agreement about the nature, length, and resources required of a good experiment, managers put on their facilitator's hat. The best ideas can fail if managers do not fully support them. Wearing the facilitator's hat, managers have to "customize ideas, win top-down support for them, and devote considerable effort to making them work" (Byrne, 1997, p. 47).

Experimental adoption does not mean that implementation can be partial, half-hearted, or tentative. A decision to adopt an innovation is a mandate for management commitment and follow-up. Management failure is more likely to be caused by deficiencies in implementation rather than lack of vision. There will always be setbacks and unanticipated problems. Managers are like scientists who follow an experimental protocol. Even in the absence of immediate success, the experiment should continue to enjoy full support unless it is having such dramatically negative results that the institution is threatened. Giving up too quickly means that we learn nothing of value. "Our tendency, however, is to try out things capriciously. When a new idea fails, we give up instead of investigating the causes of failure and addressing them systematically" (Pascale, 1991, p. 21).

Build in Assessment

An integrated, comprehensive evaluation system is an essential element of an experimental view toward a management innovation (Allen and Chaffee, 1981; Staw and Ross, 1980). An effective assessment process in an academic institution has to accept that any change may be interpreted differently by different interest groups, and innovations may have both direct and indirect effects. This suggests that representatives of groups that will be most affected by the change, and whose active support, tacit endorsement, or agreement not to oppose overtly is essential for its successful implementation, should be involved in planning, conducting, and interpreting the assessment. Assessment should begin by specifying prior to implementation what outcomes might be expected within a given time frame and how data will be collected and assessed. This is *not* to suggest that a fad is successful only if its predicted effects are seen, or that it is unsuccessful if they are not. Fads may have indirect costs or benefits not foreseen by their implementors, and good experimenters will be sensitive to both. However, identifying predicted changes will mediate the tendency to determine success only on post hoc criteria and avoid examining potentially discrediting evidence.

Getting Past the Rhetoric

I recently heard a college president tell of a faculty member who refused to serve on the institution's strategic planning committee while delaring, "I *am* the institution's strategic plan." The president was irate at this example of arrogance and irresponsibility, but the faculty member had a point. Planning committees and planning documents, management schemes for rationalizing processes and structures, and formulas for giving concrete form to the ephemeral come and go, and few institutions have much to show for them. But every time an institution hires or dismisses a new faculty member, starts a new program or curtails an old one, decides to recruit students or staff in one way rather than another, it is creating a strategic plan through its actions. The greatest influence managers have over their institutions is through the daily choices in what Baldridge and Okimi (1982) once called "jugular vein decisions," which "build the institution's internal strength and condition it to respond favorably to opportunities or threats. Cumulative, everyday decisions can have a lot more impact on an institution's destiny than any master plan" (Baldridge and Okimi, 1982, p. 18). These decisions, thoughtfully made, create "emergent strategies" (Mintzberg, 1994) that "converge in time in some sort of consistency or pattern" (Hardy, Langley, Mintzberg, and Rose, 1983, p. 407). Strategies happen in environments that encourage new ideas. The root of leadership is to recognize the emergence of these new strategies and encourage the ones with potential (Mintzberg, 1994).

Many aspects of campus life shape institutional character and directions: creating a climate of trust among constituencies, integrating planning into regular decision processes in a way consistent with institutional values and traditions, focusing on specific issues, discussing emerging trends, remaining flexible, having realistic expectations, and simplifying processes. As Schmidtlein says (1990, p. 174), "Although institutions that dealt with current issues and concerns about the future in such a variety of ways may not appear to be 'planning' in the traditional sense, they may in fact better accomplish the purposes and functions of planning."

Higher education does not need to invent more change. Change in higher education is constant. Change is what is happening while we sit in our planning sessions bemoaning the lack of change. Change can be beneficial, but of equal or greater importance is the recognition of what should *never* change (Collins, 1995).

Higher education does not need more good management techniques; it needs more good managers. Good managers may come from several sources. They may include those with professional training in graduate programs of higher education, business, or related fields, who have served apprenticeships in various academic institutions and have demonstrated their understanding of and sensitivity to the values of their institutions. They may come from those in the professorial ranks who have developed appropriate management skills through experience or additional professional education (Allen and Chaffee, 1981).

Managing in a complex, knowledge-based, interpretive institution is difficult, frustrating, and imprecise. But good management is essential for institutional success, and to be a good manager is a goal worthy of the time and effort of administrators and faculty who are committed to the enduring purposes of higher education. Good academic management is not the same as good business management, and uncritical acceptance of management innovations and fads invented to met the needs of government, business, or the military is more likely to harm than benefit colleges and universities. On the other hand, thinking about how elements of fads might provide new insights into improving institutional management can be very valuable. The critical need is to get beyond the rhetoric. Marchese (1996, p. 4) had it right when he said goodbye to CQI: "Let us put away the three-letter banners and get on with the important task of learning how to get smarter and better at the important missions in our care."

So forget the letters, the mantras, and the can't-miss scheme of the month. Pull back when it is evident that process has taken over purpose, when the process is being guarded by a priesthood, or when purpose cannot provide standards for measuring the success of process (Shapiro, 1995, pp. 178–181). The essential elements of most fads are commonsensical to most experienced managers in business, education, or any other setting: "Decentralization of authority, producing quality products, providing responsive customer service, formulating strategy in a way that takes into account distinctive internal capabilities, rewarding performance fairly, and running a socially responsible enterprise. Who could argue with such advice? When did managers think—let alone say—they were doing otherwise?" (Eccles and Nohria, 1992, p. 5).

The management problems of higher education today are not the result of fads, but of the social forces that give rise to fads because of our overreliance on decision rationality and devotion to efficiency. Fads are the instruments of these forces. Fads can cause mischief, but at the same time they offer opportunities for institutional renewal. They can reinforce the tendency to turn education into a commodity whose components can be bought and sold to the highest bidder, but they also can help institutions reflect on their purposes and processes. We should be concerned about academic management fads more for what they represent than for what they actually do.

Academic management fads are potentially disruptive in the hands of insecure or inexperienced managers who adopt them because they do not know what else to do. Academic management fads are potentially useful when managers who have internalized the critical norms and values of their institutions add the kernel of truth in each fad to their store of knowledge and behavioral repertoires.

References

Abrahamson, E. "Managerial Fads and Fashions: The Diffusion and Rejection of Innovation." *Academy of Management Review*, 1991, *16*(3), 586–612.

Albert, S., and Whetten, D. A. "Organizational Identity." *Research in Organizational Behavior*, 1985, *7*, 263–295.

Allen, R., and Chaffee, E. "Management Fads in Higher Education." Paper presented at the Annual Forum of the Association for Institutional Research. Minneapolis, Minn., May 1981.

Allen, W. H. *Self-Surveys by Colleges and Universities*. Yonkers-on-Hudson, N.Y.: World Book Company, 1917.

Alstete, J. W. *Benchmarking in Higher Education: Adapting Best Practices to Improve Quality*. ASHE-ERIC Higher Education Reports, no. 5. Washington, D.C.: George Washington Graduate School of Education and Human Development, 1995.

Anderson, R. E. *Strategic Policy Changes at Private Colleges*. New York: Teachers College Press, 1977.

Anderson, S., and others. "A Decade of Executive Excess: The 1990s." In United for a Fair Economy Sixth Annual Compensation Survey. Available: [http://www.stw.org/html/decade'of'executive'excess.html]. Sept. 1, 1999.

Anthony, R. N. "Zero-Base Budgeting Is a Fraud." *Wall Street Journal*, Apr. 27, 1977, p. 26.

Arns, R. G. "Strategic Choice in Higher Education." Paper presented at the Twenty-Second Annual Forum of the Association for Institutional Research, Denver, Colo., May 17, 1982.

Axland, S. "A Higher Degree of Quality." *Quality Progress*, Oct. 1992, pp. 41–42.

Backoff, R. W., and Mitnick, B. M. "The Systems Approach, Incentive Rela-tions, and University Management." In J. A. Wilson (ed.), *Management Science Applications to Academic Administration*. San Francisco: Jossey-Bass, 1981.

Bailey, S. K. "Combatting the Efficiency Cultists." *Change*, June 1973, pp. 8–9.

Baker, J. T. "We're Lost, But We're Making Great Time." *Industrial Management*, 1991, *33*(6), 6–7.

Balderston, F. E. *Managing Today's University*. San Francisco: Jossey-Bass, 1974.

Balderston, F. E., and Weathersby, G. B. *PPBS in Higher Education Planning and Management: From PPBS to Policy Analysis*. Ford Foundation Sponsored Research Program, no. P-31. Berkeley: University of California, 1972.

Baldridge, J. V. "Impacts on College Administration: Management Information Systems and Management by Objectives Systems." *Research in Higher Education*, 1979, *10*(3), 263–282.

Baldridge, J. V., and Okimi, P. H. "Strategic Planning in Higher Education: New Tool—or New Gimmick?" *AAHE Bulletin*, 1982, *35*(6), 15–18.

Baldrige National Quality Program: Educational Criteria for Performance Excellence. Washington, D.C.: National Institute of Standards and Technology, 1999.

Barrett, F. D. "Everyman's Guide to M.B.O." *Business Quarterly*, Summer 1973, pp. 65–82.

Becker, S. W. "TQM Does Work: Ten Reasons Why Misguided Attempts Fail." *Management Review*, 1993, *82*(5), 30, 32–33.

Bemowski, K. "Restoring the Pillars of Higher Education." *Quality Progress*, October 1991, pp. 37–42.

Bensimon, E. M. (1987). *The Discovery Stage of Presidential Leadership*. College Park, Md.: Center for Higher Education Governance and Leadership.

Bensimon, E. M. "Total Quality Management in the Academy: A Rebellious Reading." *Harvard Educational Review*, 1995, *65*(4), 593–611.

Binzen, P. "New President Looks to Reposition Drexel in the Ideas Market." *Philadelphia Inquirer*, May 20, 1996, p. C3.

Birnbaum, R. "Leadership and Learning: The College President as Intuitive Scientist." *Review of Higher Education*, 1986, *9*(4), 381–395.

Birnbaum, R. *How Colleges Work: The Cybernetics of Academic Organization and Leadership*. San Francisco: Jossey-Bass, 1988.

Birnbaum, R. "Responsibility Without Authority: The Impossible Job of the College President." In J. C. Smart (ed.), *Higher Education Handbook of Theory and Research*. New York: Agathon Press, 1989.

Birnbaum, R. *How Academic Leadership Works: Understanding Success and Failure in the College Presidency*. San Francisco: Jossey-Bass, 1992.

Birnbaum, R., and Deshotels, J. M. "Has the Academy Adopted TQM? Total Quality Myths/Continuous Quality Illusions." *Planning for Higher Education*, 1999, 28(1), 29–37.

Birnbaum, R., and Shushok, F. J. "The Crisis in Higher Education." In P. G. Altbach, P. J. Gumport, and D. B. Johnstone (eds.), *In Defense of the American University*. Baltimore, Md.: Johns Hopkins University Press, forthcoming.

Bleakley, F. R. "The Best Laid Plans: Many Companies Try Management Fads, Only to See Them Flop." *Wall Street Journal*, Jul. 6, 1993, pp. A1, A66.

Bleed, R. "Community Colleges: Using Information Technologies to Harness the Winds of Change." In R. C. Heterick, Jr. (ed.), *Reengineering Teaching and Learning in Higher Education: Sheltered Groves, Camelot, Windmills, and Malls*. Boulder, Colo.: Cause, 1993.

Blumenstyk, G. "Colleges Look to 'Benchmarking' to Measure How Efficient and Productive They Are." *Chronicle of Higher Education,* Sept. 1, 1993, pp. A41-A42.

Bogard, L. "Management in Institutions of Higher Education." In A. M. Mood and others (eds.), *Papers on Efficiency in the Management of Higher Education*. Berkeley, Calif.: Carnegie Foundation for the Advancement of Teaching, 1972.

Bohl, D. L., and Luthans, F. "To Our Readers." *Organizational Dynamics*, Winter 1996, pp. 2–3.

Bok, D. "Reclaiming the Public Trust." *Change*, 1992, 24(4), 13–19.

Boulding, K. "In Praise of Inefficiency." *AGB Reports*, Jan.–Feb. 1978, pp. 44–48.

Bowen, H. R. *Investment in Learning: The Individual and Social Value of American Higher Education*. San Francisco: Jossey-Bass, 1977.

Bowen, H. R. "Society, Students and Parents—A Joint Responsibility: Finance and Aims of American Higher Education." In D. W. Breneman, L. L. Leslie, and R. E. Anderson (eds.), *ASHE Reader on Finance in Higher Education*. New York: Simon & Schuster, 1993.

Brigham, S. E. "TQM: Ten Lessons We Can Learn from Industry." *Change*, 1993, 25, 42–48.

Brigham, S. "CQI Successes: Fourteen Examples of How Campuses Have Applied CQI to Solve Problems and Improve Processes." *AAHE Bulletin*, Apr. 1995, pp. 6–9.

Brinkman, P. T., and Morgan, A. W. "Changing Fiscal Strategies for Planning." In M. W. Peterson and others (eds.), *Planning and Management for a Changing Environment: A Handbook on Redesigning Postsecondary Institutions*. San Francisco: Jossey-Bass, 1997.

Brock, D. M., and Harvey, W. B. "The Applicability of Corporate Strategic Principles to Diversified University Campuses." *Journal for Higher Education Management*, 1993, 8(2), 43–56.

Brown, W. A. "The Best Medicine? Placebo Effect." *Psychology Today*, 1997, 30(5), 56.

Brown, W. A. "The Placebo Effect." *Scientific American*, 1998, 278(1), 90–95.

Bruegman, D. C. "An Organizational Model for the 21st Century: Adopting the Corporate Model for Higher Education." *Business Officer*, 1995, 29(5), 28–31.

Brunsson, N. "The Irrationality of Action and Action Rationality: Decisions, Ideologies and Organizational Actors." *Journal of Management Studies*, 1982, 19, 29–44.

Bryant, A. "Beyond BPR: Confronting the Organizational Legacy." *Management Decision*, 1998, 36(1), 25–31.

Burke, J. C. "Performance Funding; Arguments and Answers." In J. C. Burke and A. M. Serban (eds.), *Performance Funding for Public Higher Education: Fad or Trend?* New Directions for Institutional Research, no. 97. San Francisco: Jossey-Bass, 1998.

Butler, D. "Here Today, Wrong Tomorrow." *Accountancy (International)*, 1998, 121, 40–41.

Byrne, J. A. "Strategic Planning." *Business Week*, Aug. 26, 1996, pp. 46–52.

Byrne, J. A. "Management Theory—or Fad of the Month?" *Business Week*, June 2, 1997, p. 47.

"A Call to Meeting." *Policy Perspectives*, 1993, 4(4), 1a-10a.

Callahan, R. E. *Education and the Cult of Efficiency: A Study of the Social Forces That Have Shaped the Administration of the Public Schools*. Chicago: University of Chicago Press, 1962.

Camp, R. C. "Benchmarking: The Search for Best Practices That Lead to Superior Performance." *Quality Progress*, 1989a, 22(1), 61–68.

Camp, R. C. "Benchmarking: The Search for Best Practices That Lead to Superior Performance." *Quality Progress*, 1989b, 22(2), 70–75.

Camp, R. C. "Benchmarking: The Search for Best Practices That Lead to Superior Performance." *Quality Progress*, 1989c, 22(5), 66–68.

Camp, R. C. *Business Process Benchmarking: Finding and Implementing Best Practices*. Milwaukee, Wis.: ASQC Quality Press, 1995.

Caplan, F. "The National Educational Quality Initiative." *Quality Progress*, Oct. 1992, pp. 63–65.

Carnevale, A. P., Johnson, N. C., and Edwards, A. R. "Performance-Based Appropriations: Fad or Wave of the Future?" *Chronicle of Higher Education*, Apr. 10, 1998, pp. B6-B7.

Carter, J. "Jimmy Carter Tells Why He Will Use Zero-Base Budgeting." *Nation's Business*, Jan. 1977, pp. 24–27.

Caruthers, J. K., and Orwig, M. *Budgeting in Higher Education*. ASHE-ERIC Higher Education Research Reports, no. 3. Washington, D.C.: American Association for Higher Education, 1979.

Casey, J. M. "A Strategic Business Improvement Model for Higher Education: Move Over TQM—Here Comes BPR." Paper presented at the 44th Annual Conference of the Southeastern Regional Association of Physical Plant Administrators of Universities and Colleges, Norfolk, Va., 1995.

Chabotar, K. J., and Knutel, P. "Reengineering: A View from the Frontlines." *Planning for Higher Education*, 1996–1997, *25*, 11–17.

Chaffee, E. E. "The Role of Rationality in University Budgeting." *Research in Higher Education*, 1983, *19*(4), 387–406.

Chaffee, E. E. "Successful Strategic Management in Small Private Colleges." *Journal of Higher Education*, 1984, *55*(2), 212–241.

Chaffee, E. E. "The Concept of Strategy: From Business to Higher Education." In J. C. Smart (ed.), *Higher Education: Handbook of Theory and Research* (pp. 133–172). New York: Agathon Press, 1985.

Chaffee, E. E., and Sherr, L. A. *Quality: Transforming Postsecondary Education*. ASHE-ERIC Higher Education Reports, no. 2. Washington, D.C.: George Washington University, 1992.

Chandler, A. D. *Strategy and Structure*. Cambridge, Mass.: MIT Press, 1962.

Cheek, L. M. *Zero-Base Budgeting Comes of Age*. New York: AMACOM, 1979.

Cheit, E. F. "Challenges Inherent in the Systematic Approach." *New Directions in Institutional Research*, 1977, *15*, 57–77.

Chiarelott, L., Reed, P., and Russell, S. C. "Lessons in Strategic Planning Learned the Hard Way." *Educational Leadership*, 1991, *48*(7), 36–39.

Christensen, C. *The Innovator's Dilemma: When New Technologies Cause Great Firms to Fail*. Boston: Harvard Business School Press, 1997.

Chronister, J. L. "Implementing Management by Objectives." *Community College Review*, Spring 1974, pp. 61–69.

Cigler, B. A. "Management by Objectives: Practice, Pitfalls and Utility for Small Colleges." *Planning for Higher Education*, 1979, *7*(5), 1–7.

Clark, B. R. *The Higher Education System: Academic Organization in Cross-National Perspective*. Berkeley: University of California Press, 1983.

Clayman, M. "In Search of Excellence: The Investor's Viewpoint." *Financial Analysts Journal*, May–June 1987, pp. 54–63.

Cohen, M. D., and March, J. G. *Leadership and Ambiguity: the American College President*. New York: McGraw-Hill, 1974.

Collins, J. C. "Change Is Good—But First, Know What Should Never Change." *Fortune,* May 29, 1995, pp. 141.

Collins, J. "Railing Against Oppressive, Inhuman Structures." *Inc.,* 1996, *18*(18), 63.

Connors, E. T., Franklin, H., and Kaskey, C. "Zero-Base: A New Look at Budgeting for Education." *Journal of Education Finance,* 1978, *4*(2), 248–259.

Cooke, M. L. *Academic and Industrial Efficiency: A Report to the Carnegie Foundation for the Advancement of Teaching.* New York: Merrymount Press, 1910.

Cope, R. G. *Strategic Planning, Management, and Decision Making.* ASHE-ERIC Higher Education Research Report, no. 9. Washington, D.C.: American Association for Higher Education, 1981.

Cope, R. G. *Opportunity from Strength: Strategic Planning Clarified with Case Examples.* ASHE-ERIC Higher Education Research Reports, no. 8. Washington, D.C.: Association for the Study of Higher Education, 1987.

Cornford, F. M. *Microcosmographia Academica: Being a Guide for the Young Academic Politician.* New York: Halcyon-Commonwealth Foundation, 1964. (Originally published 1908.)

Crowe, W. J. "Zero-Base Budgeting for Libraries: A Second Look." *College and Research Libraries,* 1982, *43*(1), 47–50.

Cuban, L. "Reforming Again, Again, and Again." *Educational Researcher,* Jan. 1990, pp. 3–13.

Davenport, T. H. "The Fad That Forgot People." [http://www.fastcompany.com/online/01/reengin.html]. 1995.

Davis, J. R. "Reengineering Teaching for 21st Century Learning." *Educational Record,* Fall 1995, pp. 16–22.

Deegan, A. X., and Fritz, R. J. *MBO Goes to College.* Boulder: University of Colorado Division of Continuing Education, 1975.

Defee, D. T. "Management by Objectives: When and How Does It Work?" *Personnel Journal,* Jan. 1977, pp. 37–42.

Dennis, D. "Brave New Reductionism: TQM as Ethnocentrism." *Education Policy Analysis Archives,* 3(9). [http://olam.ed.asu.edu/epaa/v3n9.html May 3, 1995].

deSaintonge, D.M.C., and Herxheimer, A. "Harnessing Placebo Effects in Health Care." *Lancet,* Sept. 8, 1994, pp. 995–998.

Dickeson, R. C. *Prioritizing Academic Programs and Services: Reallocating Resources to Achieve Strategic Balance.* San Francisco: Jossey-Bass, 1999.

Dill, D. D. "Quality by Design: Toward a Framework for Academic Quality Management." In J. Smart (ed.), *Higher Education: Handbook of Theory and Research.* New York: Agathon Press, 1992.

Diran, K. M. "Management Information Systems: The Human Factor." *Journal of Higher Education*, 1978, *49*(3), 273–282.

Dirsmith, S. F., Jablonsky, S. F., and Luzi, A. D. "Planning and Control in the U.S. Federal Government: A Critical Analysis of PPB, MBO and ZBB." *Strategic Management Journal*, 1980, *1*(4), 303–329.

Dolence, M. G., Rowley, D. J., and Lujan, H. D. *Working Toward Strategic Change: A Step-by-Step Guide to the Planning Process.* San Francisco: Jossey-Bass, 1997.

Donaldson, L., and Hilmer, F. G. "Management Redeemed: The Case Against Fads That Harm Management." *Organizational Dynamics*, Spring 1998, pp. 7–20.

Doucette, D. "Reengineering or Just Tinkering?" In R. C. Heterick, Jr. (ed.), *Reengineering Teaching and Learning in Higher Education: Sheltered Groves, Camelot, Windmills, and Malls.* Boulder, Colo.: Cause, 1993.

Dougherty, J. D. *Business Process Redesign for Higher Education.* Washington, D.C.: National Association of College and University Business Officers, 1994.

Douglas, D. P., Shaw, P. G., and Shepko, R. "Seventh Inning Stretch: A Retrospective of the NACUBO Benchmarking Program." *NACUBO Business Officer*, Dec. 1997, pp. 28–33.

Dresch, S. P. "A Critique of Planning Models for Postsecondary Education: Current Feasibility, Potential Relevance, and a Prospectus for Future Research." *Journal of Higher Education*, 1975, *46*(1), 245–286.

Drucker, P. F. *The Practice of Management.* New York: HarperCollins, 1954.

Eccles, R. G., and Nohria, N. *Beyond the Hype: Rediscovering the Essence of Management.* Boston: Harvard Business School Press, 1992.

Eckle, P. "How Institutions Discontinue Academic Programs: Making Potentially Adverse Decisions in an Environment of Shared Decision Making." Unpublished doctoral dissertation, University of Maryland, 1998.

Eddy, J., and DeCosmo, R. "MBO or Systematic Work with College Students." *Kappa Delta Pi Record*, 1977, *13*(3), 78–83.

Einhorn, H. J. "Learning from Experience and Suboptimal Rules in Decision Making." In D. Kahneman, P. Slovic, and A. Tversky (eds.), *Judgment Under Uncertainty: Heuristics and Biases.* New York: Cambridge University Press, 1982.

El-Khawas, E. *Campus Trends 1993.* Washington, D.C.: American Council on Education, 1993.

El-Khawas, E. *Campus Trends 1994.* Washington, D.C.: American Council on Education, 1994.

El-Khawas, E. "Strong State Action But Limited Results: Perspectives on University Resistance." *European Journal of Education*, 1998, *33*(3), 317–330.

Elkin, R., and Molitor, M. *Management Indicators in Nonprofit Corporations.* Baltimore: University of Maryland School of Social Work and Community Planning, 1984.

Enarson, H. L. "The Art of Planning." *Educational Record,* Summer 1975, pp. 170–175.

Engelkemeyer, S. W. "What Happened to CQI?" *AAHE Bulletin,* 1998, *50*(7), 11–16.

Entin, D. H. "Boston: Less Than Meets the Eye." *Change,* 1993, *25,* 28–31.

Entin, D. H. "A Second Look: TQM in Ten Boston-Area Colleges, One Year Later." *AAHE Bulletin,* 1994, *46*(9), 3–7.

Etzioni, A. *Modern Organizations.* Englewood Cliffs, N.J.: Prentice Hall, 1964.

Ewell, P. T. "Total Quality and Academic Practice: The Idea We've Been Waiting For?" *Change,* 1993, *25,* 49–55.

Ewell, P. T. "Imitation as Art: Borrowed Management Techniques in Higher Education." *Change,* 1999, *31*(6), 11–15.

Farmer, J. *Why Planning, Programming, Budgeting Systems for Higher Education?* Boulder, Colo.: Western Interstate Commission for Higher Education, 1970.

Farnham, A. "In Search of Suckers." *Fortune,* Oct. 14, 1996, pp. 119–126.

Fecher, R. J. (ed.). *Applying Corporate Management Strategies.* New Directions for Higher Education, no. 50. San Francisco: Jossey-Bass, 1985.

Ferguson, A. "Goodbye, Brave Newt World." *Time,* Nov. 16, 1998, p. 134.

Festinger, L., Riecken, H. W., and Schachter, S. *When Prophecy Fails.* New York: HarperCollins, 1956.

Fisher, J. L. "TQM: A Warning for Higher Education." *Educational Record,* Spring 1993, pp. 15–19.

Flack, H. "Three Critical Elements in Strategic Planning." *Planning for Higher Education,* 1994, *22,* 25–31.

Floristano, P. S. "Accountability Guidelines." Memorandum, Jul. 1, 1996.

Fox, F. V., and Staw, B. M. "The Trapped Administrator: Effects of Job Insecurity and Policy Resistance upon Commitment to a Course of Action." *Administrative Science Quarterly,* 1979, *24*(3), 449–471.

Freed, J. E., and Klugman, M. R. *Quality Principles and Practices in Higher Education: Different Questions for Different Times.* Phoenix, Ariz.: American Council on Education and Oryx Press, 1997.

Freeman, J. E. "Whatever Happened to PPBS?" *Planning for Higher Education,* 1978, *7*(1), 37–43.

Friedland, E. N. *Introduction to the Concept of Rationality in Political Science.* Morristown, N.J.: General Learning Press, 1974.

Friedman, J. "Introduction: Economic Approaches to Politics." In J. Friedman (ed.), *The Rational Choice Controversy*. New Haven, Conn.: Yale University Press, 1995.

Frost, P. J., and Egri, C. P. "The Political Process of Innovation." In L. L. Cummings and B. M. Staw (eds.), *Research in Organizational Behavior* (Vol. 13, pp. 229–295). Greenwich, Conn.: JAI Press, 1991.

Gaither, G., Nedwek, B. P., and Neal, J. E. *Measuring Up: The Promises and Pitfalls of Performance Indicators in Higher Education*. ASHE-ERIC Higher Education Reports, no. 5. Washington, D.C.: George Washington University, Graduate School of Education and Human Development, 1994.

Getz, M., Siegfried, J. J., and Anderson, K. H. "Adoption of Innovations in Higher Education." *Quarterly Review of Economics and Finance, 37*(3), 1997, 605–631.

Gilovich, T. *How We Know What Isn't So*. New York: Free Press, 1991.

Gimpl, M. L., and Dakin, S. R. "Management and Magic." *California Management Review*, 1984, *27*(1), 125–136.

Godbey, G. "Beyond TQM: Competition and Cooperation Create the Agile Institution." *Educational Record*, Spring 1993, pp. 37–42.

Goffman, E. *The Presentation of Self in Everyday Life*. New York: Doubleday, 1959.

Goleman, D. "Placebo Effect Is Shown to Be Twice as Powerful as Expected." *New York Times*, Aug. 17, 1993, p. C3.

Gouillart, F. J. "The Self-Transformation of Corporations: A Lesson from Industry?" In J. W. Meyerson and W. F. Massy (eds.), *Measuring Institutional Performance in Higher Education* (pp. 55–70). Princeton, N.J.: Peterson's, 1994.

Green, D. P., and Shapiro, I. *Pathologies of Rational Choice Theory: A Critique of Applications in Political Science*. New Haven, Conn.: Yale University Press, 1994.

Greenhouse, S. M. "The Planning-Programming-Budgeting System: Rationale, Language and Idea-Relationships." *Public Administration Review*, 1966, *26*(4), 271–277.

Gross, B. M. "PPBS Reexamined: The New Systems Budgeting." *Public Administration Review*, 1969, *29*(2), 113–137.

Gumport, P. J. "Academic Restructuring: Organizational Change and Institutional Imperatives." *Higher Education*, 2000, *39*(1), 67–91.

Håkansson, H., and Snehota, I. *Developing Relations in Business Networks*. New York: Routledge, 1995.

Hammer, M. "Reengineering Work: Don't Automate, Obliterate." *Harvard Business Review*, Jul.–Aug. 1990, pp. 104–112.

Hammer, M., and Champy, J. *Reengineering the Corporation: A Manifesto for Business Revolution*. New York: HarperCollins, 1993.

Hammond, T. H., and Knott, J. H. *A Zero-Based Look at Zero-Base Budgeting*. New Brunswick, N.J.: Transaction Books, 1980.

Harari, O. "Ten Reasons Why TQM Doesn't Work." *Management Review*, 1993a, 82(1), 33–38.

Harari, O. "The Eleventh Reason Why TQM Doesn't Work." *Management Review*, 1993b, pp. 31, 34–36.

Hardin, B., and Lee, R. "Zero Base Budgeting—A Catalyst for Improved Management." *Community College Review*, 1979, 7(2), 51–55.

Hardy, C., Langley, A., Mintzberg, H., and Rose, J. "Strategy Formation in the University Setting." *Review of Higher Education*, 1983, 6(4), 407–433.

Harel, E. C., and Partipilo, G. L. "Post Audit Automation: Reengineering Beyond the Illusion of Control." [http://www.ucla/edu/ais]. 1995.

Harper, E. L., Kramer, F. A., and Rouse, A. M. "Implementation and Use of PPB in Sixteen Federal Agencies." In A. Schick (ed.), *Perspectives on Budgeting*. Washington, D.C.: American Society for Public Administration, 1980.

Hartley, H. J. *Educational Planning, Programming, Budgeting: A Systems Approach*. Englewood Cliffs, N.J.: Prentice Hall, 1968.

Harvey, J. *College and University Planning*. Currents '71, no. 2. Washington, D.C.: ERIC Clearinghouse on Higher Education, 1971.

Harvey, L. J. *Zero-Base Budgeting in College and Universities: A Concise Guide to Understanding and Implementing ZBB in Higher Education*. Littleton, Colo.: Ireland Educational Corporation, 1977.

Hauptman, A. M. (1993). "The Economic Prospects for American Higher Education." In D. W. Breneman, L. L. Leslie, and R. E. Anderson (eds.), *ASHE Reader in Finance in Higher Education*. New York: Simon & Schuster, 1993.

Hayes, R. H. "Strategic Planning—Forward in Reverse?" *Harvard Business Review*, 1985, 6, 111–119.

Hearn, J. C., Clugston, R. M., and Heydinger, R. B. "Five Years of Strategic Environmental Efforts at a Research University: A Case Study of an Organizational Innovation." *Innovative Higher Education*, 1993, 18(1), 7–36.

Heifetz, R. A. *Leadership Without Easy Answers*. Boston: Harvard University Press, 1994.

Heilpern, J. D., and Nadler, D. A. "Implementing Total Quality Management: A Process of Cultural Change." In D. A. Nadler and others (eds.), *Organi-*

zational Architecture: Designs for Changing Organizations. San Francisco: Jossey-Bass, 1992.

Herrmann, T. J., Pyhrr, P. A., Thomas, J. D., and Gronvall, J. A. "A Zero-Base Approach to Medical School Planning and Budgeting." *Journal of Medical Education*, 1981, 56(8), 623–633.

Heterick, R. C., Jr. (ed.). *Reengineering Teaching and Learning in Higher Education: Sheltered Groves, Camelot, Windmills, and Malls*. Boulder, Colo.: Cause, 1993.

Hilmer, F. G., and Donaldson, L. *Management Redeemed: Debunking the Fads That Undermine Corporate Performance*. New York: Free Press, 1996.

Hitch, C. J., and McKean, R. N. *The Economics of Defense in the Nuclear Age*. Santa Monica, Calif.: Rand Corporation, 1960.

Hitt, M. A., and Ireland, R. D. "Peters and Waterman Revisited: The Unending Quest for Excellence." *Academy of Management Executive*, 1987, 1(2), 91–98.

Hittman, J. A. "TQM and CQI in Postsecondary Education." *Quality Progress*, Oct. 1993, pp. 77–80.

Hoffman, A. M., and Julius, D. J. (eds.). *Total Quality Management: Implications for Higher Education*. Maryville, Mo.: Prescott, 1995.

Hoffman, A. M., and Summers, R. "TQM: Implications for Higher Education— A Look Back to the Future." In A. M. Hoffman and D. J. Julius (eds.), *Total Quality Management: Implications for Higher Education*. Maryville, Mo.: Prescott, 1995.

Hollowood, J. R. "College and University Strategic Planning: A Methodological Approach." *Planning for Higher Education*, 1981, 9(4), 8–18.

Honan, J. P. "Monitoring Institutional Performance." *AGB Priorities*, Fall 1995, p. 5.

Horn, R. N., and Jerome, R. T. "When Corporate Restructuring Meets Higher Education." *Academe*, May-June 1996, pp. 34–36.

Hungate, T. L. *Management in Higher Education*. New York: Bureau of Publications, Teachers College, Columbia University, 1965.

Hurst, D. K. "Why Strategic Management Is Bankrupt." *Organizational Dynamics*, 1986, 15, 4–27.

Immerwahr, J. "Taking Responsibility: Leaders' Expectations of Higher Education." [http://www.highereducation.org/reports/responsibility/responsibility.html]. Jan. 1999.

Iosue, R. V. "Crossing Cultures: From College Pres to CEO." *AAHE Bulletin*, Mar. 1997, pp. 10–12.

Jacob, R. "TQM: More Than a Dying Fad?" *Fortune*, Oct. 18, 1993, pp. 66–72.

Jelinek, S. M., Foster, R.S.J., and Sauser, W. I., Jr. "A Rose by Any Other Name: Applying Total Quality Management to Higher Education." In S. J. Sims and R. R. Sims (eds.), *Total Quality Management in Higher Education.* New York: Praeger, 1995.

Johnson, V. R., and Smith, K. R. "Continuous Organizational Renewal Is Total Quality at the University of Arizona." In A. M. Hoffman and D. J. Julius (eds.), *Total Quality Management: Implications for Higher Education.* Maryville, Mo.: Prescott, 1995.

Johnston, O. "Delivering the Goods in Services: Productivity Gains Prove Hard to Gauge." *Washington Post,* Feb. 26, 1989, p. H2.

Kahneman, D., and Tversky, A. "Introduction." In D. Kahneman, P. Slovic, and A. Tversky (eds.), *Judgment Under Uncertainty: Heuristics and Biases.* New York: Cambridge University Press, 1982.

Kanigel, R. *The One Best Way: Frederick Winslow Taylor and the Enigma of Efficiency.* New York: Viking, 1997.

Katz, R. N. "Silicon in the Grove: Computing, Teaching, and Learning in the American Research University." In R. C. Heterick, Jr. (ed.), *Reengineering Teaching and Learning in Higher Education: Sheltered Groves, Camelot, Windmills, and Malls.* Boulder, Colo.: Cause, 1993.

Keller, G. *Academic Strategy: The Management Revolution in American Higher Education.* Baltimore, Md.: Johns Hopkins University Press, 1983.

Keller, G. "Academic Strategy: Five Years Later." *AAHE Bulletin,* Feb. 1988.

Keller, G. "Increasing Quality on Campus: What Should Colleges Do About the TQM Mania?" *Change,* May–June 1992, pp. 48–51.

Keller, G. "Examining What Works in Strategic Planning." In M. W. Peterson and others (eds.), *Planning and Management for a Changing Environment: A Handbook on Redesigning Postsecondary Institutions.* San Francisco: Jossey-Bass, 1997.

Kennedy, D. "Another Century's End, Another Revolution for Higher Education." *Change,* 1996, *27*(3), 8–16.

Kirst, M. W. "The Rise and Fall of PPBS in California." *Phi Delta Kappan,* Apr. 1975, pp. 535–538.

Klein, K. J., and Sorra, J. S. "The Challenge of Innovation Implementation." *Academy of Management Review,* 1996, *31*(4), 1055–1080.

Knowles, A. A. *Handbook of College and University Administration.* New York: McGraw-Hill, 1970.

Koenig, M.E.D., and Alperin, V. "ZBB and PPBS: What's Left Now That the Trendiness Has Gone?" *Drexel Library Quarterly,* 1985, *21*(3), 19–38.

Kosko, B. *Fuzzy Thinking: The New Science of Fuzzy Logic.* New York: Hyperion, 1993.

Kotler, P., and Murphy, P. E. "Strategic Planning for Higher Education." *Journal of Higher Education*, 1981, *52*(5), 470–489.

Kuhn, T. S. *The Structure of Scientific Revolutions*. (2nd ed., enl.) Chicago: University of Chicago Press, 1970.

Lahti, R. E. "Management by Objectives." *College and University Business*, 1971, *51*, 31–33.

Lahti, R. E. *Innovative College Management*. San Francisco: Jossey-Bass, 1973.

Langenberg, D. N. "Chancellor Says 'Learning' Is University's Sole Product." *Faculty Voice*, 1996, *10*(6), 2.

Lasher, H. J. "Is MBO Appropriate in the Academic Setting?" *Improving College and University Teaching*, 1978, *26*(2), 107–112.

Lauth, T. P. "Zero-Base Budgeting in Georgia State Government: Myth and Reality." In A. Schick (ed.), *Perspectives on Budgeting*. Washington, D.C.: American Society for Public Administration, 1980.

Lawler, E.E.I. *From the Ground Up: Six Principles for Building the New Logic Corporation*. San Francisco: Jossey-Bass, 1996.

Lawrence, G. B., and Service, A. L. *Quantitative Approaches to Higher Education Management: Potential, Limits, and Challenge*. ERIC/Higher Education Research Report, no. 4. Washington, D.C.: American Association for Higher Education, 1977.

Leslie, D. W. "Strategic Governance: The Wrong Questions?" *Review of Higher Education*, 1996, *20*(1), 101–112.

Leslie, D. W., and Fretwell, E. K. *Wise Moves in Hard Times: Creating and Managing Resilient Colleges and Universities*. San Francisco: Jossey-Bass, 1996.

Levin, B. "Criticizing the Schools: Then and Now." *Education Policy Analysis Archives*, Aug. 20, 1998. [http://olam.ed.asu.edu/epaa/v6n16.html].

Levinson, H. "Management by Whose Objectives?" *Harvard Business Review*, 1970, *48*, 125–134.

Lindblom, C. E. "The Science of 'Muddling Through.'" *Public Administration Review*, 1959, *19*, 78–88.

Loose, C. "Retirees Going Back to School—to Live." *Washington Post*, Nov. 9, 1998, pp. A1, A4.

Lueddeke, G. R. "Toward a Constructural Framework for Guiding Change and Innovation in Higher Education." *Journal of Higher Education*, 1999, *70*(3), 235–260.

Lynch, A. *Thought Contagion: How Beliefs Spread Through Society*. New York: Basic Books, 1996.

Mahoney, R. J. "'Reinventing' the University: Object Lessons from Big Business." *Chronicle of Higher Education*, Oct. 17, 1997, pp. B4-B5.

Malhotra, Y. "Business Process Redesign: An Overview."
    [http://www.brint.com/papers/bpr.htm]. 1996.
Malone, M. S. "A Way Too Short History of Fads." *Forbes*, Apr. 7, 1997, p. 72.
Mangan, K. S. "TQM: Colleges Embrace the Concept of 'Total Quality Manage-
    ment.'" *Chronicle of Higher Education*, Aug. 12, 1992, pp. A25-A26.
March, J. G. "How We Talk and How We Act: Administrative Theory and
    Administrative Life." In T. J. Sergiovanni and J. E. Corbally (eds.),
    Leadership and Organizational Culture (pp. 18–35). Urbana: University
    of Illinois Press, 1984.
March, J. G. *A Primer on Decision Making: How Decisions Happen*. New York:
    Free Press, 1994.
Marchese, T. "TQM Reaches the Academy." *AAHE Bulletin*, Nov. 1991,
    pp. 3–9.
Marchese, T. "TQM: A Time for Ideas." *Change*, 1993, *25*, 10–13.
Marchese, T. "Understanding Benchmarking." *AAHE Bulletin*, Apr. 1995,
    pp. 3–5.
Marchese, T. "Bye, Bye CQI for Now." *Change*, May–June, 1996, p. 4.
Marchese, T. J. "Sustaining Quality Enhancement in Academic and Managerial
    Life." In M. W. Peterson and others (eds.), *Planning and Management for
    a Changing Environment: A Handbook on Redesigning Postsecondary Institu-
    tions*. San Francisco: Jossey-Bass, 1997.
Marcus, L. R. "The Micropolitics of Planning." *Review of Higher Education*, 1999,
    23(1), 45–64.
Margolis, M. "Brave New Universities." *Firstmonday*, 3.
    http://firstmonday.org/issues/issue3_/margolis/index.html]. 1998.
Marks, D. "Is the University a Firm?" *Tertiary Education and Management*, 1998,
    4(4), 245–254.
Masland, A. T. "Simulators, Myth, and Ritual in Higher Education." *Research in
    Higher Education*, 1983, *18*(2), 161–177.
Mathews, J. "Totaled Quality Management: Consultants Flourish Helping Firms
    Repair the Results of a Business Fad." *Washington Post*, June 6, 1993,
    pp. H1, H16.
McClure, P. A. "'Growing' Our Academic Productivity." In R. C. Heterick, Jr.
    (ed.), *Reengineering Teaching and Learning in Higher Education: Sheltered
    Groves, Camelot, Windmills, and Malls*. Boulder, Colo.: Cause, 1993.
McGuinness, A.C.J., and Ewell, P. T. "Improving Productivity in Higher Educa-
    tion." *AGB Priorities*, 1994, *2*.
McManis, G. L., and Parker, W. C. *Implementing Management Information Systems
    in Colleges and Universities*. Littleton, Colo.: Ireland Educational Corpora-
    tion, 1978.

Melan, E. H. "Quality Improvement in Higher Education: TQM in Administrative Functions." In B. D. Ruben (ed.), *Quality in Higher Education*. New Brunswick, N.J.: Transaction Publishers, 1995.

Melissaratos, A., and Arendt, C. "TQM: The Westinghouse Experience." In A. M. Hoffman and D. J. Julius (eds.), *Total Quality Management: Implications for Higher Education* (pp. 17–30). Maryville, Mo.: Prescott, 1995.

Meredith, M. "What Works (and Doesn't) in Planning." *Planning for Higher Education*, Fall 1993, pp. 28–30.

Meyer, J. W. "The Politics of Educational Crisis in the United States." In W. K. Cummings and others (eds.), *Educational Policies in Crisis*. New York: Praeger, 1986.

Meyer, J. W. "Innovation and Knowledge Use in American Public Education." In J. W. Meyer and R. W. Scott (eds.), *Organizational Environments: Ritual and Rationality*. Thousand Oaks, Calif.: Sage, 1992.

Meyer, J. W., and Rowan, B. "The Structure of Educational Organizations." In J. W. Meyer and R. W. Scott (eds.), *Organizational Environments: Ritual and Rationality*. Thousand Oaks, Calif.: Sage, 1992.

Micklethwait, J., and Wooldridge, A. *The Witch Doctors: Making Sense of the Management Gurus*. New York: Random House, 1996.

Milbank, D. "Academe Gets Lessons from Big Business." *Wall Street Journal*, Dec. 15, 1992, pp. B1-B2.

Mingle, J. R. "Foreword." In R. C. Heterick, Jr. (ed.), *Reengineering Teaching and Learning in Higher Education: Sheltered Groves, Camelot, Windmills, and Malls*. Boulder, Colo.: Cause, 1993.

Minimer, G. S. *An Evaluation of the Zero-Base Budgeting System in Governmental Institutions*. Research Monograph, no. 68. Atlanta: Georgia State University, 1975.

Mintzberg, H. "Patterns in Strategy Formation." *Management Science*, 1978, 24, 934–948.

Mintzberg, H. *The Rise and Fall of Strategic Planning: Reconceiving Roles for Planning, Plans, Planners*. New York: Free Press, 1994.

Mintzberg, H., and Van der Heyden, L. "Organigraphs: Drawing How Companies Really Work." *Harvard Business Review*, Sept.–Oct. 1999, pp. 87–94.

Morgan, G. *Images of Organization*. Thousand Oaks, Calif.: Sage, 1986.

Morrison, J. L., Renfro, W. L., and Boucher, W. I. *Futures Research and the Strategic Planning Process: Implications for Higher Education*. ASHE-ERIC Higher Education Research Reports, no. 9. Washington, D.C.: Association for the Study of Higher Education, 1984.

NACUBO Benchmark Program. [http://www.nacubo.org/website/benchmarking/program.html]. 1997–1998.

National Association of College and University Business Officers. *A College Planning Cycle: People, Resources, Process.* Washington, D.C.: National Association of College and University Business Officers, 1975.

Nelson, C. "The War Against the Faculty." *Chronicle of Higher Education,* Apr. 16, 1999, pp. B4-B5.

Neustadt, R. E. *Presidential Power and the Modern Presidents: The Politics of Leadership from Roosevelt to Reagan.* (3rd ed.) New York: Free Press, 1990.

"A New Aim." *Change,* 1993, *25,* 47.

Newton, R. D. *PPBS in Higher Education: The Impossible Dream?* University, Pa.: Center for the Study of Higher Education, Pennsylvania State University, 1976. (ED 140 719)

Nicklin, J. L. "The Hum of Corporate Buzzwords." *Chronicle of Higher Education,* Jan. 27, 1995, pp. A33-A34.

Nisbett, R., and Ross, L. *Human Inference: Strategies and Shortcomings of Social Judgment.* Englewood Cliffs, N.J.: Prentice Hall, 1980.

Njoku, E. S. "Introducing Management by Objectives in Higher Education." *West African Journal of Education,* 1977, *19*(2), 199-212.

Noble, D. F. "Digital Diploma Mills: The Automation of Higher Education." *Firstmonday* 3. [http://firstmonday.org/issues/issue3_/noble/index.html]. 1998.

Nohria, N., and Berkley, J. D. "Whatever Happened to the Take-Charge Manager?" *Harvard Business Review,* Jan.-Feb. 1994, pp. 128-137.

Norris, D. M. "Turning Idea into Expeditions: Expeditionary Strategy and Products for the Knowledge Age." *AAHE Bulletin,* May 1998, pp. 12-16.

O'Neill, P., and Sohal, A. S. "Business Process Reengineering: A Review of Recent Literature." *Technovation,* 1999, *19,* 571-581.

O'Shea, J., and Madigan, C. *Dangerous Company: The Consulting Powerhouses and the Businesses They Save and Ruin.* New York: Random House, 1997.

Odiorne, G. S. *Management by Objectives: A System of Managerial Leadership.* New York: Pitman, 1965.

Odiorne, G. S. "Management by Objectives." *College and University Journal,* 1971, *10,* 13-15.

Ohio Board of Regents. *Planning Universities.* Columbus: Ohio Board of Regents, 1973a.

Ohio Board of Regents. *Program Budgeting.* Columbus: Ohio Board of Regents, 1973b.

Oldenburg, D. "The Last Reunion: College Grads Act on Their Grave Concerns." *Washington Post,* Oct. 17, 1996, p. E5.

Pallas, A. M., and Neumann, A. "Blinded by the Light: The Applicability of Total Quality Management to Educational Organizations." Paper presented at the Annual Meeting of the American Educational Research Association. Atlanta, Ga., Apr. 1993.

Parden, R. J. "Rationalizing Management Information System Costs." *Cause/Effect*, 1978, *1*(4), 10–19.

Pascale, R. T. *Managing on the Edge: How the Smartest Companies Use Conflict to Stay Ahead*. New York: Simon & Schuster, 1991.

Penrod, J. I., and Dolence, M. G. "Concepts for Reengineering Higher Education." *Cause/Effect*, 1991, *14*(2).

Penrod, J. I., and Dolence, M. G. *Reengineering: A Process for Transforming Higher Education*. Boulder, Colo.: Cause, 1992.

Peters, T. J., and Waterman, R.H.J. *In Search of Excellence: Lessons from America's Best-Run Companies*. New York: HarperCollins, 1982.

Peterson, M. W. "The Potential Impact of PPBS on Colleges and Universities." *Journal of Higher Education*, 1971, *42*(1), 1–20.

Peterson, M. W. "Analyzing Alternative Approaches to Planning." In P. Jedamus and others (eds.), *Improving Academic Management: A Handbook of Planning and Institutional Research* (pp. 113–163). San Francisco: Jossey-Bass, 1980.

Pfiffner, J. M. "Administrative Rationality." *Public Administration Review*, 1960, *20*(3), 125–132.

Pham, A. "Reengineering Guru to Launch Consulting Firm." *Boston Globe*, Aug. 21, 1996.

Pinola, M., and Knirk, F. G. "A Well-Designed Budget Yields Long-Term Rewards." *Instructional Innovator*, 1984, *29*(7–8), 10–15.

Plous, S. *The Psychology of Judgment and Decision Making*. Philadelphia: Temple University Press, 1993.

Pool, R. *Beyond Engineering: How Society Shapes Technology*. New York: Oxford University Press, 1997.

Porter, J. H. "Business Reengineering in Higher Education: Promise and Reality." *Cause/Effect*, 1993, *16*(4), 48–53.

Postman, N. *The End of Education: Redefining the Value of School*. New York: Knopf, 1995.

Presley, J. B., and Leslie, D. W. "Understanding Strategy: An Assessment of Theory and Practice." In J. Smart (ed.), *Higher Education: Handbook of Theory and Research*. New York: Agathon Press, 1998.

Principal Universities and Colleges of the United States. Table One. In *World Almanac and Encyclopedia*. New York: Press Publishing Company, 1901.

Pritchett, M. "Reengineering in Higher Education." *On the Horizon*, 1994–1995, *3*(2), 7–8.

Pyhrr, P. A. "Zero-Base Budgeting." *Harvard Business Review*, Nov.-Dec. 1970, pp. 111–121.

Pyhrr, P. A. "The Zero-Base Approach to Government Budgeting." *Public Administration Review*, 1977, *37*(1), 1–8.

Radin, B. A., and Coffee, J. N. "A Critique of TQM: Problems of Implementation in the Public Sector." *Public Administration Quarterly*, 1993, *17*(1), 42–54.

Rahul, J. "TQM: More Than a Dying Fad?" *Fortune*, Oct. 18, 1993, pp. 66–68, 72.

Raia, A. P. "Goal Setting and Self Control." *Journal of Management Studies*, 1965, *2*(1), 34–53.

Reddin, W. J. *Effective Management by Objectives: The 3-D Method of MBO.* New York: McGraw-Hill, 1970.

"Repositioning Reengineering." [http://www.businessarch.com/papers/repos.asp]. N.d.

Rifkin, G. "When Is a Fad Not a Fad?" *Harvard Business Review*, Sept.–Oct. 1994, p. 11.

Rifkin, G. "Re-Engineering Firm Tries Some of Its Own Medicine." *New York Times*, Dec. 16, 1996, p. C6.

Rigby, D. *Management Tools and Techniques.* Boston: Bain and Company, 1998.

Roach, S. S. "The Hollow Ring of the Productivity Revival." *Harvard Business Review*, 1996, *74*(6), 81–89.

Robbins, H., and Finley, M. *Why Change Doesn't Work: Why Initiatives Go Wrong and How to Try Again—and Succeed.* Princeton, N.J.: Peterson's, 1996.

Roe, E. *Narrative Policy Analysis: Theory and Practice.* Durham, N.C.: Duke University Press, 1994.

Rogers, E. M. *Diffusion of Innovations* (4th ed.) New York: Free Press, 1995.

Rose, R. "Implementation and Evaporation: The Record of MBO." In A. Schick (ed.), *Perspectives on Budgeting* (pp. 103–113). Washington, D.C.: American Society for Public Administration, 1980.

Ross, J., and Staw, B. M. "Expo 86: An Escalation Prototype." *Administrative Science Quarterly*, 1986, *31*(2), 274–297.

Ross, J., and Staw, B. M. "Organizational Escalation and Exit: Lessons from the Shoreham Nuclear Power Plant." *Academy of Management Journal*, 1993, *36*(4), 701–732.

Ross, L., and Anderson, C. A. "Shortcomings in the Attribution Process: On the Origins and Maintenance of Erroneous Social Assessments." In D. Kahneman, P. Slovic, and A. Tversky (eds.), *Judgment Under Uncertainty: Heuristics and Biases.* New York: Cambridge University Press, 1982.

Rourke, F. E., and Brooks, G. E. *The Managerial Revolution in Higher Education.* Baltimore, Md.: Johns Hopkins Press, 1966.

Rowley, D. J., Lujan, H. D., and Dolence, M. G. *Strategic Change in Colleges and Universities: Planning to Survive and Prosper*. San Francisco: Jossey-Bass, 1997.

Rush, S. C. "Benchmarking: How Good Is Good?" In J. W. Meyerson and W. F. Massey (eds.), *Measuring Institutional Performance in Higher Education*. Princeton, N.J.: Peterson's, 1994.

Salipante, P. F., and Golden-Biddle, K. "Managing Traditionality and Strategic Change in Nonprofit Organizations." *Nonprofit Management and Leadership*, 1995, 6(1), 3–20.

Samuelson, R. J. "Why I Am Not a Manager." *Washington Post*, Mar. 18, 1999, pp. A-21.

Saurman, K. B., and Nash, R. J. "M.B.O., Student Development and Accountability: A Critical Look." *NASPA Journal*, 1975, 12(3), 179–189.

Schargel, F. P. "Total Quality in Education." *Quality Progress*, Oct. 1993, pp. 67–70.

Schick, A. *Budget Innovation in the States*. Washington, D.C.: Brookings Institution, 1971.

Schick, A. "Budgeting as an Administrative Process." In A. Schick (ed.), *Perspectives on Budgeting*. Washington, D.C.: American Society for Public Administration, 1980.

Schmidt, P. "Rancor and Confusion Greet a Change in South Carolina's Budgeting System." *Chronicle of Higher Education*, Apr. 4, 1997, pp. A26-A27.

Schmidt, W. H., and Finnigan, J. P. *The Race Without a Finish Line: America's Quest for Total Quality*. San Francisco: Jossey-Bass, 1992.

Schmidtlein, F. A. "Decision Process Paradigms in Education." *Educational Researcher*, 1974, 3(5), 4–11.

Schmidtlein, F. A. "Why Linking Budgets to Plans Has Proven Difficult in Higher Education." *Planning for Higher Education*, 1989–1990, 18(2), 9–23.

Schmidtlein, F. A. "Planning for Quality: Perils and Possibilities." Paper presented at Quality and Communication for Improvement, the 12th European Association for Institutional Research Forum, Lyon, France, Sept. 1990.

Schmidtlein, F. A. "Assumptions Underlying Performance-Based Budgeting." *Tertiary Evaluation and Management*, 1999, 5, 159–174.

Schmidtlein, F. A., and Milton, T. H. "College and University Planning: Perspectives from a Nation-Wide Study." *Planning for Higher Education*, 1988–1989, 17(3), 1–19.

Schuster, J. H., Smith, D. G., Corak, K. A., and Yamada, M. *Strategic Governance: How to Make Big Decisions Better*. Phoenix, Ariz.: American Council on Education/Oryx Press, 1994.

Scott, W. R. *Institutions and Organizations*. Thousand Oaks, Calif.: Sage, 1995.

Secor, J. R. "TQM: A Flavor-of-the-Month Buzzword or Step One to Designing Processes That Deliver Continuous Value to the Customer?" In *Total Quality Management in Academic Libraries: Initial Implementation Efforts*. (Proceedings of the International Conference on TQM and Academic Libraries, Apr. 20–22, 1994.) Washington D.C.: Association of Research Libraries, 1995.

Serban, A. M. "Opinions and Attitudes of State and Campus Policy Makers." In J. C. Burke and A. M. Serban (eds.), *Performance Funding for Public Higher Education: Fad or Trend?* New Directions for Institutional Research, no. 97. San Francisco: Jossey-Bass, 1998.

Sergiovanni, T. J. "Schools Are Special Places." *Education Week on the Web*, May 10, 1995.

Seymour, D. T. "TQM on Campus: What the Pioneers Are Finding." *AAHE Bulletin*, Nov. 1991, pp. 10–13, 18.

Seymour, D. T. *On Q: Causing Quality in Higher Education*. New York: American Council on Education/Macmillan, 1992.

Seymour, D. "Quality on Campus: Three Institutions, Three Beginnings." *Change*, 1993, *25*, 14–27.

Seymour, D. "The Baldridge Cometh." *Change*, Jan.-Feb. 1994, pp. 16–27.

Seymour, D. *Once upon a Campus*. Phoenix, Ariz.: Oryx, 1995.

Shapiro, E. C. *Fad Surfing in the Boardroom: Reclaiming the Courage to Manage in the Age of Instant Answers*. Reading, Mass.: Addison-Wesley, 1995.

Shapiro, E. "Managing in the Age of Gurus." *Harvard Business Review*, Mar.-Apr. 1997, pp. 142–147.

Sherwood, F. P., and Page, W. J., Jr. "MBO and Public Management." *Public Administration Review*, 1976, *36*, 5–12.

Shetty, Y. K., and Carlisle, H. M. "A Study of Management by Objectives in a Professional Organization." *Journal of Management Studies*, 1975, *12*(1), 1–11.

Shils, E. *Tradition*. Chicago: University of Chicago Press, 1981.

Shirley, R. C. "Strategic Planning: An Overview." In D. W. Steeples (ed.), *Successful Strategic Planning: Case Studies*. New Directions for Higher Education, no. 64. San Francisco: Jossey-Bass, 1988.

Sims, R. R., and Sims, S. J. "Toward an Understanding of Total Quality Management: Its Relevance and Contribution to Higher Education." In S. J. Sims and R. R. Sims (eds.), *Total Quality Management in Higher Education*. New York: Praeger, 1995.

Slaughter, S. "Criteria for Restructuring Postsecondary Education." *Journal for Higher Education Management*, 1995, *10*(2), 31–44.

Slaughter, S., and Leslie, L. L. *Academic Capitalism: Politics, Policies and the Entre-preneurial University*. Baltimore, Md.: Johns Hopkins University Press, 1997.

Slavin, R. E. "Pet and the Pendulum: Faddism in Education and How to Stop It." *Phi Delta Kappan*, 1989, *20*(10), 752–758.

Sloan, V. "Total Quality Management in the Culture of Higher Education." *Review of Higher Education*, 1994, *17*(4), 447–464.

Slocum, D. L., and Rooney, P. M. "Responding to Resource Constraints: A Departmentally Based System of Responsibility Center Management." *Change*, 1997, *29*(5), 51–57.

Smallen, D. L. "Reengineering of Student Learning? A Second Opinion from Camelot." In R. C. Heterick, Jr. (ed.), *Reengineering Teaching and Learning in Higher Education: Sheltered Groves, Camelot, Windmills, and Malls*. Boulder, Colo.: Cause, 1993.

Spanbauer, S. J. *A Quality System for Education: Using Quality and Productivity Techniques to Save Our Schools*. Milwaukee, Wis.: ASQC Quality Press, 1992.

Spencer, W. L. "What Do Upper Executives Want from MIS?" *Administrative Management*, Jul. 1978, pp. 26–27, 66–68.

Stahlke, H.F.W., and Nyce, J. M. "Reengineering Higher Education: Reinventing Teaching and Learning." *Cause/Effect*, Winter 1996, pp. 44–51.

Staw, B. M. "The Escalation of Commitment to a Course of Action." *Academy of Management Review*, 1981, *6*(4), 577–587.

Staw, B. M. "The Escalation of Commitment: An Update and Appraisal." In Z. Shapira (ed.), *Organizational Decision Making*. New York: Cambridge University Press, 1997.

Staw, B. M., and Ross, J. "Commitment in an Experimenting Society: A Study of the Attribution of Leadership." *Journal of Applied Psychology*, 1980, *85*(3), 249–260.

Steeples, D. W. (ed.). *Successful Strategic Planning: Case Studies*. New Directions for Higher Education, no. 64. San Francisco: Jossey-Bass, 1988.

Stone, D. A. *Policy Paradox and Political Reason*. Glenview, Ill.: Scott, Foresman, 1988.

Strassmann, P. A. "The Hocus-Pocus of Reengineering." [http://www.strassmann.com/pubs/hocuspocus.html]. June 1994.

Strassmann, P. A. "In Search of 'Best Practices.'" *Computerworld*. [http://www.strassmann.com/pubs/cw/best-practices.html]. Feb. 1995.

Suver, J. D., and Brown, R. L. "Where Does Zero-Base Budgeting Work?" *Harvard Business Review*, 55(6), 1977, 76–84.

Swenk, J. M. "Strategic Planning and Fiscal Benefits: Is There a Link?" Paper presented at the Annual Conference, Association for the Study of Higher Education, Miami, Fla., Nov. 1998.

Swenk, J. "Planning Failures: Decision Cultural Clashes." *Review of Higher Education*, 1999, *23*(1), 1–21.

Tan, D. L. "Strategic Planning in Higher Education: Varying Definitions, Key Characteristics, Benefits, Pitfalls, and Good Approaches." Paper presented at the Southwest Society for College and University Planning, Tucson, Ariz., Mar. 1990.

Taylor, B. E., Jr. "Keeping BPR from Being TQMed." [http://ni.umd.edu/~billy/writings/er/9412-01c.html]. 1995.

Taylor, B. E., and Massy, W. F. *Strategic Indicators for Higher Education: Vital Benchmarks and Information to Help You Evaluate and Improve Your Institution's Performance*. Princeton, N.J.: Peterson's, 1996.

Temple, C. M. "Management by Objectives at the University of Tennessee." *Intellect*, 1973, *102*, 98–100.

Tenner, E. *Why Things Bite Back: Technology and the Revenge of Unanticipated Consequences*. New York: Knopf, 1996.

Thomas, K. B. "The Placebo Effect in General Practice." *Lancet*, Sept. 15, 1994, pp. 1066–1067.

Thomas, M. "What You Need to Know About: Business Process Re-engineering." *Personnel Management*, 1994, *26*, 28–31.

Thompson, D. L. "PPBS: The Need for Experience." *Journal of Higher Education*, 1971, *42*, 678–691.

Thurow, L. C. "Building Wealth: The New Rules for Individuals, Companies and Nations." *Atlantic Monthly*, June 1999, pp. 57–69.

Tornatzky, L. G., and Fleischer, M. *Technological Innovation*. San Francisco: New Lexington Press, 1990.

Trombley, W. "Performance-Based Budgeting: South Carolina's New Plan Mired in Detail and Confusion." *National Crosstalk*, 1998, *6*(1), 1, 14–16.

Trombley, W., and Sevener, D. "Budgeting for Results: Use of Performance Indicators Increases in Popularity." *National Crosstalk*, 1998, *6*(1), 14.

Turner, J. A., and others. "The Importance of Placebo Effects in Pain Treatment and Research." *Journal of the American Medical Association*, May 25, 1994, pp. 1609–1614.

Twigg, C. A. "Information Technology—Enabling Transformation." In R. C. Heterick, Jr. (ed.), *Reengineering Teaching and Learning in Higher Education: Sheltered Groves, Camelot, Windmills, and Malls*. Boulder, Colo.: Cause, 1993.

Tyack, D., and Cuban, L. *Tinkering Toward Utopia: A Century of Public School Reform.* Cambridge, Mass.: Harvard University Press, 1995.

"University and Corporate Representatives Determine Focus of CUPA-Led Benchmarking Study." *CUPA News,* Apr. 6, 1998, pp. 1–2.

Veblen, T. *The Higher Learning in America: A Memorandum on the Conduct of Universities by Business Men.* New York: Sagamore Press, 1957. (Originally published 1918.)

Wade, N. "Method and Madness: The Spin Doctors." *New York Times,* Jan. 7, 1996, p. 16.

Wanat, J. *Introduction to Budgeting.* Boston: PWS-Kent, 1978.

Waters, L. A. "Higher Education and Total Quality Management: Taking Lessons from Government and Business Ventures." In S. J. Sims and R. R. Sims (eds.), *Total Quality Management in Higher Education.* New York: Praeger, 1995.

Weaver, P. H. "Excellence in Search of Impermanence." *Wall Street Journal,* Oct. 14, 1987, p. 1.

Weick, K. E. "Educational Organizations as Loosely Coupled Systems. *Administrative Science Quarterly,* 1976, *21,* 1–19.

Weick, K. E. *The Social Psychology of Organizing.* (2nd ed.) Reading, Mass.: Addison-Wesley, 1979.

Weick, K. E. *Sensemaking in Organizations.* Thousand Oaks, Calif.: Sage, 1995.

West, G. E. "Bureaupathology and the Failure of MBO." *Human Resource Management,* 1977, *16*(2), 33–40.

West, T. W., and Daigle, S. L. "Comprehensive Universities Refocusing for the Next Century." In R. C. Heterick, Jr. (ed.), *Reengineering Teaching and Learning in Higher Education: Sheltered Groves, Camelot, Windmills, and Malls.* Boulder, Colo.: Cause, 1993.

"What Is a Nocebo?" *Harvard Mental Health Letter,* 1997, *14*(1), 8.

"What You Really Think About Reengineering." *CF,* May 1995, pp. 53–57.

Wheatley, W. J. "Impediments to Overcome If Academia Is Going to Successfully Embrace Total Quality Management." In S. J. Sims and R. R. Sims (eds.), *Total Quality Management in Higher Education.* New York: Praeger, 1995.

White, J. B. "R-Engineering Gurus Take Steps to Remodel Their Stalling Vehicles." *Wall Street Journal,* Nov. 26, 1996, pp. 1, 13.

"Who's Excellent Now? Some of the Best-Seller's Picks Haven't Been Doing So Well Lately." *Business Week,* Nov. 5, 1984, pp. 76–78.

Wildavsky, A. "If Planning Is Everything, Maybe It's Nothing." *Policy Sciences,* 1973, *4,* 127–153.

Wildavsky, A. *The Politics of the Budgetary Process*. (2nd ed.) Boston: Little, Brown, 1974.

Wildavsky, A., and Hammond, A. "Comprehensive Versus Incremental Budgeting in the Department of Agriculture." *Administrative Science Quarterly*, 1965, *10*, 321–346.

Williams, H. *Planning for Effective Resource Allocation in Universities*. Washington, D.C.: American Council on Education, 1966.

Wilson, D. C. *A Strategy of Change: Concepts and Controversies in the Management of Change*. New York: Routledge, 1992.

Wilson, J. A. (ed.). *Management Science: Applications to Academic Administration*. San Francisco: Jossey-Bass, 1981.

Willis, C. *Bellwether*. New York: Bantam Books, 1996.

Winston, G. C. "Hostility, Maximization, and the Public Trust: Economics and Higher Education." In D. W. Breneman, L. L. Leslie, and R. E. Anderson (eds.), *ASHE Reader on Finance in Higher Education*. New York: Simon & Schuster, 1993.

Winston, G. C. "Why Can't a College Be More Like a Firm?" *Change*, 1997, *29*(5), 33–38.

Wiseman, C. "New Foundations for Planning Models." *Journal of Higher Education*, 1979, *50*(6), 726–744.

Woodbury, R. L. "Why Not Run a Business Like a Good University?" *Christian Science Monitor*, Mar. 23, 1993, p. 19.

Work Environment Research Group. *Total Quality Management in Higher Education: From Assessment to Improvement*. Ann Arbor, Mich.: Center for the Study of Higher and Postsecondary Education, 1995.

Yin, R. K. *Case Study Research: Design and Methods*. Thousand Oaks, Calif.: Sage, 1984.

Name Index

A

Abrahamson, E., 146, 152, 157, 170
Albert, S., 220, 223
Allen, R., 5, 70, 147, 180, 219, 230, 238, 240
Allen, W. H., 17
Alperin, V., 41, 58, 60, 61
Alstete, J. W., 77, 79, 80, 82, 86, 87, 88, 156, 209
Anderson, C. A., 131, 165, 171, 174–175, 176, 177, 179, 189
Anderson, K. H., 139, 145
Anderson, R. E., 73
Anthony, R. N., 53, 54, 55, 195
Arendt, C., 92, 94, 99
Arms, R. G., 64, 69
Arnold, M., 75
Axland, S., 98

B

Backoff, R. W., 41
Bailey, S. K., 215, 228
Baker, J. T., 4
Balderston, F. E., 22, 36, 37, 39, 40, 42, 60, 229
Baldridge, J. V., 10, 67, 73, 185, 239
Barrett, F. D., 44, 45
Becker, S. W., 161
Bemowski, K., 98, 101
Bensimon, E. M., 107, 172
Berkley, J. D., 4, 8, 9, 12, 141, 143, 145, 147, 180, 195, 202, 235, 236, 241
Binzen, P., 173
Birnbaum, R., 88, 102, 137, 143, 151, 170, 171, 172, 175, 207, 210, 223, 225
Bleakley, F. R., 95, 119, 131, 163, 169, 178, 195, 229
Bleed, R., 116
Blumenstyk, G., 82
Bogard, L., 23, 37, 38
Bohl, D. L., 142, 196, 206
Bok, D., 144
Boucher, W. I., 65
Boulding, K., 199, 217
Bowen, H. R., 198, 228
Brigham, S. E., 93, 96, 99, 101, 163
Brinkman, P. T., 229
Brooks, G. E., 14, 24, 25, 154
Brown, R. L., 56, 58, 202
Brown, W. A., 187
Bruegman, D. C., 222
Brunsson, N., 27, 28
Bryant, A., 108, 110, 113, 119, 120
Burke, J. C., 88
Butler, D., 7, 8
Byrne, J. A., 67, 97, 237

C

Callahan, R. E., 14, 17, 181–182, 218
Camp, R. C., 76, 77, 78, 79, 94

Caplan, F., 100
Carnevale, A. P., 88, 229
Carter, J., 53–54, 55, 169, 184
Caruthers, J. K., 20, 23, 34, 36, 38
Casey, J. M., 108, 119
Chabotar, K. J., 117
Chaffee, E., 5, 10, 64, 67, 70, 73, 75, 93, 147, 156, 180, 196, 208, 219, 230, 238, 240
Champy, J., 77, 109–113, 114–115, 119, 120, 161–162, 195, 203
Chandler, A. D., 64
Cheek, L. M., 53, 54, 59
Cheit, E. F., 24, 25, 198
Chiarelott, L., 205
Christensen, C., 234
Cigler, B. A., 50
Clark, B. R., 145
Clayman, M., 7
Clugston, R. M., 70
Coffee, J. N., 95
Cohen, M. D., 151, 159, 171, 183
Collins, J., 7, 239
Connors, E. T., 53
Cooke, M. L., 16
Cope, R. G., 64, 65, 66, 67, 69, 70, 71
Corak, K. A., 71
Crowe, W. J., 58
Cuban, L., 18, 138, 147, 150, 164, 235

D

Daigle, S. L., 116
Dakin, S. R., 9, 155, 160, 162, 212
Davenport, T. H., 118, 119, 196
Davis, J. R., 118
DeCosmo, R., 50
Deegan, A. X., 44, 45, 47–48, 50
Defee, D. T., 44
Deming, W. E., 93
Dennis, D., 107
Deshotels, J. M., 102, 137, 170
Dickeson, R. C., 6, 138
Dill, D. D., 93
Diran, K. M., 210
Dirsmith, S. F., 60, 155

Dolence, M. G., 72, 73, 74, 108, 110, 117
Donaldson, L., 5, 80, 120, 172, 194, 201, 231, 236
Doucette, D., 114
Dougherty, J. D., 108, 110, 111, 113, 115, 119
Douglas, D. P., 82, 83
Dresch, S. P., 29, 156
Drucker, P. F., 43

E

Eccles, R. G., 4, 8, 9, 12, 145, 147, 180, 236, 241
Eddy, J., 50
Edwards, A. R., 88, 229
Egri, C. P., 11, 29, 167
Einhorn, H. J., 180
El-Khawas, E., 85, 99, 118, 137, 203, 236
Elkin, R., 81
Enarson, H. L., 88, 201
Engelkemeyer, S. W., 103
Entin, D. H., 101–102, 106, 160
Etzioni, A., 197
Ewell, P. T., 85, 93, 94, 105, 161, 222, 231

F

Farmer, J., 37, 38, 40
Farnham, A., 149
Fecher, R. J., 24
Ferguson, A., 92
Festinger, L., 132, 148, 187
Finley, M., 44, 153, 174
Finnigan, J. P., 92, 94, 95, 96, 104, 105, 106
Fisher, J. L., 107
Fleischer, M., 10, 161, 206
Floristano, P. S., 85
Foster, R.S.J., 98
Freed, J. E., 103
Freeman, J. E., 36, 40, 43
Fretwell, E. K., 201, 221
Friedland, E. N., 28
Friedman, J., 164

Fritz, R. J., 44, 45, 47–48, 50
Frost, P. J., 11, 29, 167

G

Gaither, G., 81–82, 84, 85, 86, 88, 147
Getz, M., 139, 145
Gilovich, T., 11, 167, 177, 178, 179, 189
Gimpl, M. L., 9, 155, 160, 162, 212
Gingrich, N., 92
Godbey, G., 229
Goffman, E., 173, 182
Golden-Biddle, K., 152, 200, 220, 222
Goleman, D., 188
Gouillart, F. J., 186
Green, D. P., 164
Greenhouse, S. M., 39
Gronvall, J. A., 58
Gross, B. M., 34, 35, 40, 41
Gumport, P. J., 226

H

Håkansson, H., 146
Hammer, M., 77, 109–113, 114–115, 119, 120, 161–162, 195, 202, 203
Hammond, A., 41, 42, 56, 155
Hammond, T. H., 13, 54, 55, 58, 59, 60, 61, 169, 170, 172–173, 180, 184, 185, 203
Harari, O., 96, 106, 164, 184
Hardin, B., 57
Hardy, C., 74, 239
Harel, E. C., 117
Harper, E. L., 36
Hartley, H. J., 36, 38
Harvey, L. J., 46, 52, 56, 59, 60, 195, 196, 208
Hauptman, A. M., 70
Hayes, R. H., 66
Hearn, J. C., 70
Heifetz, R. A., 201
Heilpern, J. D., 94, 104, 105
Herrmann, T. J., 58
Heterick, R. C., Jr., 115
Heydinger, R. B., 70

Hilmer, F. G., 5, 80, 120, 172, 194, 201, 231, 236
Hitch, C. J., 34, 40
Hitt, M. A., 7, 230, 231, 234
Hittman, J. A., 101, 107
Hoffman, A. M., 95, 101
Hollowood, J. R., 70
Honan, J. P., 81, 82, 86
Horn, R. N., 118
Hurst, D. K., 66, 67

I

Immerwahr, J., 215
Iosue, R. V., 216
Ireland, R. D., 7, 230, 231, 234

J

Jablonsky, S. F., 60, 155
Jacob, R., 96, 104
Jelinek, S. M., 98
Jerome, R. T., 118
Johnson, L. B., 34, 35–36
Johnson, N. C., 88, 229
Johnson, V. R., 173
Johnston, O., 87
Julius, D. J., 101

K

Kahneman, D., 177
Kanigel, R., 14
Katz, R. N., 116
Keller, G., 64, 65, 67, 68–69, 70, 71, 72, 74, 96, 98, 105, 106, 112, 145, 152, 165, 203
Kennedy, D., 222
Kirst, M. W., 41
Klein, K. J., 166
Klugman, M. R., 103
Knirk, F. G., 57
Knott, J. H., 13, 54, 55, 58, 59, 60, 61, 169, 170, 172–173, 180, 184, 185, 203
Knowles, A. A., 19
Knutel, P., 117
Koenig, M.E.D., 41, 58, 60, 61
Kosko, B., 213

Kotler, P., 6, 67, 68
Kramer, F. A., 36
Kuhn, T. S., 140, 223

L

Lahti, R. E., 47, 49
Langenberg, D. N., 84
Langley, A., 74, 239
Lasher, H. J., 49, 50
Lauth, T. P., 53, 208
Lawler, E. E., 229
Lawrence, G. B., 24, 25, 26
Lee, R., 57
Leslie, D. W., 67, 71, 75, 201, 221, 236
Leslie, L. L., 218
Levin, B., 103
Levinson, H., 51
Lindblom, C. E., 28–29
Loose, C., 221
Lueddeke, G. R., 198
Lujan, H. D., 72, 73, 74
Luthans, F., 142, 196, 206
Luzi, A. D., 60, 155
Lynch, A., 11, 158, 159

M

Madigan, C., 4, 6, 149, 184
Mahoney, R. J., 217
Malhotra, Y., 112
Malone, M. S., 5
Mangan, K. S., 98
March, J. G., 138, 148, 151, 159, 171, 177, 179, 181, 183, 211, 212, 218, 219, 220
Marchese, T., 77, 78, 80, 93, 94, 97, 99, 102, 103–104, 105, 106, 107, 110, 112, 134, 137, 140, 144, 196–197, 205, 222, 240
Marcus, L. R., 184
Margolis, M., 92
Masland, A. T., 27, 155
Massy, W. F., 83
Mathews, J., 96
McClure, P. A., 116
McGuiness, A.C.J., 161

McKean, R. N., 34
McManis, G. L., 24
McNamara, R., 34
Melan, E. H., 106
Melissaratos, A., 92, 94, 99
Meredith, M., 72, 163
Meyer, J. W., 128, 129–130, 144, 145, 149, 150, 151, 154, 198
Micklethwait, J., 110, 113, 120, 148, 155, 182, 183, 184, 203, 230, 232
Milbank, D., 100
Milton, T. H., 66, 69, 72, 73, 74, 147, 166, 173, 236
Mingle, J. R., 116
Minimer, G. S., 55
Mintzberg, H., 9, 64, 65, 66, 67, 74, 75, 79, 150, 163, 166, 167, 173, 185, 203, 213, 224, 225, 239
Mitnick, B. M., 41
Molitor, M., 81
Morgan, A. W., 229
Morgan, G., 162, 183
Morrison, J. L., 65
Murphy, P. E., 6, 67, 68

N

Nadler, D. A., 94, 104, 105
Nash, R. J., 51, 205
Neal, J. E., 81–82, 84, 85, 86, 88, 147
Nedwek, B. P., 81–82, 84, 85, 86, 88, 147
Nelson, C., 227
Neumann, A., 107, 222
Neustadt, R. E., 224
Newton, R. D., 42
Nicklin, J. L., 3, 99, 105, 118, 119, 165
Nisbett, R., 131, 165, 171, 174–175, 176, 177, 179, 189
Nixon, R., 46
Njoku, E. S., 49, 169
Noble, D. F., 92
Nohria, N., 4, 8, 9, 12, 141, 143, 145, 147, 180, 195, 202, 235, 236, 241

Norris, D. M., 229
Nyce, J. M., 115, 119

O
Odiorne, G. S., 43, 45, 48, 49
Okimi, P. H., 10, 67, 73, 239
Oldenburg, D., 221
O'Neill, P., 111
Orwig, M., 20, 23, 34, 36, 38
O'Shea, J., 4, 6, 149, 184

P
Page, W. J., Jr., 46, 51
Pallas, A. M., 107, 222
Parden, R. J., 25
Parker, W. C., 24
Partipilo, G. L., 117
Pascale, R. T., 4, 209, 238
Penrod, J. L., 108, 110, 113, 114, 115, 117
Peters, T. J., 7
Peterson, M. W., 13, 38, 39, 70, 154
Pfiffner, J. M., 225
Pham, A., 112
Pinola, M., 57
Plous, S., 170, 179
Pool, R., 156
Porter, J. H., 116
Postman, N., 226
Presley, J. B., 67, 75, 236
Pritchett, M., 117
Pyhrr, P. A., 52, 53, 56, 58, 59

R
Radin, B. A., 95
Rahul, J., 97
Raia, A. P., 51
Reed, P., 205
Renfro, W. L., 65
Riecken, H. W., 132, 148, 187
Rifkin, G., 113, 141, 206
Rigby, D., 4, 169, 177, 197
Roach, S. S., 113
Robbins, H., 44, 153, 174
Roe, E., 9, 128, 144, 227

Rogers, E. M., 10, 128, 132, 133, 134, 136, 147, 156, 157, 160
Rooney, P. M., 229
Rose, J., 74, 239
Rose, R., 46, 196
Ross, J., 174, 186, 237, 238
Ross, L., 131, 165, 171, 174–175, 176, 177, 179, 189
Rourke, F. E., 14, 24, 25, 154
Rouse, A. M., 36
Rowan, B., 128, 129–130, 149, 150, 154, 198
Rowley, D. J., 72, 73, 74
Rush, S. C., 81
Russell, S. C., 205

S
Salipante, P. F., 152, 200, 220, 222
Samuelson, R. J., 183
Saurman, K. B., 51, 205
Sauser, W. I., Jr., 98
Schachter, S., 132, 148, 187
Schargel, F. P., 100
Schick, A., 22, 34, 35, 36, 41–42, 193, 236
Schmidt, W. H., 92, 94, 95, 96, 104, 105, 106
Schmidtlein, F. A., 28, 66, 69, 72, 73, 74, 88, 147, 165, 166, 173, 202, 206, 236, 239
Schuster, J. H., 71
Scott, W. R., 13, 137, 146, 220
Secor, J. R., 104, 161
Serban, A. M., 88
Service, A. L., 24, 25, 26
Sevener, D., 86, 148
Seymour, D. T., 91, 93, 98–99, 100, 101, 103, 108, 165, 221
Shapiro, E. C., 5, 112, 223, 236, 240
Shapiro, I., 164
Shaw, P. G., 82, 83
Shepko, R., 82, 83
Shert, L. A., 93, 156
Sherwood, F. P., 46, 51
Shils, E., 220
Shirley, R. C., 71, 154

Shushok, F. J., 143
Siegfried, J. J., 139, 145
Sims, R. R., 93, 132, 221
Sims, S. J., 93, 132, 221
Slaughter, S., 218
Slavin, R. E., 5
Sloan, V., 107
Slocum, D. L., 229
Smallen, D. L., 116
Smith, D. G., 71
Smith, K. R., 173
Snehota, I., 146
Sohal, A. S., 111
Sorra, J. S., 166
Spanbauer, S. J., 102
Spencer, W. L., 26
Stahlke, H.E.W., 115, 119
Staw, B. M., 174, 186, 237, 238
Steeples, D. W., 69, 71
Stone, D. A., 8, 227
Strassmann, P. A., 77, 79, 110, 121, 184
Summers, R., 95
Sutton, W., 141
Suver, J. D., 56, 58, 202
Swenk, J., 64, 71, 236

T

Tan, D. L., 70, 156
Taylor, B. E., 5, 83
Taylor, F. W., 14
Temple, C. M., 49
Tenner, E., 194
Thomas, J. D., 58
Thomas, K. B., 188
Thomas, M., 111
Thompson, D. L., 38, 40
Thurow, L. C., 220

Tornatzky, L. G., 10, 161, 206
Trombley, W., 85, 86, 87, 148, 173, 199, 204, 208
Turner, J. A., 188
Tversky, A., 177
Twigg, C. A., 117
Tyack, D., 18, 164, 235

V

Veblen, T., 17

W

Wade, N., 188
Wanat, J., 18, 35
Waterman, R.H.J., 7
Waters, L. A., 100
Weathersby, G. B., 36, 37, 39, 40, 42
Weaver, P. H., 7
Weick, K. E., 150, 179, 200, 209, 212
West, G. E., 47
West, T. W., 116
Wheatley, W. J., 221, 222
Whetten, D. A., 220, 223
White, J. B., 112, 167
Wildavsky, A., 23, 41, 42, 56, 73, 155, 160, 163, 184, 195
Williams, H., 37
Wilson, D. C., 8
Wilson, J. A., 24
Winston, G. C., 216, 218
Wiseman, C., 225
Wooldridge, A., 110, 113, 120, 148, 155, 182, 183, 184, 203, 230, 232

Y

Yamada, M., 71
Yin, R. K., 125

Subject Index

A

"A Box" Fallacy, the, 175–177

AAHE (American Association for Higher Education), 97, 99, 148

Academic fads. *See* Higher education management fads

Academic sector. *See* Higher education; Sectors, organizational

Academics. *See* Faculty

Accountability in public institutions: and assessment, 81–82; and continuity, 152; demand for, 19, 23–24, 85, 228. *See also* Mandates, government-imposed innovation

Administration, reengineering university, 115–116

Administrators, professionalization of, 18. *See also* Managers and subordinates

Adoption and failure. *See* Failure of fads

Adoption of innovation, 175–178; accounting for, 139–142, 169–170; anticipating resistance to, 120, 233; and contagion of ideas, 158–159; criteria and conditions for, 61, 105, 140–141; doing research before, 231–232; on an experimental basis, 236–237; facilitation of, 237–238; factors affecting, 143, 156–157, 170; after failure of past fads, 61, 128, 195–196; between organizational sectors, 133–134, 135; rates of, 157, 169; starting small with, 234; strategies for constructive, 228–238; timing of, 232; virtual or symbolic, 138, 149, 150, 154, 174, 182, 218

Adoption of people by ideas, 158–159

Adoption statistics. *See* Statistics

Advocacy of fads: avoiding bandwagon, 232; contagiousness and, 158–159; upon failure of past fads, 128, 195–196; and idealization, 164–165; and imitation, 148, 152–153, 180–182; and overpromising, 128, 235; reasons for, 60–61, 105, 140–141, 159–160, 179; and self-efficacy, 182–185; without supporting evidence, 37, 44, 47, 49–50, 54, 58, 86, 103, 139, 158, 180, 199; tautologies and oxymorons, 69, 86–87; typical statements made in, 230–231

Advocates and champions of fads: or of academic institutions, 237; academic managers, 151–152, 171–189; biases influencing, 171–189; businesspeople, 148; early majority, 134, 136; initial or leading, 40, 43, 52, 56, 97, 126; intersector carriers, 133–134; lack of management

Advocates and champions of fads
(*cont.*)
experience of, 60; managers with
new jobs, 172–173, 185; the nature
of, 165–167, 178; and opponents,
119, 120, 166–167, 233; professional associations as, 67–68, 82,
97, 148, 232; subjective judgment
characteristic of, 134, 181; U.S.
presidents as, 33, 34, 35–36, 46,
60–61, 184. *See also* Networks,
organizational; Opponents of
innovation
American Association for Higher
Education (AAHE), 97, 99, 148
Analysis: cost-benefit, 29, 52;
KPI/SWOT cross-impact, 75;
revisionist, 130–131; TQM
statistically based, 93, 106–107.
See also Program analysis,
institutional
Anarchies, organized, 151
Animals: comparing, 215, 222;
reading entrails of, 199
Applicability of innovations.
See Higher education
Appropriateness, logic of, 181
Assessment of management tech-
niques: building in, 238; and
cognitive bias, 178–180; factors
hindering, 193–195; quantitative,
197–198. *See also* Program analysis,
institutional
Association of Governing Boards
(AGB), 82, 83, 84
Associations, professional: as advo-
cates of fads, 67–68, 82, 97, 148,
232; networking through, 148, 232
Availability heuristic, 179

B

Bandwagon advocacy of fads, 68–69,
232
Base funding. *See* Budgeting
Benchmarking, 4, 75–89; definition
of, 76; development of, 76–80;

future of, 88–89; in higher education, 80–85, 155–156, 199, 204,
208, 211; what happened to, 85–88
Biases, manager. *See* Managers and
fads
Blame for failure of innovations, placing: on the institutions, 104; not
applied to fad itself, 85, 87, 120,
163–164, 167, 200; on not following their rules, 161–162; on people,
119–120, 165–167, 202–203; on
wrong methodology, 71, 86, 104.
See also Failure of fads
Books, management innovation, 4,
43, 68, 109; and articles, 53, 67, 97;
business consultants and, 149; and
handbooks, 37, 47–48, 56. *See also*
Research studies
Boston Consulting Group, 6
BPR. *See* Business Process
Reengineering (BPR)
Budgeting: absence of, 16, 18; and
base funding, 20, 22, 55; current
and upcoming fads in, 229; ideal,
42–43; for inputs not outputs, 23;
line-item (incremental), 19–20,
22–23, 53, 55, 183; versus multiyear planning, 22; portfolio matrix,
6; PPBS system of, 34–43; ZBB
system of, 52–60, 183–184
Business consultants. *See* Consultants,
management innovation
Business fads history. *See* History
of business management fads
Business management fads: cycles of,
4–6; examples of, 6–8, 229; First
Revolution in, 14–23; one-way
migration of, to education, 10,
125–126, 141; Second Revolution
in, 23–27. *See also names of specific
innovations*
Business principles, applicability of,
to higher education, 17, 26, 91–92,
107, 148, 217–218
Business Process Reengineering
(BPR), 4, 108–121; definition of,

109; development of, 109–113; in
higher education, 113–118, 208;
rules for success of, 7, 161–162,
195–196, 236; what happened to,
118–121
Business products, fads as, 8, 141
Business sector: compared to universities, 99, 215–216, 220; cooperation
with higher education, 100; customers, 216, 225–226; fad diffusion
to education from, 10, 141;
networks, 147–148
Buzzwords, management. *See* Terms
and buzzwords, fad

C

Carnegie Commission on Higher Education, 38
Cat on the Toilet Seat Fallacy,
177–178
Cats and dogs, comparing, 215, 222
Causality: fad assumptions of, 164,
194; and managerial roles,
171–174; organizational paradigm
emphasis on, 140
CAUSE, 115–116
Cautions. *See* Warnings and cautions
Centralization of bureaucracy,
203–204
Certainty, the illusion of, 110, 155, 198
Change: as adventure, 174; constructive strategies for managing fads
and, 228–238; continuity versus,
152, 220–223; destructive imposition of, 120–121, 147, 222–223;
effects of fads and constant, 200;
forecasting, 65; as improvement
or progress, 28, 138–139, 219, 221;
ongoing institutional, 117–118,
144, 236, 239; the pace of, 144;
radical or revolutionary, 110, 120,
121; variety essential to, 209–210
Chaos or anarchy, calculated, 104,
151, 224–225
Characteristics of fads. *See* Fads, the
nature of

Chronology of fads. *See* Fad cycles
Coercive processes of fad diffusion, 146
College and University Personnel
Association (CUPA), 82
Colleges. *See* Environment, the
higher education; Higher education
Commitment: bias and escalation of,
185–187; to goals of higher educa-
tion, 204–205
Communication of fads: and the
nature of people, 165–167; between
sectors, 133–134, 135. *See also*
Networks, organizational
Comparison: of business and educa-
tional organizations, 99, 215–216,
220; of cats and dogs, 215, 222.
See also Benchmarking
Competence of managers, 223–225,
239–241; and fads, 200–201, 208,
210
Competitive benchmarking. *See*
Benchmarking
Confidence in higher education, 198,
220–221; crisis of, 205–206; and
managers, 201
Consequences. *See* Legacy of fads,
residual
Consortium for Higher Education
Benchmarking Associations
(CHEBA), 89
Consultants, management innova-
tion, 69, 134; business priority of,
141; conflicting interests of, 126,
149; networking by, 148–149;
results that justify hiring, 119; as
statisticians, 84, 106, 204; as witch
doctors, 155, 199
Contagion of ideas, 11, 158–159
Context of management: customiza-
tion to, 235–236; disconnection
from, 12, 224–225. *See also* Environment, the higher education
Continuous Quality Improvement.
See Total Quality Management/
Continuous Quality Improvement
(TQM/CQI)

Control by managers, the illusion of, 182–185, 212. *See also* Managers and subordinates

Cost-benefit analysis: effectiveness of, 29; ZBB emphasis on, 52

Costs, educational: controlling rising, 47–48; joint or stand-alone, 59–60

Costs of implementing management fads, 141, 219; benchmarks data subscription, 83; difficulty of estimating, 186; exceeding benefits, 36, 58; high, 41, 116, 201, 204; significant commitment to, 49, 186, 201; summary and trial balance of, 218–228

CQI. *See* Total Quality Management/Continuous Quality Improvement (TQM/CQI)

Creation, fad. *See* Fad cycles

Creation stage, fad, 126–128, 186

Crisis in higher education: claims of, 68, 115, 126, 143–144; self-fulfilling prophecy of, 205–206

Criteria: fad identification test, 230–231; of a perfect management system, 29–30

Criteria for adoption. *See* Adoption of innovation

Criticism of innovations: from external groups, 205, 227; from proponents, 107–108, 111–112; widespread, 195–196. *See also* Opponents of innovation

Culture lag between organizational sectors, 58, 133–134, 135

Culture of higher education. *See* Environment, the higher education

Curriculum. *See* Program analysis, institutional

Customer satisfaction, TQM/CQI, 93–94, 98

"Customers," higher education: ambiguity about, 105; commodification for, 92, 107; compared to business customers, 216, 225–226

Customizing innovations, culturally, 235–236

Cycles, fad. *See* Fad cycles

Cynicism about management, 202–203

D

Data: confirming or denying fad validity, 138, 183; hard or soft, 224; line-item budgeting, 20; and measuring higher education outputs, 39, 84, 197–198, 228; quantitative versus qualitative, 24–25, 79, 87, 136–137; and the tyranny of numbers, 197–198

Data collection, 201, 204; fad recommendations on, 70, 78–79; importance of, 207; organizational sector differences in, 136–137; performance indicators, 82–85; problems in higher education, 39. *See also* Management information systems (MIS)

Decision making, institutional: avoiding rhetoric in, 238–241; centralization of, 203–204; and cognitive bias, 174–180; and commitment bias, 185–187; constructive, 236; data-based, 18, 39; and decision rationality, 27–28, 60, 61, 148, 199, 224–225; democratic, 74; and fuzzy logic, 213; and the illusion of certainty, 110, 155, 198–199; and management fads, 27–29; MBO participative, 44–45, 51; and MIS systems, 24–27, 204; promise of shared, 44–45, 51, 74; strategic, 74; subjectivity of, 79; symbolic, 138, 149, 182. *See also* Adoption of innovation; Managers and fads

Decision units and budget levels, ZBB, 56–57

Democratic decision making, 44–45, 51, 74

Departments, academic. *See* Faculty

Development of fads. *See names of specific innovations*

Development stages, fad. *See* Fad cycles

Diffusion processes, fad: one-way business-to-education, 10, 125–126, 141; types of, 146, 148

Discontinuation factors, innovation, 157

Dissonance, innovation cycle resolution of, 131–132, 178

Divination, animal entrails, 199

Documentation, line-item budgeting, 20

Downsizing, company, 112, 113, 119, 120

E

Early majority. *See* Advocates and champions

Education management fads. *See* Higher education management fads

Efficiency and productivity: and institutional legitimacy, 153–154, 198, 227; positive residuals of fads on, 206–213; in the service sector, 87; and Taylorism, 14–16; and technical inefficiency, 61, 201, 217

Enrollment, postwar growth in, 21

Environment, the higher education, 143–145; chaos in, 104, 151, 224–225; claims of crisis in, 68, 126, 143–144; complexity and nonlinearity of systems in, 194; customizing innovations to, 235–236; disconnection from context of, 12, 224–225; fads and, 12–13, 104, 138, 140, 143, 182, 194, 219–223; and the illusion of control, 182–185, 212; organizational characteristics in, 149–156, 194–195, 235; and scientific management, 16–18. *See also* Higher education

Errors, cognitive, 175–178

Evaluation as a fad, test for, 230–231

Evaluation system, management innovation, 238

Evidence supporting innovations: lack of, 37, 44, 47, 49–50, 54, 58, 103, 116, 139, 158, 180, 199; obtaining, 232, 238. *See also* Research studies

Evolution, Darwinian, 209

Evolution of fads. *See* Fad cycle stages

Excellence movement, the, 7–8, 92–108, 137, 208

Expectancy bias, 187–189

Experimenting with innovation, 236–237

F

Factory systems: metaphors, 94, 99; scientific management of, 14–16

Faculty, 39; attitudes, 202; past and present narratives of, 225–228; roles of, 205; standards for, 16–17, 115–116, 120

Fad, the management: accounting for, 139–142; as business product, 8, 141; concepts versus actual practice, 42, 47, 53, 55, 138–139, 149, 182; dating a, 31; definition of, 3; identifying a, 230–231; as magic, 9, 155; as managerial judgment alternative, 12, 155, 223–225; as meme, 11, 158–159; as narrative, 8–9, 128–130, 141, 225–228; new and upcoming, 229; as placebo, 11, 187–189; as political process, 11, 29, 155–156; as post hoc social construction, 12, 119, 163–164, 238; as rejected innovation, 10, 60–61, 195–196; as rhetoric, 9, 159; as solution to problems, 140, 189; as substitute for problems, 155, 201, 223, 234; as technology transfer, 9–10, 108–109, 128; as uninstitutionalized innovation, 10–11, 219–223

Fad adoption. *See* Adoption of innovation

Fad advocates. *See* Advocates and champions of fads

Fad cycle stages, 126–132; Creation or Initiation, 126–128, 186; diagram of, 127; Narrative Devolution, 130–131, 136; Narrative Evolution, 128–130, 133–134; Resolution of Dissonance, 131–132; Time Lag, 58, 130, 136

Fad cycles, 4–6, 10; abandonment phase examples, 36, 40–43; academic management, 125–142, 203; accounting for, 139–142; chronology of, 30–31, 133–134, 135; constructive strategies during, 228–238; as essential to higher education, 197, 206–213; and evolution of organizations, 209–210; failure in, 195–196; longevity of, 230; and migration across sectors, 58, 133–134, 135; new and upcoming, 229; review process, 231–233; stage process diagram, 127; stages of, 126–132. *See also* Legacy of fads, residual

Fad reinvention. *See* Reinvention of fads

Fad sponsorship. *See* Advocates and champions of fads

Fad test, the, 230–231

Fads, constructive use of, 228–238; evaluation phase, 238; exploration phase, 230–233; implementation phase, 233–238

Fads, the nature of, 156–165; adoptability, 156–157; complexity, 5, 8, 161–162, 184, 200, 227; comprehensiveness, 105, 161–162; contagiousness, 158–159; credibility, 199; definition of, 3; failure endemic to, 195–196; and fit with employee values, 166–167, 198; as idealized, 164–165; impurity of adaptation, 193–194; lacking a priori criteria, 194; nonfalsifiability, 162–164; reasonableness, 159–160; simplicity, 5, 8, 184, 200, 227; as sustaining or disruptive, 234; undefinability, 70, 120, 160–161, 194. *See also* Legacy of fads, residual

Failure of fads: advocacy despite, 55, 60–61, 86, 131, 185–187, 189; complexity an excuse for, 161–162; and conceptual assumptions, 14, 44, 49, 59–60, 87–88, 163–164, 167; discontinuation factors, 157; escalation of commitment despite, 185–187; and Narrative Devolution, 130–131, 136; negative consequences after, 197–206; and nonfalsifiability, 162–164; organizational factors affecting, 143; persistence of paradigms despite, 140–141, 158, 186, 187–189; positive consequences despite, 43, 141–142, 206–213; post hoc explanations for, 119, 163–164, 238; and radical change, 110, 120, 121; rationalizations for, 132, 162–163, 200; reasons for, 41–42, 47, 50–51, 59, 60, 104, 157, 161–162; Resolution of Dissonance after, 131–132; in state governments, 53, 55, 59; on their own terms, 195–196; to be implemented, 42, 47, 53, 55–56, 116, 138; undefinability and inconclusiveness of, 70, 120, 160–161, 194. *See also* Blame for failure of innovations, placing

Fallacies, cognitive: "A Box" Fallacy, 175–177; and bias, 174–180; Cat on the Toilet Seat, 177–178; on causality, 140, 164, 171–174, 194; and cognitive errors, 175–178; of comparing business and education organizations, 99, 215–216, 220; in specific innovations, 73–74

Fate of profiled fads: benchmarking, 85–88; BPR, 118–121; MBO, 50–52; PPBS, 40–42; strategic planning, 72–75; TQM/CQI, 96–97, 104–108, 208; ZBB, 58–60. *See also* Failure of fads; *names of specific innovations*

Feedback on innovations, seeking, 238

Financial status, portfolio matrix, 6

Ford Foundation, 37

Forecasting: change, 65; turbulence, 69

Fourteen Points, TQM, 93

Funding: altruism or academic capitalism sources of, 218; base, 20, 22, 55; performance, 80–81

Fuzzy logic, 213

G

Generalizations, logically unsupportable, 177–178

Georgia, ZBB in, 53, 55, 169, 208

GI Bill, 20–21

Giving up too quickly, 237–238

Goals, institutional: consensus lacking on, 51; performance indicators and unclear, 84; quantitative approach to assessment of, 24–25, 84, 136, 197–198

Goals, organizational: emphasis on, 140; MBO approach to, 44–45; PPBS analysis of national and, 35–36

Good management, 239–241

Government sponsorship of fads: failure despite, 46, 53, 55, 59–60; influence of, 146–147; reasons for, 60–61; by U.S. presidents, 33, 34, 35–36, 46, 60–61, 184. *See also* Mandates, government-imposed innovation

H

Heroes. *See* Advocates and champions of fads

Hierarchies: and centralization of bureaucracy, 203–204; control, 44–45, 51, 111, 114–115, 166, 172–173, 182–185; MBO, 46, 49, 51

Higher education: absence of uniformity in, 16–17, 18, 107, 140, 194; applicability of business principles to, 17, 26, 91–92, 107, 148, 217–218; as being in crisis, 68, 126, 143–144; commodification of, 91–92, 107; confidence in, 198, 201, 205–206, 220–221; constancy versus change in, 151–152, 220–221; distrust of, 147; fad cycles essential to, 197, 206–213; joint costs and benefits in, 59–60; purposes of, 106–107, 119, 228; social support and respect for, 147, 198, 201, 220–221; three trends threatening, 219–228; types of innovation in, 145, 150–151; weakening commitment to, 204–205. *See also* Environment, the higher education

Higher education institutions: business cooperation with, 100; business organizations compared with, 215–217, 220–221; centralization of bureaucracy in, 203–204; change in, 209–210, 236, 239; external legitimacy of, 147, 154–155, 185, 198, 220–221; imitation of other, 148, 152–153; internal legitimacy of, 155–156, 186; managers and management in, 151–152, 169–189, 223–225; the narrative of, 225–228; as normative, 220; obliteration or automation of, 110; ongoing restructuring in, 118; organizational characteristics of, 149–156, 194; public, 73; redundancies of, 217; structure of, 26–27, 150–151, 182, 203–204, 211–213; successful change within, 236; types of resources in, 53, 55, 235; variety and change in, 209–210; weakening of, 110, 219–223

Higher education management fads, 4–12; chronology of, 30–31, 133–134, 135; consistent failure of, 195–196; current and upcoming, 229; cycles of, 10, 126–132, 135; difficulty of applying, 42–43, 57, 59; indirect consequences of, 12–13, 38, 194, 238; inheriting, 203; nature and characteristics of, 156–165; negative consequences after, 197–206; organizational and governance problems caused by, 38, 189, 200–201; positive consequences despite failures of, 43, 141–142, 160; summary and trial balance, 218–228; virtual adoption of, 138, 149, 150, 154, 174, 182, 218. *See also* Management revolutions; *names of specific innovations*

Higher education trends. *See* Trends in higher education

History of a fad. *See* Fad cycle stages

History of academic management fads, 3–4, 12–13, 31–32; benchmarking, 80–89; BPR, 113–121; from the business sector, 10, 125–126, 141; characteristics and, 156–165; the continuing, 228–230; evolution and hybridization, 193–195; and imitation, 148, 153; MBO, 47–52; PPBS, 36–40; strategic planning, 67–75; TQM/CQI, 97–108; ZBB, 56–60. *See also* Legacy of fads, residual

History of business management fads, 3–4, 30–31, 147; benchmarking, 76–80; BPR, 109–113; exported to higher education, 10, 125–126, 141; failures and criticisms, 107–108, 195–196; MBO, 43–47; number and, 169–170; PPBS, 33–36; strategic planning, 64–67; TQM/CQI, 93–97; ZBB, 52–56

Human resources: BPR and downsizing of, 112, 113, 119, 120; commitment of, 201; devaluation of, 201. *See also* Managers and subordinates; People

I

Idealization of innovations, 101, 164–165, 176–177

Ideas, adoption of. *See* Adoption of innovation

Identifying a fad, 230–231

Identity erosion, educational institution, 73, 225–228

Illusion: of certainty, 110, 155, 198; of control, 182–185, 212

Implementation of innovations. *See* Failure of fads; Successful implementation

Incremental budgeting. *See* Budgeting, line-item

Incrementalism, blaming management, 166

Indicators, performance. *See* Performance indicators, key (KPI)

Industry management practices. *See* Business management fads; Scientific management

Inefficiency, technical, 61, 201, 217

Influence. *See* Legacy of fads, residual

Information technology (IT). *See* Management information systems (MIS)

Inheriting fads, 203

Innovation adoption. *See* Adoption of innovation; Successful implementation

Innovations, educational: difference between fads and, 195–196; fads as uninstitutionalized, 10–11; management fads as, 5. *See also* History of academic management fads

Innovations, fads as rejected organizational, 10, 60–61. *See also* Business management fads; History of business management fads

Institutionalization, the power of, 220–221, 239

Investigating management innovations, 231–232

J

Joint big decision committees (JBDC), 71

Judgment, managerial, fad as alternative to, 12

"Jugular vein decisions," 239

K

Key performance indicators. *See* Performance indicators, key (KPI)

Knowledge institutions. *See* Higher education institutions

Knowledge of management, investment in, 231–232

KPI. *See* Performance indicators, key (KPI)

KPI/SWOT cross-impact analysis, 75

L

Language of fads. *See* Terms and buzzwords, fad

Leadership in educational institutions, 151–152; compared to business CEOs, 216; and employees, 165–167. *See also* Managers and subordinates

Leadership of fads. *See* Advocates and champions of fads

Legacy of fads, residual, 142, 196–213; core ideas, 207–208; factors hindering judgment of, 193–195; indirect consequences as, 12–13, 38, 194, 238; negative residuals, 197–206; new techniques, 208–209; positive residuals, 206–213; secondary benefits, 43, 141–142, 160. *See also* Fads, the nature of; Successful implementation

Legitimacy, social and institutional, 153–156, 186, 198, 201, 220–221

Libraries, ZBB in, 58

Life cycle of fads. *See* Fad cycles

Line-item budgeting. *See* Budgeting

Literature on higher education management: lack of, 23, 30, 72; perusing, 231–232. *See also* Books, management innovation

Longevity: of fad cycles, 230; of universities versus businesses, 220

M

Magic: fad as, 9; Taylorism as, 14

Malcolm Baldrige National Quality Award, 78, 95, 99; for educational institutions, 103

Management, strategic. *See* Strategic planning

Management by Objectives (MBO), 43–52, 208; development of, 43–47; in higher education, 47–50; premises, 44, 49; what happened to, 50–52

Management by walking around (MBWA), 7

Management information systems (MIS): BPR emphasis on information technology and, 108–109; and computer-based planning models, 26–27; introduction and effects of, 24–27, 204; and quantitative versus qualitative data, 24–25

Management revolutions, twentieth-century, 13–31; impact on schools, 218; and management fads, 27–29; and the perfect management system, 29–31; the Triumph of Managerialism (first), 14–23; the Triumph of Rationality (second), 23–27, 199, 223–224. *See also* Higher education management fads

Managerialism, the Triumph of, 14–23

Managers and fads, 169–189; and cognitive bias, 174–180; and commitment bias, 185–187, 201, 235, 236–237; and constructive use strategies, 228–238; and cynicism, 202–203; and expectancy bias, 187–189; and managerial competence, 200–201, 208, 210, 223–225, 239–241; and normative bias, 180–182; overview of, 169–170; and role bias, 171–174; and self-efficacy bias, 182–185; and skeptical interest, 230–231. *See also* Decision making, institutional

Managers and subordinates: adopting fads, 169–170; and cynicism, 202–203; fads and the nature of, 165–167; and hierarchical control, 44–45, 51, 111, 114–115, 166, 172–173, 182–185; morale of, 206; and Taylorism, 14–16

Managers with new jobs, 172–173, 185

Mandates, government-imposed innovation, 170; abandonment or lapsing of, 41; for federal agencies, 34, 45–46, 54, 55–56; for state budgets, 53, 59; for statewide education systems, 21, 39, 40, 41, 82, 85, 147, 153. *See also* Government sponsorship of fads; Sectors, organizational

Marketing: by consultants, 126, 149; of ineffective innovations, 61

Master planning, educational institution: and computer modeling, 26–27; and MIS data, 24–25; statewide, 21, 153

MBO. *See* Management by Objectives (MBO)

Measuring higher education outputs, 39, 84, 197–198, 228

Memes, fad contagion through, 11, 158–159

Mimetic processes of fad diffusion, 146, 148

Mission, institutional, 73, 75, 78, 106–107, 119; and values, 220, 228

Myths, organizational: and institutional legitimacy, 153–156, 198, 220–221; reinforcement of, 210–211

N

NACUBO (National Association of College and University Business Officers), 37, 82–83, 84, 148

Names of fads, 5, 7, 104, 195; applied to change, 117; applied to dissimilar processes, 194; current and upcoming, 229; revising the, 61, 157, 229

Narrative, fad as, 8–9, 128–131, 133–134, 136; creation stage of, 126, 128; and organizational paradigms, 140–141; of success, not failure, 164–165. *See also* Rhetoric

Narrative Devolution stage, 130–131, 136

Narrative Evolution stage, 128–130, 133–134

Narrative of higher education, erosion of, 73, 225–228

National Association of College and University Business Officers (NACUBO), 37, 82–83, 84, 148

National Center for Higher Education Management Systems (NCHEMS), 37, 67

National Educational Quality Initiative (NEQI), 100

Nature of fads. *See* Fads, the nature of

Negative residuals of fads, 197–206; centralization of bureaucracy, 203–204; and continual change, 200; cynicism about management, 202–203; illusion of certainty, 155, 198–199; reduction of managerial competence, 200–201; self-fulfilling prophesies, 205–206; simplicity, complexity, and change, 200, 227; tyranny of numbers, 197–198; weakening commitment to education, 204–205

Negotiation process, manager and subordinate, 44–45, 51, 165–167

Networks, organizational, 128, 146–149; associations, 67–68, 97, 148, 232; business and education, 147–148; of consultants, 148–149; and external agendas, 146, 185, 232; government, 146–147; new groupings in, 211–212. *See also* Advocates and champions of fads

New jobs, managers with, 172–173, 185

Nocebo effect, 189

Nonacademic sector. *See* Business management fads; Sectors, organizational

Normative, higher education institutions as, 220

Normative biases, 180–182

Normative processes of fad diffusion, 146

Numbers, the tyranny of, 197–198

O

Objectives, management by. *See* Management by Objectives (MBO)

Ohio Board of Regents, 39, 43

Opponents of innovation: resistance from, 119, 120; and skepticism, 130–131, 202–203, 230–231, 237; as villains, 166–167; working with,

233. *See also* Criticism of innovations; Warnings and cautions

Organizational networks. *See* Networks, organizational

Outcomes, negative and positive. *See* Negative residuals of fads; Positive residuals of fads

Outcomes of innovation: "A Box" Fallacy of, 175–177; encouraging action, 212; lack of agreement on, 86, 194; MBO focus on, 45, 48, 49; nonfalsifiability of, 162–164; positive feedback about, 180; post hoc explanations for, 119, 163–164, 238; reasons not to assess, 183; specifying expected, 238; per unit of cost, 116

Outputs, higher education: difficulty of identifying, 38, 116; difficulty of measuring, 39, 87, 197–198, 228; multiple, 216; quantification of, 197–198. *See also* Benchmarking; Program analysis, institutional

P

Paperwork, line-item budgeting, 20

Parsimony, the law of, 200

Participative philosophy, MBO, 44–45, 51

People: biases of institutional management, 171–189; committed to educational institutions, 221; company downsizing of, 112, 113, 119, 120; cynicism toward managerial, 202–203; fad stimulation of action by, 212; higher education changes, 228; innovations that ignore, 112–113, 118; managerial competence of, 200–201, 208, 210, 223–225, 239–241; the nature of, 165–167; with new leadership jobs, 172–173, 185. *See also* Advocates and champions of fads; Managers and subordinates

Perfect management system, criteria for a, 29–30

Performance budgeting, 21–22, 85–86, 229

Performance comparisons. *See* Benchmarking

Performance funding, 80–81

Performance indicators, key (KPI), 75, 81–85, 204, 208; confusion between benchmarks and, 80–81

Pilot testing management innovations, 234

Placebo, fad as, 11, 187–189

Planning Programming Budgeting System (PPBS), 3, 33–43; development of, 34–36; in higher education, 36–40, 153, 154; positive consequences of, 43, 207–208; what happened to, 40–42

Planning systems: PPBS, 34–35; strategic planning, 63–75. *See also* Master planning, educational institution

Political process: deep structure, 29; fad as, 11, 29, 155–156; management fads as ignoring, 36, 51, 59, 225

Poor management as a stereotype of higher education, 152

Portfolio matrix concept, 6

Positive residuals of fads, 206–213; emphasis on alternative values, 207–209; the importance of data, 207; production of variety, 209–210

Post hoc social construction, fad as, 12, 119, 163–164, 238

PPBS. *See* Planning Programming Budgeting System (PPBS)

Practice benchmarks, best. *See* Benchmarking

Presidents (college), 171, 173

Presidents (U.S.). *See* Advocates and champions of fads

Product benchmarks. *See* Benchmarking

Production line metaphors, 94, 99

Productivity. *See* Efficiency and productivity

Products, fads as, 8

Professionalism, respect for, 200–201, 225–228

Program analysis, institutional: common classification structures for, 26–27; difficulty of, 39, 42–43, 57, 107; interdependent or discrete, 59–60; management system effects on technology and, 13; portfolio matrix, 6; and program budgeting, 39; and zero budgets, 60. See also Outputs, higher education

Program failure. See Failure of fads

Progress: change seen as, 28, 138–139, 219, 221; professional and generational, 144. See also Change

Propagation of fads, 4, 11, 158–159

Public educational institutions, 73, 95. See also Accountability in public institutions

Public mandates. See Mandates, government-imposed innovation

Public relations, 129, 131

Purchasing system, university, 117

Purposes of higher education, 106–107, 119, 228

Q

Quality improvement. See Total Quality Management/Continuous Quality Improvement (TQM/CQI)

Quantification. See Data; Rationality

Questions, the fad test, 230–231

R

Rand Corporation, 34

Ranking process, decision unit, 57; as nonsense, 60

Rational choice theory, problems of, 63, 163–164, 198–199

Rationality: and cognitive biases, 174–180; definitions and concepts of, 27–29, 199, 207; and ends sacrificed to means, 42, 219; in government budgeting, 54–55, 60, 61; the image of quantitative, 154, 156, 197–198; ineffective innovations based on, 61, 201, 207; and measuring higher education outputs, 39, 84, 197–198, 228; the myth of, 154, 155, 199; persistence of paradigm of, 140–141; scientific, 175, 199. See also Fallacies, cognitive

Rationality, the Triumph of, 23–27, 199, 223–224. See also Management revolutions, twentieth-century

Rationalizations of failure. See Failure of fads

Reality, distortion of, 200

Reallocation of resources, ZBB and, 53, 55

Reasons for failures. See Failure of fads

Redundancies of higher education, 217

Reengineering. See Business Process Reengineering (BPR)

Reform, pressures for educational, 145, 217–218

Regents. See Statewide master plans

Reinvention of fads, 132, 140; failure of previous fads and, 195–196; and renaming, 61, 65–66, 101, 157; undefinability and, 160–161. See also Fad cycles

Rejection of fads: in higher education, 10; by later fad proponents, 195–196. See also Fate of profiled fads

Research studies: lack of comparative, 167; lack of successful implementation evidence for, 42, 49–50, 53; lacking on higher education management, 23, 30, 72; on results of fad implementation, 36, 55, 180. See also Books, management innovation

Residual legacy. See Legacy of fads, residual

Resistance to innovations, 119, 120, 233

Resolution of Dissonance. See Fad cycles

Resources, educational institution, 235; reallocation of, 53, 55. See also Human resources

Responsibility center fads, 229

Revolutions, management. *See* Management revolutions, twentieth-century

Rhetoric: fad as, 9, 31, 159; getting past the, 238–241. *See also* Narrative, fad as

Ritual: fad implementation, 155; versus rationality, 29, 210–211

Role biases. *See* Managers and fads

Rules for success of fads, following the, 7, 161–162, 195–196, 236

S

Scanning, environmental, 65

Schools, applicability of Taylorism to, 17–18

Scientific management: and education, 16–18; illusion of, 199; intuitive, 174–180; and Taylorism in business, 14–16. *See also* Management revolutions, twentieth-century

Scientists, managers as intuitive, 174–180

Sectors, organizational: fad stages in academic and nonacademic, 135; meanings of adoption in, 137–138; movement of fads between, 58, 132–134, 141, 145–146; similarities and differences between, 99–100, 134–139. *See also* Mandates, government-imposed innovation

Self-efficacy biases, 182–185

Self-fulfilling prophesies, 205–206

Service sector productivity. *See* Efficiency and productivity

Simplicity and complexity of fads, 5, 8, 128, 184, 200, 227; and change, 209–210; warnings on, 104, 161–162

Site visits, innovation, 232, 233

Skepticism toward innovations, 230–231, 237; and cynicism, 202–203; narrative of, 130–131. *See also* Opponents of innovation

Skills, insufficient, 86–87

Small, starting, 115, 234

Social technology implementation: constructive strategies for, 228–238; and ideology, 107; unintended consequences of, 12–13, 38, 147, 194

Society for College and University Planning (SCUP), 68

Sponsorship. *See* Advocates and champions of fads; Government sponsorship of fads

Stages of fads. *See* Fad cycle stages

Stagnation, claims of institutional, 144

State governments, failure of management fads in, 53, 55, 59

Statewide master plans: California, 21, 153; Georgia and ZBB, 53, 55, 169, 208; New York, 21; Ohio, 39, 153; South Carolina, 199

Statisticians, 84, 106, 204

Statistics: Baldrige Award application, 95, 103; business consultant spending, 148; decision unit ranking process, 57; educational institutions' demise prediction, 68, 70; on fad adoption and implementation, 47, 56, 66, 69, 72, 78, 99, 111, 137, 157, 169; on fad effectiveness and satisfaction levels, 178; "institution which," 177–178; on longevity of universities and businesses, 220; and performance indicators, 81–85, 88; TQM based on quality processes and, 93, 106–107; TQM/CQI activity, 101–102; on use of management techniques, 169

Status quo, challenging or improving the, 108

Stories, success: Cat on the Toilet Seat Fallacy, 177–178; focus on, 101, 128–130, 164–165, 176–177; and individual case studies, 71, 72; and revisionist analyses, 130–131. *See also* Narrative, fad as

Strategic planning, 63–75; development of, 64–67; in higher education, 67–72, 153, 154, 208, 211, 212; what happened to, 72–75

Strategic planning engine, 74–75

Strategies for constructive adoption of innovations, 228–238

Strength, weakness, opportunity, threat analysis (SWOT), 75

Students: as customers, 105, 216, 225–226; enrollment growth, 21; specifications to be met by, 99

Subjective biases. *See* Managers and fads

Subjectivity: of decision making, 79; of innovation advocates, 134, 181

Successful implementation of fads: "A Box" Fallacy of, 175–177; Cat on the Toilet Seat Fallacy of, 177–178; complexity of requirements for, 161–162; constructive strategies for, 233–238; exceptional, 139–140; factors hindering judgment of, 88, 193–195; follow-up study of, 102, 119; idealization of, 101, 164–165, 176–177; invoking examples of, 140–141, 177–178, 189; lack of actual adoption and evidence of, 42, 44, 49–50, 53–55, 139, 180, 195; lack of disproof of, 162–163; lack of empirical findings on, 72, 79, 82; management commitment to, 237–238; and the nature of people, 165–167; and nonfalsifiability, 162–164; and the placebo effect, 11, 187–189; and statistics on adoption, 47, 56, 66, 69, 72, 78, 99, 111, 137, 157, 169; undefinability and the, 88, 120, 160–161. *See also* Legacy of fads, residual

Succession, management, 172–173, 174, 185

Summary and trial balance of fads, 218–228

Surfing, fad, 203

SWOT analysis, 75

Symbolic adoption. *See* Adoption of innovation

T

Tautologies and oxymorons, fad advocacy, 69, 86–87

Taylorism. *See* Scientific management

Teaching and learning: generational improvement of, 144; reengineering of, 115–116, 120

Technology of education. *See* Program analysis, institutional

Technology transfer: fad as, 9–10, 108–109, 128; questions about, 145–146

Terms and buzzwords, fad, 6, 229; confusion in, 82; corporate, 203–204; fuzzy logic, 213; and higher education narrative, 225–226; and innovation as meme, 11, 158–159; management, 3; tautologies and oxymorons, 69, 86–87; undefinability of, 70, 120, 160–161, 194

Test, the fad, 230–231

Texas Instruments, 52, 54–55

Time Lag stage, innovation, 58, 130, 136. *See also* Fad cycles

Total Quality Management/Continuous Quality Improvement (TQM/CQI), 92–108; development of, 93–97; in higher education, 97–104, 137, 140, 153, 157, 170, 211; implementation statistics, 137; public sector, 95; questions about, 161; rationalizing the failure of, 163; reinvention of TQM as CQI, 101, 117; undefinability of, 160; what happened to, 96–97, 104–108, 208

Trapped managers, 185–187, 235, 236–237

Trends in higher education, fad effects on, 219–228; erosion of higher education narrative, 73, 225–228; impairment of academic management, 223–225; weakening of colleges and universities as institutions, 219–223

Truth: versus evidence, 199; or hypothesis, 8; the kernel of, 196, 207–208; or narrative, 227

U

Undefinability of fads, 70, 120, 160–161, 194
Universities. *See* Environment, the higher education; Higher education
University of California, 40
University of Tennessee, 49
Ur-Management in higher education, 18–19; benefits of, 21–22; deficiencies of, 22–23; fads no improvement on, 223–224; and line-item budgeting, 19–20; and planning, 20–21
U.S. Bureau of the Budget, 36
U.S. Department of Defense, and PPBS, 34–36
U.S. Office of Education (USOE), 37
U.S. Office of Management and Budget (OMB), 46
U.S. presidents as advocates, 33, 34, 35–36, 46, 60–61, 184

V

Values, institutional, 166–167, 198; degradation of, 225–228; and educational purposes, 106–107, 119, 228; emphasizing alternative, 207–209; mission-driven, 73, 75, 78, 220, 228; weakening commitment to, 204–205, 222–223
Villains, fad opponents as, 166–167
Virtual adoption of fads. *See* Adoption of innovation

W

Warnings and cautions: fad complexity, 104, 161–162; fad implementation, 38, 63, 79–80, 205; from the past, 60–61, 130
Weakening of higher education institutions, 219–223
Wisdom, conventional. *See* Narrative Evolution stage
Words looking for hosts, 159

X

Xerox Corporation, 76

Z

Zero-Base Budgeting (ZBB), 52–60; development of, 52–56; in higher education, 56–58, 154–155; and the illusion of control, 183–184; positive consequences of, 208; premises, 59–60; what happened to, 58–60